GREAT MYSTERIES
OF THE 20th CENTURY

GREAT MYSTERIES OF THE 20th CENTURY

FOREWORD

As the millennium draws to a close, **THE EVENTFUL CENTURY** series presents the vast panorama of the last hundred years – a century which has witnessed the transition from horse-drawn transport to space travel, and from the first telephones to the information superhighway.

THE EVENTFUL CENTURY chronicles epoch-making events like the outbreak of the two world wars, the Russian Revolution and the rise and fall of communism. But major events are only part of this glittering kaleidoscope. It also describes the everyday background – the way people lived, how they worked, what they ate and drank, how much they earned, the way they spent their leisure time, the books they read, and the crimes, scandals and unsolved mysteries that set them talking. Here are fads and crazes like the Hula-Hoop and Rubik's Cube . . . fashions like the New Look and the miniskirt . . . breakthroughs in entertainment, such as the birth of the movies . . . medical milestones such as the discovery of penicillin . . . and marvels of modern architecture and engineering.

GREAT MYSTERIES OF THE 20th CENTURY presents the most profound puzzles of the century. Deaths in mysterious circumstances, such as that of the Italian banker Roberto Calvi . . . unexplained evidence at the heart of such historic events as the assassination of President Kennedy . . . strange disappearances, including that of Agatha Christie – a story worthy of one of her own novels . . . paranormal phenomena, like the heavenly vision that appeared to three Portuguese children at Fatima . . . and mysteries of modern science. It might be possible to dismiss all paranormal reports as products of the fallible human mind, were it not that modern science itself challenges every commonsense belief about space and time. Black holes, it appears, may act as conduits into another dimension. Time, it seems, does not run in a ruler-straight line; past, present and future may exist simultaneously. The great mysteries of the 20th century warn at every turn against the closed mind; the best we can do is to sift the evidence and acknowledge all realms of possibility.

GREAT MYSTERIES
OF THE 20th CENTURY

Reader's
Digest

PUBLISHED BY
THE READER'S DIGEST ASSOCIATION LIMITED
LONDON NEW YORK SYDNEY MONTREAL CAPE TOWN

GREAT MYSTERIES OF THE 20th CENTURY
Edited and designed by Toucan Books Limited
Written by Tim Healey
Edited by Mandie Rickaby, Robert Sackville West
and Jo Wells
Designed by Bradbury and Williams
Picture research by Vickie Walters and
Christine Vincent

FOR READER'S DIGEST
Series Editor Christine Noble
Editorial Assistant Alison Candlin
Production Controller Lorine Stapleton

READER'S DIGEST GENERAL BOOKS
Editorial Director Cortina Butler
Art Director Nick Clark

First English edition copyright © 1996
The Reader's Digest Association Limited,
11 Westferry Circus, Canary Wharf,
London E14 4HE

Reprinted with amendments 1997

Copyright © 1996
Reader's Digest Association Far East Limited
Philippines copyright © 1996
Reader's Digest Association Far East Limited
All rights reserved

No part of this book may be reproduced, stored in a
retrieval system or transmitted in any form or by any
means, electronic, electrostatic, magnetic tape,
mechanical, photocopying, recording or otherwise,
without permission in writing from the publishers.

® Reader's Digest, The Digest and the Pegasus logo
are registered trademarks of The Reader's Digest
Association, Inc, of Pleasantville, New York, USA

Printing and binding: Printer Industria Gráfica,
Barcelona
Separations: Litho Origination, London
Paper: Perigord-Condat, France

ISBN 0 276 42260 0

FRONT COVER
Background picture: A Kirlian photograph of a
human hand, top; water, bottom.
From left to right: Death mask, Tutankhamun;
London newsboy with details of *Titanic* disaster,
1912; luggage label from the *Hindenberg*, 1930s;
Lord Lucan.

BACK COVER
Clockwise from top left: Joseph Stalin; Agatha
Christie; Glenn Miller; Albert Einstein.

Page 3 (from left to right): Sir Harry Oakes, the
millionaire who was murdered in the Bahamas in
1943; a 1939 propaganda poster for Stalin's rule; the
remains of an unknown animal, thought
by some to be those of a yeti; Our Lady of the
Rosary appears before three shepherd children
at Fatima, 1917.

Background pictures:
Page 13: A fingerprint.
Page 51: Crowds await news of survivors of the
Titanic, April 1912.
Page 89: Water.
Page 113: An aerial view of a crop formation near
Hungerford, Berkshire, England, in the 1980s.
Page 141: A Kirlian photograph of a human hand.

CONTENTS

MYSTERY IN MODERN TIMES

THE MYSTERIES OF THE 20TH CENTURY TEACH US TO KEEP AN OPEN MIND AND TO ACKNOWLEDGE ALL REALMS OF POSSIBILITY

FIRST FAMILY John Kennedy (centre) and his brother Robert (centre right), photographed in 1960, were both alleged to have had affairs with Marilyn Monroe.

The tremendous advances of scientific understanding in the 20th century sometimes lead us to believe that we have answers to all the questions, and yet there is much that continues to baffle the modern mind, whether in the annals of statecraft or crime, the records of the natural world or of the cosmos. Bizarre phenomena, strange deaths, inexplicable disappearances and miraculous cures…all in their different ways open windows into the unknown, challenging

THE MISFIT The actress Marilyn Monroe appears on location in 1960 during the making of *The Misfits*, a film written by her third husband, Arthur Miller. The marriage came to an end not long afterwards.

orthodox assumptions about the world and the recent past.

At the time of Marilyn Monroe's death in 1962, few doubted that the Hollywood superstar died of a self-administered drug overdose in her mock-adobe hacienda at Fifth Helena Drive in the Los Angeles suburb of Brentwood. Today, more than 30 years later, stories of her affair with President Kennedy – and discrepancies in the official reports concerning her death – prompt widespread rumour and speculation. The circumstances of Kennedy's own sensational death have long provoked debate and disquiet. Was the president really shot from behind by a lone gunman in the Texas School Book Depository? What of the witnesses

who reported that the shots came from an area known as the 'grassy knoll', in front of the president's car?

Elements of mystery surround a wealth of historic events, and in some cases the fates of nations have hung on their outcomes. Other less portentous enigmas are no less intriguing for the human dramas which they

MISSING MAN There have been hundreds of so-called 'sightings' of Lord Lucan since his disappearance in 1974.

evoke. Who killed the vicar and choir-mistress in the New Jersey lovers' lane killings of 1922? What happened to the pioneer woman aviator Amelia Earhart, whose plane vanished in 1937 over the Pacific? Where is the suave English aristocrat Lord Lucan, missing since the night in 1974 when he became implicated in the murder of his children's nanny? And why did the murder of a four-year-old boy in 1984 tear a remote French community apart?

Hi-tech investigation

Mystery hunters have acquired a wealth of hi-tech aids to investigation in recent years. Undersea search equipment has located the remains of the ill-fated luxury liner *Titanic*, and genetic fingerprinting has identified the

THE FATE OF THE FAMILY Tsar Nicholas II and his family enjoy a holiday in Sweden in 1909. Did any of them survive the brutal massacre nine years later?

remains of the last Russian Tsar's family. Push-button electronic indexing allows detectives to computer-match fingerprints at rates of tens of thousands per second, while spectrographic analysis permits police laboratories to identify a culprit by a single hair from his or her head.

Yet for every puzzle that is solved by science it seems that a new one emerges. In 1988 newspapers reported that the Turin Shroud, a relic that was said to bear the imprint of Christ, had been exposed through radio-carbon analysis as a medieval fake. But how did a 14th-century forger achieve such astonishing photo-like results? In 1996 a computer for the first time beat a world champion at two games of chess. Does that mean that electronic brains are attaining levels of true consciousness? Can machines really think?

How did life begin?

The biggest enigmas surround the origins and destiny of life and the cosmos. In centuries past, creation myths from around the world told how gods with very human attributes shaped our planet and caused living things to flourish upon it. Modern scientists have challenged scriptural accounts of the Creation, proposing alternative models that are harder for the layman to grasp. Many scientists believe that life on Earth began in what is called a 'cosmic soup' of chance chemical reactions in the gases surrounding the primeval planet. Lightning, meteorites and cosmic radiation bombarded the fog and produced amino acids, which make up

the proteins on which all life is based. This theory is supported by some experimental evidence. Since the 1950s scientists have found it possible to manufacture amino acids in the laboratory by passing heat or electricity through mixtures of methane, hydrogen, ammonia and water vapour. They have also created amino acids by bombarding a mix-

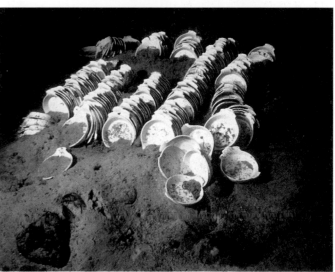

MARVELS OF MODERN SCIENCE Gary Kasparov, the world chess champion, defeated IBM's Deep Blue computer in 1996 (top) but not in 1997. Thanks to hi-tech underwater cameras, thousands of artefacts from the wreck of the *Titanic* (above) have been identified and salvaged.

ture of carbon monoxide, water and nitrogen with high-energy atomic particles, to simulate the radiation that issues from solar flares. One way or another, it appears, intense energy acting on the Earth's ancient

CREATIVE CHEMISTRY Scientists probe into the origins of life by producing amino acids in a flask containing water, hydrogen, methane and ammonia (left). Sir Fred Hoyle (below) argued that amino acids may be distributed throughout the Universe.

fog could have created the organic molecules necessary to form primitive life forms. And from primeval seas of bacteria and blue-green algae, evolutionary forces are thought to have shaped the Earth's incredible menagerie: octopus, eagle, primrose – and man.

That, at least, is the theory most widely accepted among scientists. But an alternative model has been proposed by the British astronomer Sir Fred Hoyle, following the discovery that organic molecules do exist – albeit thinly distributed – in interstellar space. Hoyle has theorised that life-carrying amino acids travel through space aboard comets and meteorites. According to Hoyle, the seeds of life were sown on the Earth, and may also be sown when they reach any planet with a suitably hospitable atmosphere. In 1996 examination of meteorites from Mars suggested that primitive single-celled life forms have existed there.

The Big Bang

How did the Universe itself begin? Hoyle was among a group of cosmologists who in 1948 advanced a 'Steady State' theory, which holds that the Universe is eternal and has always existed. More widely held, though, is the so-called 'Big Bang' theory. This suggests that, about 15 000 million years ago, there was a gigantic explosion whose outrush of

gases formed the galaxies, stars and planets of today. The belief derives from the discoveries of the American astronomer Edwin Hubble. Working in the 1920s, he discovered that the galaxies are moving away from one another and that the more distant galaxies are rushing away faster than those nearer at hand. By dividing the galaxies' distance by their speeds, Hubble could work out when the great cosmic explosion took place. The answer (by the best available calculations) is somewhere between 10 000 and 20 000 million years ago.

But although many astronomers agree about how the universe was born, there is much debate on how it will end. Some believe that the momentum from the Big Bang will keep the galaxies flying apart for many millions of years, when the stars will at last burn out and collapse to become black holes or dark, solid objects known as black dwarfs. So the universe will die. Another theory proposes that the exploding galaxies will

HUBBLE'S LAW Edwin Hubble, shown in front of the telescope at Mount Wilson Observatory in California, provided the first direct evidence for an expanding Universe.

eventually start to come together again under the force of their mutual gravity, impacting in a Big Crunch. Such a collision could cause another Big Bang – and trigger a new Universe.

The inner mysteries

If an aura of mystery surrounds the gigantic issues of life and the cosmos, it clings no less to the minutiae of everyday life. Doctors who can now transplant human hearts and perform eye surgery with lasers are still no closer to finding a cure for that unglamorous, familiar infection – the common cold.

And if the galaxies seem infinite in their grandeur and complexities, so too are the mysteries of the human brain. In the bundle of nervous tissue lying within the skull is a cosmos composed of 100 000 million nerve cells, each of which has 10 000 connections. Here is the control centre for all our bodily movements, a communications HQ to process information from the senses, and a storehouse for all our memories. Today, the PET (positron emission tomography) scan provides us with TV-type images of the brain at work, while the EEG (electroencephalograph) traces fluctuations in its electrical activity.

The brain functions with astonishing clarity and efficiency to order our daily lives. It governs the craftsman's eye, the hands of the concert pianist and the limbs of the gymnast. Yet its control collapses every night as each of us plunges into the mysterious otherworld of dreams – and no one knows quite why.

In our dreams we fly through the air, meet alligators in the street, or take tea with Queen Elizabeth. Forested with strangely connected ideas and images, dreams are experienced by everyone. Research shows that they occur particularly in what is called 'paradoxical sleep', when the EEG apparatus records

BRAIN SCAN A PET scan of the human brain (right) shows a person reading aloud (top) and silently (bottom), while an EEG print-out (below) reveals electrical activity in the brain.

bursts of brain activity and the eyeballs can be seen darting about behind the lids. In REM (Rapid Eye Movement) sleep, as it is also known, the dreamer is evidently responding to particularly vivid visual events. Most people experience REM sleep four or five times a night, in 20-minute episodes. Whether or not the dreams are remembered depends on how quickly after the episode the sleeper wakes up.

Dream symbols

In societies of past times, dreams were always regarded as intensely significant phenomena, loaded with omens and prophecies. Entire nations might be guided by the dreams of their leaders, as interpreted by diviners such as Joseph in the Old Testament. In the 20th century there is no scientific consensus on the relevance of dreams to waking life. The Austrian psychiatrist Sigmund Freud analysed dream contents in terms of unconscious erotic desires and suppressed memories of sexual experiences, often dating from childhood. However, Freud's one-time pupil, the Swiss psychologist Carl Jung, came to believe that the master had placed far too much emphasis on the sexual urges buried in the subconscious. Jung thought that dreams had a more profound religious and magical significance, both to the lives of the individual and to his or her social group.

Neither Freud's nor Jung's ideas are accepted wholesale today. Many modern scientists have come to doubt whether dreams have any profound meaning; according to one school of thought, they reflect little

EXPLORING THE MIND Carl Jung was one of the founding fathers of modern psychology.

more than the random processing of sights and sounds from the dreamer's waking life.

Whatever theory they adhere to, all investigators agree that there are different types of dream. Some seem to be compensatory; people deprived of food, for example, are often tormented by dreams of luscious meals. Other dreams clearly recall stressful real-life experiences. For example, soldiers who have just gone through intense battle ordeals may relive their combat terrors in nightmare dreams. And there are dreams which very clearly reflect facets of the dreamer's own culture. In Western society, for example, a common dream is of appearing naked and embarrassed among strangers.

In other respects, however, dreams are so private, disjointed and transient that they resist scientific analysis. All that can be said with certainty is that we need these nightly mysterious excursions for our own good health. Studies have shown that if subjects are repeatedly deprived of the opportunity to dream (by being woken when REM begins) they become irritable and inefficient, and eventually succumb to hallucinations.

Just as the 20th-century citizen still needs to dream, so 20th-century society seems still to need the supernatural. In a scientific age, we have not lost our fascination with ghosts, premonitions and miracles.

At a solemn ceremony held in November 1993, the Duke and Duchess of Norfolk and the Earl and Countess of Arundel joined staff from nearby Coutts Bank for a ceremony at Corpus Christi Church in Covent Garden, London. The purpose was to appease the unquiet spirit of their ancestor Thomas Howard, 4th Duke of Norfolk, who had been executed for treason four centuries earlier. He was beheaded in 1572 near the Tower of London, where he had been imprisoned. But his spirit was by all accounts distressed by the false accusations which sent him to the block, and appeared before receptionists at the great steel-and-glass headquarters of Coutts Bank in the Strand – headless and in Elizabethan dress. Other strange happenings, such as lights going off of their own accord, were also reported in the building, which stands near the site of a former Howard residence. Lady Mary Mumford, daughter of the late 16th Duke of Norfolk, who organised the service, told a reporter for *The Times* that it was 'the least we can do for poor Thomas. I hope he's happy now.' And indeed the apparitions seemed to stop after the service.

Science and superstition

This very English haunting has its counterpart in newspaper stories of apparitions and miracles which continue to be reported all around the computer-age world. In 1994 the American media proclaimed an epidemic of visions of the Blessed Virgin Mary. For a brief period in September 1995, India was brought to a standstill as the country's 800 million Hindus were seized by devotional frenzies following reports that statues of the gods were drinking milk in the temples.

An interest in the supernatural is not necessarily a hangover from the pre-scientific

MIND BENDER Uri Geller surveys a collection of spoons that have been bent by force of mind.

GHOST STORY The Duke of Norfolk attends a ceremony of exorcism at Corpus Christi Church in London.

age. Many 20th-century thinkers, including Carl Jung, have sought to marry their scientific interests with a belief in other realities. Even the most hardened sceptic may, at some time in his or her life, experience a perfectly extraordinary coincidence which prompts him or her to wonder whether life is not, after all, governed by unseen powers.

Jung coined the word 'synchronicity' to describe significant, coincidental events which seem to violate the laws of cause and effect. Indeed, 20th-century physics, at the subatomic level, challenges the very idea of simple causal connections; the idea of scientific predictability has given way to the notion of statistical probability.

There are other respects in which 20th-century science hints at realities that defy common sense. Einstein proposed that journeys at very high speeds ought to make time travel possible. Scientists have suggested that black holes in space may lead through to other dimensions. And they have postulated a Multiverse principle, by which ours may be just one of an infinite number of parallel universes. It could be that uncanny happenings sometimes leak into our everyday existence from an alternative reality.

Smart, modern aficionados of the paranormal do not fear the claims of science; in fact, they have embraced scientific findings. Hi-tech astrologers, casting horoscopes, use the latest results of space research to determine the supposed influence of the heavenly bodies on their human clients. In 1996 the Israeli superstar Uri Geller announced a thoroughly up-to-date challenge to the world's psychics: to bend a spoon over the Internet and win $1 million. The challenge involved trying to bend an Internet video image of a spoon which was placed inside a see-through safe in Geller's home. If the piece of cutlery suddenly bent, anyone who was logged on at the time would be invited to repeat the feat in front of a panel of judges.

Prophet of the unexplained

Among 20th-century students of bizarre phenomena, none has been more assiduous than the wealthy New York eccentric, Charles Hoy Fort. From 1916, he accumulated newspaper reports on all kinds of remarkable occurrences, such as frogs falling from the sky, mysterious disappearances, wild children and weird coincidences. It was Fort who coined the word 'teleportation' to describe cases where people or objects had reportedly been transported through space and time. Dubbed by cynics 'the patron saint of cranks', Fort was fascinated by the fact that although newspapers and scientific journals often reported strange phenomena, they generally failed to provide any kind of explanation. In *The Book of the Damned* (1919) and three further volumes, he collected thousands of unexplained occurrences and, despite a quirky, hard-to-read style, he

established himself as a notable prophet of the unexplained.

The classic Fortean phenomenon is the fall of strange objects from the skies. Remarkable showers of living creatures from above have often been reported by newspapers

WEIRD AND WONDERFUL Charles Hoy Fort (above) inspired massive public interest in strange phenomena, such as frogs falling from the sky – featured on the cover of a magazine in 1958 (right).

with little attempt at explanation; fish, worms and frogs are typical subjects. Sceptics often propose in such cases that the creatures do not fall from above but emerge from dormancy in the earth with the sudden rainfall. But this theory can hardly be used to explain a case, in June 1954, when witnesses in Birmingham, England, saw hundreds of little frogs bouncing off people's heads.

Fort heard the dark laughter of the gods in such events. Falling objects, he suggested,

might come from 'a region somewhere above the earth's surface in which gravitation is inoperative'. Into this mysterious zone, he theorised, objects were sucked from the ground to be shaken down later by storms. The more prosaic scientific explanations suggest freak whirlwinds, although it has also been proposed that dew, sea or lake water rising through evaporation on hot days may carry lightweight fish or frogspawn up into the clouds, which then fall when different atmospheric conditions prevail.

Fort preferred mystery zones and extraterrestrial forces. After his death in 1932, his achievements were neglected by all but a handful of admirers who formed a Fortean Society to carry on his work. But his reputation gained ground with the worldwide UFO mania which spread after Kenneth Arnold's Flying Saucer sighting of 1947. Fort had been among the first to suggest that mysterious lights seen in the sky might be craft from outer space. He had also speculated

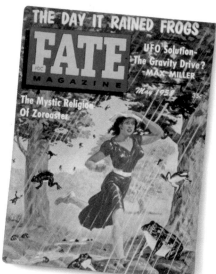

on alien landings. Above all, he criticised scientists' doctrinaire hostility to life's marvellous possibilities, noting how often scientists themselves argued according to their own narrow beliefs, tending to suppress or discredit any data that challenged cold materialism. Colin Wilson, a modern writer on the paranormal, has explained Fort's fundamental principle thus: it may

FACT OR FANTASY? So-called UFOs hover in the sky above a Yorkshire town in a photo of 1966 (above). Are they any more real than the artist's reconstruction on a magazine cover of 1939 (top right)?

well be that some people have a psychological need to believe in marvels, but it is also true that the orthodox scientist has a psychological need not to believe in marvels.

Marvels in the modern age

Suppose that supernatural powers – even alien landings – were a reality and that the authorities were aware of the fact. Might they not suppress the evidence in the interests of public tranquillity? *Project Blue Book*, the US Air Force's official investigation of UFOs, provoked strong criticism that it censored the truth about flying saucers in order to reassure the alarmed population.

Suspicion of government and big business has been a feature of Western thought in the late 20th century. It has recently been revealed that, during the early 1970s, America's Central Intelligence Agency (CIA) contracted the Stanford Research Institute in California to begin a study of controlled clairvoyance – known as *Project Scanate*. The context was the Cold War, and the aim was to discover whether the apparent psychic ability of some people to visualise hidden objects could be employed in espionage against Soviet installations.

Renamed Operation Stargate, the project was for nearly 20 years based at Fort Meade, Maryland, headquarters of the NSA (National Security Agency). The 'Mystics of Fort Meade' were alleged to have identified a major

LIFT-OFF Worshippers at a temple in the north of England appear to levitate.

Soviet submarine project in 1979 and a suspected Libyan training facility for PLO terrorists ten years later. However, in 1996 the CIA recommended to Congress that it discontinue funding for Operation Stargate.

For all the money that has been spent on research into ESP (extrasensory perception), no evidence has ever been accepted by the scientific community as a whole. Investigators have never caged a ghost; Loch Ness refuses to yield up a Monster; no one has levitated in a laboratory – not, at least, to the satisfaction of watching scientists. Sceptics argue that research into the supernatural is doomed to disappoint. Yet the urge to dream mad dreams, that possesses us in our sleep, seems to animate society in its waking life. It appears that 20th-century men and women need mysteries as much as our prehistoric ancestors who drew their magic on the walls of caves.

DEATHS IN MYSTERIOUS CIRCUMSTANCES

ACCORDING TO THE JACOBEAN PLAYWRIGHT PHILIP MASSINGER, 'DEATH HAS A THOUSAND DOORS TO LET OUT LIFE'. WHEN A BODY IS FOUND OVERDOSED WITH SLEEPING PILLS OR FLOATING IN THE SEA, IT IS NOT ALWAYS EASY TO DETERMINE WHETHER THE CAUSE OF DEATH WAS SUICIDE, ACCIDENT OR MURDER. AND EVEN WHERE EVIDENCE OF FOUL PLAY IS COMPELLING, A QUESTION OFTEN ENDURES – WHODUNNIT?

DEATH OF A CARD PLAYER

THE BAFFLING MURDER OF A FAMOUS BRIDGE EXPERT AND PLAYBOY AT HIS NEW YORK HOME

The discovery of the body of Joseph Bowne Elwell in his elegant Manhattan home on the morning of June 11, 1920, made front page news at home and abroad. Elwell was acknowledged as a world expert on bridge, and his books *Elwell on Bridge* and *Elwell's Advanced Bridge* were both international best-sellers.

Profits from the card table, lessons to the rich and famous, royalties from book sales, and wise investments had made Elwell – a former insurance salesman who learnt to play cards at a church youth club – a wealthy man. By 1920, at the age of 47, he owned a luxurious New York home, three country retreats, a yacht, an art collection and a partnership in a stud farm.

An irresistible man

Elwell's reputation as a womaniser was enhanced after his death and probably considerably embellished by the press. Newspaper reports claimed that his address book contained the names of between 53 and 400 women, many of whom were reputedly his mistresses. His New York residence included a luxury boudoir, and the female guests whom he regularly entertained there ranged from show girls to chic divorcees and titled ladies. All became names of interest to the police after 8.10 on the morning of June 11, when Elwell's housekeeper found her employer dying, slumped in a chair and bleeding from a single fatal shot, exactly between his eyes.

It was a puzzling murder. Joseph Elwell had been shot sometime between the delivery of the morning mail at 7.10 am and his discovery an hour later. There was a letter in his lap, and several others lay unopened at his feet. Blood had stained the carpet and his pyjamas, and was spattered on the wall behind the chair where he still sat.

What baffled detectives was the fact that all the doors were locked and all the windows fastened from the inside except Elwell's own bedroom window high up on the third floor. There was no evidence of a break-in or struggle, and a search of the house ruled out burglary as a motive, since none of the many valuables or any

MAN ABOUT TOWN This picture of Joseph B. Elwell (right) was taken at Palm Beach, Florida, where he had a luxury home. Income from books on bridge helped to finance his lifestyle (far right).

cash had been touched. Suicide was also ruled out early in the investigation as the gun had been fired on an upward trajectory – virtually from the hip – from a distance of 3-4 ft (1-1.3 m). No, the evidence pointed to

LONG-LASTING INFLUENCE

One of Elwell's most famous and able pupils was Harold Vanderbilt, son of the tycoon William K. Vanderbilt. After Elwell's death Harold devised the form of contract bridge which is now widely played around the world.

murder by someone well known to the victim. Either he or she had been in the house with Elwell all night, or the victim had let him or her in early in the morning. Elwell must have felt perfectly relaxed if he continued to leaf through the morning mail, barefoot, in pyjamas, and without the toupé or false teeth he was accustomed to wear in company.

The combination of money, sex and fame proved irresistible to the press and speculation was rife. Had he been killed by a female friend who had stayed overnight?

On his last evening Elwell had dined at the Ritz-Carlton and watched a show with his recently divorced lover Viola Kraus and a

1900 Joseph Elwell marries Helen Derby Hanford

1915 Helen and Joseph begin to live apart

1920 Elwell found shot

1925 *Great Gatsby* published. May have been partly based on Elwell's life couple called Lewisohn. Elwell took a cab home alone at about 2 am after a tiff with Viola. Despite the discovery of a pink silk kimono found hanging in his wardrobe, it did not, in reality, look as if he had enjoyed a

SCENE OF THE CRIME The house at 244 West 70th Street, New York, where Elwell was shot dead in the front room.

SPORTING LIFE Joseph Elwell (on horseback) with a group of jockeys and trainers at his Kentucky stud farm.

torrid last night of love. His bed had been only lightly slept in and the telephone company records reinforced the impression that he was awake and alone for much of that night. Shortly after his arrival, he took a phone call from Viola. At 4.39 am he rang William H. Pendleton, his partner in a stud farm in Kentucky, but got no reply. At 6.09 am he rang a Long Island number, the owner of which is not known.

A crime of passion?

The postman delivered the mail at 7.10 am. According to the likeliest scenario, Elwell admitted the killer himself, then returned to his mail. After what must have been a brief conversation, the murderer fired the fatal shot.

It is not hard to picture a love quarrel as the motive. But the shot that killed Elwell was fired from a .45 calibre army revolver, a heavy weapon that was

TURFMAN On his last night Elwell tried to contact William H. Pendleton, his associate and partner in a stud farm.

scarcely a natural choice for a woman. A male assailant was just as likely: perhaps the jealous husband or lover, or outraged relative, of one of Elwell's mistresses.

The pink silk kimono in the wardrobe belonged to Viola Kraus, but the Lewisohns confirmed that she had spent the night with them. Neither William H. Pendleton nor any other business associate stood to profit from Elwell's demise. Elwell's ex-wife Helen came under some suspicion, for he had recently cut her out of his will. But she stood to lose an allowance of $2400 a year if Elwell died, and she had a strong alibi.

There remained the names in the notorious 'love file': a well-known lady of fashion, a Polish countess, an Egyptian princess . . . the police had no shortage of leads, but they were as short of evidence as suspects were well stocked with alibis. A cigarette butt found at the scene that was believed to have belonged to the killer yielded no fingerprints.

No one ever stood trial for the card player's murder – the killer took the trick.

THE VICAR AND THE CHOIRMISTRESS

A LOVERS' LANE KILLING THAT SCANDALISED NEW YORK'S COMMUTER BELT

On Saturday, September 16, 1922 a couple taking a stroll down a lovers' lane in New Brunswick, New Jersey, came upon evidence of a savage double killing. Sprawled on their backs under a crab-apple tree were the bodies of a man and a woman strewn with their own torn-up love letters. When the identity of the victims became known it created a sensation. The man was the Reverend Edward Wheeler Hall, rector of St John's Episcopal Church. The woman was Mrs Eleanor Mills, the sexton's wife and a choir singer at St John's.

Both victims had been shot, and whoever murdered them had also arranged their bodies side by side in an awkward embrace. A single bullet through the head had dispatched the minister, but the attack on the choir-singing Eleanor Mills was more ferocious. She had been shot three times in the

SLAIN LOVERS The Reverend E.W. Hall and Mrs Eleanor Mills, the sexton's wife. When their torrid correspondence appeared in the newspapers the readers were shocked.

UNEASY ACQUAINTANCES Eleanor Mills, the murdered choir singer, with an unsmiling Mrs Frances Hall, the rector's wife.

head and, for good measure, had her throat slashed and tongue and vocal chords cut out.

The love letters found at the scene of the crime and others which came to light later bore witness to a passionate illicit liaison. 'I want you – your arms to hold me close,' wrote the 34-year-old Mrs Mills. 'When my arrow enters your haven I am transported to ecstasy,' replied the balding pastor. He was her 'Babykins'. She was his 'Gay Gypsy'. They wrote to each other of deep, true and eternal love, of crushing embraces and of the pain of separation.

When published in the newspapers, the torrid correspondence helped to spread the scandal far beyond the local area. But the tormenting question remained: who killed the lovers?

The motive for double murder

Although someone had gone through the pastor's pockets and stolen his gold watch, robbery could hardly have motivated this grisly crime. Slain at their secret rendezvous, with their love letters strewn all around them, the couple seemed the obvious victims of retribution. The police naturally questioned the two spouses of the deceased. Frances Hall, the wife of the dead minister,

was a dignified, grey-haired woman who claimed to know nothing of her husband's affair with his choirmistress. She could say no more than that, on the evening of Thursday, September 14, her husband had received a telephone call and left the house, never to return.

James Mills, husband of the murdered Eleanor, told a similar tale. He knew nothing of any affair. His wife had simply gone out on the Thursday evening and not come back.

Wronged spouses become suspects

Doubt was to be cast on James Mills's version of events when he later sold a cache of love letters to the newspapers. Did the sexton really know nothing of his wife's affair?

Further doubts about both spouses were aroused when it became known that neither Mrs Hall nor James Mills had called the police to report husband or wife missing when they failed to come home on Thursday night. But as the investigation proceeded, a plausible explanation for their apparent lack of concern emerged. Rumours of the illicit liaison had, it appeared, been rife for some

WRONGED COUPLE James Mills and Mrs Frances Hall, both injured spouses, appeared to have a motive for murder.

time in the pastor's congregation. It was possible that Mrs Hall and James Mills both knew of the affair, but failed to call the police because they suspected an elopement.

It was four years before the case came to trial, at Somerville, New Jersey. And when it

THE PIG WOMAN Mrs Gibson, who was a key witness in the trial, shown here at her pig farm near the scene of the crime.

did, the prosecution case was directed against Mrs Hall, together with two of her brothers, William and Henry Stevens. The star witness for the prosecution was a 58-year-old widow, Mrs Gibson, who raised hogs on a smallholding and became celebrated in the case as the 'Pig Woman'. She testified that on the Thursday evening, the night of the murder, she had heard noises in the lane and had gone out on her mule to investigate. In the shadows of the crab-apple tree, she saw two men and two women arguing. One was a white-haired lady and the other a man with bushy hair (these the Pig Woman later identified as Mrs Hall and her brother Willy Stevens). 'Explain these letters,' the white-haired woman had cried. The name Henry was mentioned and someone shouted 'Don't, don't, don't . . .' Then four shots cracked the night air and the Pig Woman fled the scene.

It was a powerful testimony made all the more convincing by the fact that the Pig

Woman was brought into court on a stretcher because she was dying of cancer. Why would she falsely accuse Mrs Hall? Unhappily for the prosecution, the Pig Woman's mother had an answer. This vociferous old lady, tracked down by the defence counsel, turned up at the trial and caused

SICK EVIDENCE By 1927 Mrs Gibson, a key witness, was dying of cancer and had to give her testimony from a bed in the courtroom.

much consternation by interjecting 'She's a liar, a liar, a liar! That's what she is, and what she's always been.' The defence also forced James Mills to admit under questioning that he had known all along about his wife's affair with Mr Hall. Was he wholly beyond suspicion? Was it even permissible to speculate (the defence counsel went so far as to argue) that the Pig Woman did it – mistaking the lovers for thieves?

After a five-hour deliberation at the end of the long and much publicised trial, the jury brought in a verdict of not guilty. Mrs Hall and her brothers were acquitted, and Mrs Hall subsequently went into seclusion, to die in 1942.

The case continued to intrigue long after that, however; in a study of 1964, author William Kunstler proposed that the Ku Klux Klan, which had active branches in New Jersey, might have committed the murders as a warning against such a flagrant breach of Biblical teaching on adultery. True or not, the lovers' lane killer or killers were never brought to justice. The case remains one of the most intriguing in America's annals of crime.

1964 Kunstler publishes his book which points the finger of blame at the Ku Klux Klan

THE UNTIMELY DEATH OF STARR FAITHFULL

THE UNSOLVED MYSTERY OF HOW THE JAZZ-AGE PARTY GIRL MET HER WATERY END

The body of a young woman was found at dawn on June 8, 1931, on the wet sand of Long Beach only 20 miles (32 km) from the heart of New York. Dark bedraggled hair framed a beautiful face which was marked with small cuts and bruises. An expensive, brightly coloured silk dress and silk stockings – her only garments – clung to her body. Before long, millions of newsprint words would be expended on what one reporter called 'this mystery with the wonderful name'.

The corpse was identified as that of Starr Faithfull, the 25-year-old stepdaughter of a Mr Stanley E. Faithfull. High-spirited and good-looking, Starr was a typical product of America's young Jazz Age generation. She loved to dance and to drink, even though these were Prohibition days. She frequented illegal speakeasies and late-night parties on the luxury liners which glittered with lights at the docks of New York harbour.

Starr's stepfather was adamant that she had been murdered and pointed the finger

TROUBLED BEAUTY Good looks concealed a disturbed psyche. Starr had needed psychiatric help on several occasions.

PEACE AT LAST? The post-mortem recorded more than 100 injuries on the body.

BODY ON THE BEACH Police cluster around a beachcomber's grisly early-morning find on the Long Island shore – Starr Faithfull's body.

1906 Born
Starr Wyman

1924 Starr's
parents are
divorced

1931 Starr
found dead on
the beach

1949 Stanley
Faithfull dies

HANDWRITING ANALYSIS

The case of Starr Faithfull in 1931 exposed some of the problems still associated with handwriting analysis. Letters stating that she intended to end her life were declared forgeries by her family, and the case remains controversial to this day. Handwriting comparisons are problematic because the same hand may change considerably according to the writer's circumstances and state of mind. For example, in optimistic mood an individual may write with a vigorous right slant which is absent when he or she is feeling more cautious.

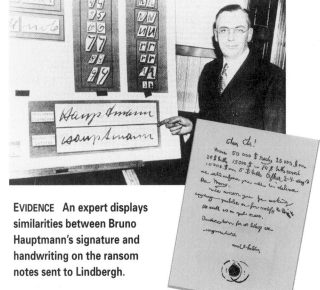

Nonetheless, when a letter flops onto the doormat, it is often easy enough to spot at a glance that it is from a particular friend or relative. Experts become skilled at recognising the multitude of distinguishing features: the size of capitals in relation to smaller letters; pen pressure; letter connections and the spacing of words; and quirks of spelling and punctuation. Disguised writing can often be spotted through a lack of fluidity in the script: little tremors, for example, and evidence that the pen has stopped and started as the forger copied a model.

Handwriting evidence can be crucial. For example, evidence from ransom notes was vital in the conviction of Bruno Hauptmann (left), in 1934, for the kidnap and murder of the baby of the aviator Charles Lindbergh.

EVIDENCE An expert displays similarities between Bruno Hauptmann's signature and handwriting on the ransom notes sent to Lindbergh.

of blame firmly at a one-time family friend of considerable social standing: Andrew J. Peters, former Congressman and former Mayor of Boston. Faithfull claimed that Peters had seduced Starr when she was only 11 years old, and that the relationship had persisted over the years. One entry in Starr's diary ran: 'Spent night A.J.P. Providence. Oh, Horror, Horror, Horror!!!' The investigation revealed that Peters had paid the Faithfull family a 'considerable sum of money'. Mr Peters denied having had improper relations with Starr Faithfull, and refused to comment about payments to her parents. His alibi was strong and he was dismissed from police enquiries.

For the young Starr Faithfull, good-time living put pressure on a damaged personality. Her party-going highs were matched by desperate lows. Her love-life was complex; only four days before her death, she was found in a hotel with a man named Joseph Collins, naked, drunk and so badly beaten that she had to be hospitalised. She also nursed a violent, unrequited love for a ship's surgeon called Jameson-Carr.

Dr Jameson-Carr returned from England about a fortnight after Starr's body was found, bearing three letters that she had written to him shortly before her death. In them she said that she was going to end her 'worthless, disorderly bore of an existence', and that she had promised herself one last delicious meal. Examination showed that Starr had eaten a large meal shortly before dying and that she had also taken enough of the barbiturate veronal to cause unconsciousness. The coroner's verdict was that Starr had drugged herself and walked into the sea – suicide.

Officially the matter was closed, but many people were dissatisfied with the verdict. After all, the body bore many marks of violence; was she killed by thugs employed by her childhood seducer? A respected investigator from the *New Yorker* magazine proposed that she was effectively 'murdered on her suicide

THE FAITHFULL FAMILY Starr's sister (left), stepfather and mother refused to accept that Starr had written the suicide notes.

night' by a casual pick-up. Another theory suggested that Starr was abducted and killed by a notorious Brooklyn bootlegger and racketeer in an attempt to obtain blackmail material against 'A.J.P'. The truth may never be known, but the legend lived on. The tragic heroine of John O'Hara's bestselling novel *Butterfield 8* was based on Starr Faithfull.

OLDER MEN A.J. Peters (left) was a suspect in the Faithfull case. Starr was infatuated with Dr G. Jameson-Carr (far left).

1960 Elizabeth Taylor wins an Oscar for her part, based on Starr Faithfull, in the film of *Butterfield 8*.

DID DILLINGER REALLY DIE?

**PUZZLES STILL SURROUND THE SHOOTING OF
A MIDWESTERN OUTLAW HERO**

On July 22, 1934, federal agents lay in wait outside Chicago's Biograph Cinema and ambushed and shot dead Public Enemy Number One – the infamous outlaw John Dillinger. But was the man who was shot that night really John Dillinger, as the government agents claimed?

The 'Dillinger Gang' robbed banks in the Midwestern states between 1933 and 1934. John Dillinger's own ability to evade capture and to escape from even the tightest security had made him something of a living legend. To many Midwestern farmers struggling through the depression, the banks which foreclosed on their loans were enemies and Dillinger was a folk hero.

Despite a spree of over a dozen robberies and several murders in three different states, local police forces alone were left to try to contain the trail of destruction. The national Bureau of Investigation (which would later become the FBI) could not act until a federal law was broken. Then, while escaping from prison, Dillinger drove a sheriff's car over a state boundary, thereby committing a

CASH INCENTIVE The Bureau of Investigation and individual states offered rewards for the capture of Dillinger in a major campaign.

DEADLY DESPERADO The infamous and much-photographed John Dillinger poses with a Colt .38 and submachine gun, shortly before his supposed death.

federal offence, and the government men were on his trail at last.

According to the official story, Anna Sage, a landlady and madam in Chicago, tipped off the Bureau that one of her tenants was dating a man calling himself Jimmie Lawrence, whom she believed to be John Dillinger. She told the Bureau agents that 'Jimmie Lawrence' had admitted to her that he was the infamous bank robber. Mrs Sage arranged to accompany 'Jimmie Lawrence' to the cinema, where federal agents could arrest him, on Sunday, July 22. At 10.30pm as the suspect emerged, he spotted the danger and sprinted for an alleyway, drawing out

1900   1950

1903 John Dillinger
born

1924 Dillinger jailed
for assault

1933 Dillinger robs his first bank
1934 Dillinger shot dead by the FBI

A JOB WELL DONE? Director of the Bureau of Investigation, J. Edgar Hoover (above). Headlines proclaim Dillinger's demise (below).

a gun. Before he could pull the trigger, he was shot dead.

The Bureau of Investigation could hardly have asked for a more newsworthy outcome. Previously the department had been dismissed as an ineffectual organisation of 'College Cops'.

A dubious trophy

Doubts exist, however, as to the identity of the Bureau's prize catch. Sensational rumours surrounded Dillinger's death, as they had his life: allegedly the fingerprints didn't match, and people who knew him didn't recognise the body. When the autopsy report was uncovered, 35 years later, it contained controversial information. The corpse was

PRYING EYES The public file past the supposed body of the outlaw as it lies in a Chicago morgue. But was the corpse really Dillinger's?

noted as having brown eyes – Dillinger's were recorded as grey on police files. None of Dillinger's identifying scars was mentioned: one on his upper lip and another on his left hand. The body was too short and too stocky, and the heart showed signs of childhood illnesses which Dillinger had never had.

If it was a case of mistaken identity, it would not have been the first. Dozens of men had been arrested during the search for Dillinger. Had the Bureau of Investigation covered up a mistake, or had the ambush been a stage-managed fraud? And if so, by whom? Why did the Bureau keep Chicago's 'Dillinger Squad' in ignorance of their plans? Was it to avoid a leak, or to keep all the glory?

One theory is that the shooting was a charade organised by Dillinger and Lewis Piquett, his mob-connected lawyer. Perhaps the 'leaping bandit' had lost his taste for crime once many of his accomplices and lovers were dead or behind bars. For years rumours that he was alive were fuelled by reported sightings. In

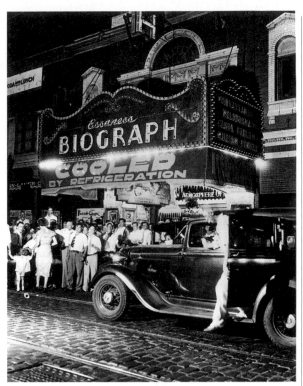

FATEFUL SPOT Dillinger was reportedly shot outside the Biograph Cinema which was showing *Manhattan Melodrama* that night.

1969 the *Indianapolis Star* received a letter from 'John Dillinger', enclosing a photograph of a man resembling a much-aged John Dillinger. There was no return address.

1969 Newspaper receives a letter from 'Dillinger'
1973 *Dillinger: Dead or Alive?* published

THE SHARK ARM AFFAIR

MACABRE AQUARIUM DISCOVERY PROVOKES A MURDER INVESTIGATION WITHOUT A BODY

For bizarre detail, nothing could match the mystery of Australia's Shark Arm Affair, which hit the headlines on Anzac Day – April 25, 1935. The identification of a tattooed arm, disgorged by a captive shark in Coogee Aquarium, led to one of the most grotesque murder cases of the 20th century.

The affair began in the seas off Sydney, where a fisherman hauled in a 14 ft (4.2 m) tiger shark. Rather than kill the saw-toothed giant, he towed it ashore and offered the live specimen to his brother, who managed an aquarium at Coogee.

Some days later, while the shark was swimming around in front of spectators at the aquarium, the creature suddenly went into a spasm and expelled its stomach contents which included a human arm. The limb trailed a piece of rope from the wrist and was found to bear the tattoo of a pair of boxers. At first, this grisly relic was assumed to have resulted from the shark biting a swimmer. But no one had reported an attack in the area, nor had any swimmer gone missing.

Police puzzlement deepened when further examination revealed that the arm had been severed with a knife.

Fingerprints identified the owner of the arm as James Smith, a 40-year-old ex-boxer with a police record. Smith had once been arrested for illegal bookmaking. Enquiries revealed that he had been missing for over

SHADY CHARACTERS   Left: Reginald Holmes, the prosecution's star witness, was murdered. Right: Prime suspect Patrick Brady.

LONELY LIMB   The tattooed arm disgorged by a captive tiger shark. Below left: James Smith, the arm's owner, who is believed to have been murdered.

two weeks. His wife, Gladys, believed that he had gone on a fishing trip. The police assumed that Smith was dead and began a major investigation.

Police make an arrest

When detectives arrested 42-year-old Patrick Brady, a criminal associate of Smith's who was wanted on forgery charges, he admitted that he had recently spent a holiday on the coast with Smith, but denied any involvement with his death. Brady did, however, implicate Smith's employer, a boatbuilder called Reg Holmes, in forgery dealings. The relationship between Holmes and Brady now became of central importance to the police investigation. Reg Holmes denied even knowing Brady, but he clearly had something to hide. After he tried to shoot himself dead aboard his speedboat in Sydney Harbour, he was apprehended and placed under police guard in hospital for four days while surgeons removed a bullet from his forehead. Holmes then changed his story and accused Brady of killing James Smith.

On May 17, Brady was charged with the murder of James Smith, but on the day before the Coroner's Inquest there was a sensational development. Reg Holmes, the key police witness, was found shot dead in his car near Sydney Harbour Bridge.

Another dramatic twist followed the next day. The coroner ruled that he could not hold an inquest without a body. And he did not have a body – he only had an arm.

Despite the coroner's objections Brady was tried for murder, but after a trial lasting just two days the judge directed the jury to bring a verdict of not guilty; the main prosecution witness was gone, and there was no proof that Smith was dead. Two men later charged with Reg Holmes's murder were also acquitted, and the whole police case collapsed. The case remains unsolved.

The police theory is that Smith and Brady were involved in an insurance fraud involving a yacht, which resulted in a quarrel. Brady murdered Smith and dismembered the body which he crammed into a tin trunk for disposal at sea. The arm would not fit in so it was lashed to the outside (hence the piece of rope trailing from the wrist). It worked loose and was swallowed by the shark, which then revealed its ghastly secret to pleasure seekers at Coogee Aquarium.

A SHOOTING IN KENYA'S 'HAPPY VALLEY'

THE GUNSHOT WHICH SHATTERED A COLONIAL HAVEN OF PARTIES AND FUN FAR FROM THE WAR

When Josslyn Hay, 22nd Earl of Erroll, was found shot dead with a bullet through his head just outside Nairobi in January 1941, the scandal rocked the upper classes throughout the English-speaking world. It was wartime, and the Blitz was still raging in London where rationing had been introduced and austerity styles held sway. Amid the white colonial community of Kenya, however, decadent pleasure-seeking and misbehaviour were rife.

Handsome 36-year-old Lord Erroll, the Military Secretary in Nairobi, was a notorious member of the 'Happy Valley Set' – a

ONE OF THE GANG Lord Erroll sports a bow tie in the back row of this picture taken in 1928 at the wedding of two of the 'Happy Valley Set'– Nina Layman and Jack Soames.

permissive elite whose homes lay along the Wanjohi river in Kenya's 'White Highlands'. There were rumours of orgies, drug-taking, wild drinking and wife-swapping.

Lord Erroll was a voracious womaniser who had been named as a 'very bad blackguard' by one shocked judge in an English divorce court. 'To hell with husbands' was the motto of this old Etonian, who seems

TROUBLED HOME The house at Karen which was leased by Jock Broughton to share with his young and beautiful new wife Diana.

particularly to have relished seducing the wives and girlfriends of his own upper-class friends and acquaintances. No one doubted the motive for the killing; 'Passionate Peer Gets His', read one headline, when news of the murder broke.

The chief suspect was quickly identified as 57-year-old Sir Henry 'Jock' Delves Broughton – the latest in a trail of wronged husbands. It was well known in Happy Valley that Jock Broughton's wife Diana had been having an affair with Erroll. At a party in the exclusive Muthaiga Country Club on December 22, 1940, the lovers had been seen dancing together locked in a passionate embrace. In the first week of January the following year they had shared a weekend together at a friend's home.

Early in January Broughton received the first of several spiteful anonymous notes: 'You seemed like a cat on hot bricks at the club last night. What about the eternal triangle? What are you going to do about it?' It would hardly be surprising if the injured husband did take violent action.

But he had never seemed greatly troubled by his wife's illicit liaison with the murdered peer. When he brought her from England to Kenya, a friend asked if he realised that every man in Nairobi was going to fall madly in love with her. Jock said, 'Oh, that's all right. I'm not the least bit jealous.'

Jock Broughton had been born into a great English landowning and horse-racing family. He had recently been divorced from his first wife and married Diana. Six weeks before they were married in a register office in Durban, Jock and Diana made a remarkable contract that if she should fall in love

with a younger man, he would not stand in the way of a divorce. Indeed, he would supply her with a gross income of £5000 a year for at least seven years. It was a peculiarly generous arrangement, which seemed to acknowledge Jock Broughton's low expectations of enduring loyalty or affection from his beautiful young wife.

When Diana's affair with Erroll became common knowledge Jock saw his lawyer about a divorce. In a letter to a friend he said: 'They say they are in love with each other and mean to get married. It is a hopeless position and I'm going to cut my losses. I think I'll go to Ceylon. There's nothing for me to live in Kenya for.'

The matter seemed to have been resolved amicably when on January 23, at a dinner at the Muthaiga Club, Jock Broughton toasted the lovers: 'I wish them every happiness, and may their union be blessed with an heir. To Diana and Joss.'

A 'blackguard' is murdered

At about 2 am the next day Broughton was driven home, reportedly rather drunk. Later Lord Erroll dropped Diana back at the Broughtons' house. Just 45 minutes later at around 3 am he was found dead in his Buick a couple of miles from the house. Erroll's body was found by two African dairy workers. The peer lay on the floor of his Buick which was plunged, with its headlights still blazing, at a steep angle into the sloping grass verge near a road junction.

At first the police could not identify the body in the Buick because it was crammed down into the space under the dashboard. When the police examined the corpse it was found to be Lord Erroll, who had been shot at point blank range with a .32 calibre revolver. Two shots had been fired in the car, and the fatal bullet had penetrated just behind the peer's left ear. The position of the wound, which was scorched with black powder, suggested that Lord Erroll had been

AN IMPERFECT MATCH The second Lady Broughton (above) was blonde with striking good looks, but she did not have a faithful heart. Months after marrying Jock Broughton (left) she fell for another man.

shot either by someone sitting in the front passenger seat, or through the open window from the running board. The precise manner in which the murder was accomplished still remains a puzzle.

When the police arrived at the Broughtons' house to take statements that morning they made no reference to murder, but said that Lord Erroll had broken his neck in a motor accident. Diana became too hysterical to face questioning, and Broughton's reaction was to ask 'Is he all right? Is he all right?'

Broughton made no attempt to hide the affair between his wife and the deceased. In fact Diana asked Jock to take something personal of hers to lay on Erroll's body, so he visited the mortuary and gave one of her handkerchiefs to one of the officers to leave on the body of his rival, with the words 'My wife was very much in love with Lord

Erroll.' However, the police were suspicious of Broughton's actions when he got home that afternoon; he built a large bonfire in the grounds of his home, and had it dowsed with petrol by his head boy. Later the charred remnant of a bloodstained golf sock was recovered from the ash.

The investigation began to focus more and more on the injured husband who had both motive and opportunity for the killing. Broughton could well have entered the Buick before Erroll drove away – whether secretly, forcibly, or quite openly, claiming that he had things to discuss with the murder victim. He could even have gone ahead to the intersection and flagged Erroll down on the road so as to murder his rival out of earshot of the house.

Suspicious behaviour

Broughton had come to the room of a houseguest, Mrs Carberry, at 3.30 am to ask if she needed anything and to say goodnight. This appeared to give him an alibi. But, had he hurried back after shooting Erroll and knocked on her door for just that reason?

Other suspicions were raised by the fact that only days before the murder, Broughton had reported a burglary to the police. He claimed that two revolvers, a cigarette case and a small sum of money had been stolen from the living room. One of the missing guns was a .32 calibre weapon

– and Erroll had been shot with a .32 calibre revolver. Was it possible that Broughton had faked the burglary in his house so that there should be no evidence of the murder weapon? This hints at a premeditation untypical of love triangle shootings. Was the

STICKY END Lord Erroll and his second wife, Molly, in London in 1937. She was one of many rich older women he courted. She died in 1939 from drink and drug abuse. He was shot dead in 1941 (left).

urbane 57-year-old Jock Broughton capable of such deviousness? The police case implied that he was.

Sir Henry Delves Broughton was arrested and charged with murder. He was tried in May 1941 at Nairobi's Central Court, and the public galleries overflowed with smartly dressed members of Kenya's elite. Diana, the grieving adulteress, came to court day after day in a succession of spectacularly elegant outfits; it was said that she never wore the same one twice. The world's

press watched too, as the prosecution witnesses locked horns in cross-examination with Broughton's brilliant South African defence counsel H.H. Morris.

In the end, the defence won the day. The police case rested strongly on ballistics evidence connecting the two murder bullets with Broughton's 'stolen' .32 calibre revolver. Experts testified that the bullets came from a gun which had scored them with five grooves and a right-hand twist. But the defence was able to prove that Broughton's two stolen guns were Colts – all Colts had six grooves and a twist to the left. Erroll had not then been shot with either of Broughton's guns.

When the verdict of 'not guilty' was announced in the packed courtroom there was an audible sigh of relief from the audience, and some clapping. But questions lingered long afterwards. If Broughton was innocent who was the killer? Another outraged husband? A scorned woman of the Happy Valley set? Or did Broughton hire an assassin to do the job for him?

After the trial Broughton took Diana on a cruise to Ceylon, but during the trip he sustained a paralysing back injury. In December 1942 he died in Liverpool, having taken a massive overdose of Medinal. Two suicide notes referred to his suffering, and the strain of the recent trial, but he did not admit to the murder. It has been reported that Broughton privately confessed his guilt to various acquaintances, but the stories do not entirely tally. In one version, Broughton planned the murder with an accomplice who had his own reasons for wanting Erroll dead, and they employed an African killer who hid in the back of the car. In another, Broughton shot Erroll himself and threw the gun away.

Later evidence suggests the killer was Diana herself, outraged at Erroll's attempt to end the relationship. A recently published book casts suspicion on Diana and suggests that Broughton covered up for her. But 'not guilty' was the verdict of the court, and a final judgment must remain suspended.

WHO KILLED SIR HARRY OAKES?

A BRUTAL MURDER IN A TROPICAL BRITISH COLONY THAT WAS DUBBED THE 'CRIME OF THE CENTURY'

THE MURDERED MILLIONAIRE Machete in hand, Sir Harry Oakes poses for a photograph. Below, the murder bedroom, with Sir Harry's body still on the bed.

winds and pelting rain. And next morning, dawn light played upon the burnt and battered corpse of Sir Harry Oakes – one of the islands' most prominent citizens.

Sir Harry's body was found in bed at his palatial home in Nassau. His skull had been fractured by four blows from a heavy object with one or more sharp points. The body had also been partially burnt, so that charred remnants of his flimsy pyjamas clung to his flesh. He was still alive – just – when he was set on fire, or the flesh would not have blistered as it did. Unaccountably, feathers from a pillow had been scattered over the corpse.

Set as it was in a millionaires' playground, the case was to become even more colourful through association with British royalty, Mafia interests, an aristocratic French playboy, black magic ritual, and a suspected Nazi spy . . . small wonder that the Oakes Case was billed in its day as the Crime of the Century.

SHUTTERED ROOM Sir Harry was killed in the room behind these shuttered windows.

Oakes was aged 69 at the time of his death. This American-born businessman had made his fortune as a gold prospector in Canada. To strengthen his connection with the country which had furnished his riches, Oakes renounced his US citizenship and became a Canadian.

The 'uncrowned king' of the Bahamas

He moved to the Bahamas, at that time a British colony, because of the tax advantages. Subsequently he poured millions of pounds into the islands, through both tourist development and charitable works. In 1939 Oakes was made a Baronet in recognition of his services to the British Empire.

He was regarded by many as the uncrowned king of the Bahamas, and when, in August 1940, the Duke of Windsor was appointed Governor-General of the islands, Sir Harry Oakes was among the first to welcome him. The duke, who was the former King Edward VIII of England, had provoked a constitutional crisis within the Empire when he abdicated his throne to marry the American divorcee Wallis Simpson. He had

White sands, turquoise seas and sparkling sunshine have made the Bahamas a paradise for millionaire tourists for many years. On the night of July 7, 1943, the thunder of a tropical storm rocked the capital Nassau, lashing the city with high

1939 Harry Oakes made a Baronet

1943 Sir Harry Oakes found murdered

GOOD FRIENDS Harry Oakes at a polo match with the Duke of Windsor (far left). The Duke called in US detectives Barker, Conway and Melchen (left) to investigate Oakes's death.

been appointed Governor-General of the Bahamas to isolate him from the intrigues and perils of wartime Europe. Sir Harry, the self-made millionaire, became good friends with the outcast duke, and they often played golf together.

On the morning that the tycoon's battered and burnt corpse was discovered, the Duke of Windsor was roused immediately from his sleep by an equerry.

The duke's actions on that fateful day were decidedly odd. He first invoked his authority under the Emergency War Powers Act to impose press censorship and try to hush the case up. In this he was frustrated, for the news had already been cabled out of the Bahamas and was making headlines around the world. Some hours afterwards – notably late in the day – he opened enquiries, not by handing the case over to the Bahamas police or to Scotland Yard, but by calling in a personal contact named Captain Edward Melchen from

the Miami police department. The duke's request was puzzling: 'I think one of our leading citizens has committed suicide. Can you come and confirm this?'

By no stretch of the imagination had Sir Harry killed himself. When Melchen arrived with a colleague named Barker to investigate

the case he came quickly to the point. 'Face up to it,' Melchen told the duke. 'This is no suicide.'

Harry Oakes had made many enemies on his road to riches, but the two American investigators settled very quickly on one man as prime suspect: Sir Harry's son-in-law, Alfred ('Freddie') de Marigny. This tall and dashing native of Mauritius had a reputation as a shiftless womaniser, and it was widely believed that he had married Sir Harry's eldest daughter only for her money. The murdered tycoon had quarrelled vigorously with the playboy on more than one occasion.

'Freddie' had been near Oakes's house late on the fateful night, while driving two dinner guests home. He had the opportunity for murder. Moreover, the American detectives discovered singed hairs on the suspect's arms, which they took to result from the fire that had burnt Sir Harry. The detectives' most damning accusation was that de Marigny's fingerprints were found on a Chinese screen in the murder bedroom.

But in the course of the ensuing much-publicised trial it became clear that the detectives had bungled badly or, more sinisterly, fabricated evidence to frame de Marigny. The significance of the singed hairs on the playboy's arms was quickly dismissed by the defence counsel with a witness's testimony that de Marigny had scorched himself while trying to

BAHAMAS QUARTET
Clockwise from top left: the accused playboy Alfred de Marigny; the Duke of Windsor; Swedish industrialist and mystery man Axel Wenner-Gren; Harold Christie, who found the body.

light a candle inside a lantern at the dinner party he had hosted that night. The defence demonstrated that the supposedly damning fingerprints could not have been taken from the Chinese screen as claimed, but must have come from a smooth, clean surface, probably a glass or cigarette packet which the detectives handed to de Marigny during questioning.

Other disquieting features of the investigation emerged. For example, it transpired that the Commissioner of the Police in the Bahamas had not believed in the case against de Marigny and had been transferred to Trinidad, with the result that he could not testify at the trial. Vital fingerprint evidence had been destroyed or ignored, including a bloody handprint on the wall; camera film of the handprint was mysteriously exposed to the light and ruined. Two watchmen who might have shed light on the murder – one

MAFIA MAN Meyer Lansky, a key figure in organised crime, has been connected with the Oakes murder case.

in the grounds of the Oakes house and another in the adjacent Nassau Country Club – had vanished without trace since the fatal event. It took the jury only two hours to reach their verdict – not guilty.

Many theories but no conclusions

No one else was ever charged with the crime. But many theories have been proposed to explain the case, and they often point to a Mafia connection through a tough, intelligent gangster called Meyer Lansky who ran the syndicate's operations in Florida and Cuba. Lansky badly wanted to open a gambling casino in Nassau, a city close to Miami and already well known to the mob's powerboat skippers, who had once used it as

a base for running bootleg alcohol into the United States. Gambling was illegal in the Bahamas, but perhaps that could be changed, through the influence of Sir Harry Oakes and the Duke of Windsor? According to one theory, Sir Harry was killed because he refused to be pushed around by the mob. In this version, the ritualistic elements of the murder – the fire and feathers – were seen as trademarks of a Mafia contract killing. It is interesting that Captain James Barker, one of the two Miami policemen brought into the case, was to die in 1952, corrupt and drug-addicted, on Meyer Lansky's payroll.

Suspicion has also fallen on Harold Christie, a Bahamian property developer who was Sir Harry Oakes's best friend. Christie had dined with Oakes on the fateful night and slept in a bedroom just down the corridor from the murder room; in fact it was he who discovered the body and raised the alarm. He and Oakes were the only two people in the house that night, and Christie swore on oath that he never left the building after going to bed at 11 pm. However, a local traffic policeman, Captain Edward Sears, testified that he saw Christie in George Street, Nassau, at 1 am on the day of the murder, travelling in a car speeding away from Nassau harbour.

Sears had known Christie all his life and had no apparent motive to lie. Although Christie was widely

FINGERPRINTING TO SOLVE MYSTERIES

A century of scientific crime detection opened in 1901 when a man named Edward Henry was put in charge of the Criminal Investigation Department at Scotland Yard. He had pioneered the classification of fingerprints as a means of identifying criminals while inspector-general of the Indian Police. Everyone, it had been discovered, had their own unique pattern of skin ridges. Henry's particular contribution was to discern, amid the infinite variety of loops, whorls, deltas and arches, five basic patterns which he then broke down into subdivisions.

Arch   Loop   Whorl   Composite

Spur   Crossover

Fork   Island

Enclosure   Ridge termination

POINTING THE FINGER In court an expert must show at least sixteen points of similarity between the prints from the scene of a crime and those of a suspect.

The first great test for Edward Henry's system of analysing fingerprints came in a case in 1905 when an elderly couple living above their shop in Deptford, London were murdered. Police managed to obtain a clear thumbprint from a cash box emptied out by the intruders. Suspicion fell on two young criminals – the Strattons – who were arrested. Their fingerprints were used as evidence in an historic trial. The prosecution pointed out eleven points of similarity between the thumb print of Alfred Stratton and that found on the cash box. The Strattons were found guilty and sent to the gallows.

Police forces worldwide soon began to build up card index files of fingerprints; these have been replaced since the 1980s with push-button electronic indexing, and computer systems that can match prints at a rate of 60,000 comparisons a second.

The traditional method for obtaining prints at the scene of a crime is to dust surfaces with a substance such as powdered aluminium, then place sticky tape over the mark to lift away an impression.

New technology has brought improvements. Since 1988 the FBI has been using laser and other devices to pick up fingerprints from such unpromising surfaces as Styrofoam cups. It has also now become possible to take a fingerprint from the body of a murder victim.

ACQUITTED De Marigny with his wife Nancy Oakes, pictured after he was found not guilty of murdering her father.

thought of as a public-spirited, kindly man, he may have had some involvement with rum-running to Florida during Prohibition. He may well have known more about the Harry Oakes case than ever emerged at the trial. One version of events proposes that he and Oakes both went to Nassau harbour on the fateful night, to meet emissaries from Meyer Lansky on a powerboat. The obdurate Oakes was beaten up there before being

TRAFFIC COP Captain Edward Sears, Bahamas chief of traffic police, gave important evidence at the de Marigny trial.

driven back to his home, with Christie shivering in the passenger seat. That could explain the mud tracks found on the stairs, and the evidence that suggested that, after being beaten, Sir Harry had been turned over or repositioned on the bed in some way. (Although the corpse was lying on its back, blood from a wound at the back of the head had run across the face, indicating that the corpse must have been face down at some time.)

Another more forthright accusation proposes that Christie killed Sir Harry because Oakes was about to ruin him financially. Some newly declassified FBI documents have been invoked to show that Nassau police believed Christie guilty at the time.

But there have been many other theories. One centres on the wealthy Swedish industrialist Axel Wenner-Gren, who had a house in the Bahamas and was well acquainted with Sir Harry Oakes and the Duke of Windsor. The Swede was also friendly with Hermann Goering and Mussolini, and was widely rumoured to be a Nazi spy. Wenner-Gren had set up a bank in Mexico, and some researchers believe that he was helping his Bahamian friends to evade wartime currency restrictions through its facilities. The big money, combined with

a pro-fascist government in Mexico, would have made Sir Harry a figure of key interest to both Allied and Axis intelligence. He could have fallen foul of either.

Other speculation focuses on the ritualistic elements of the murder. Some suggest that the fire and the feathers were linked with the Bahamian magical practice called Obeah, which is comparable in some ways to Haitian voodoo. Was Sir Harry Oakes killed by a witch-doctor hitman brought in from southern Florida? Some argue that the Duke of Windsor tried to hush up the case because the notion of such a prominent white citizen being victim of a black cult murder would inflame racial tensions on an island which had seen recent riots.

Whatever the truth, when in 1944 the Duke of Windsor was asked to reopen the case he refused. Not long after the end of the Second World War, the duke returned to Europe. He never again discussed the Oakes murder.

❝ DID THE DETECTIVES LIE?

In the trial of Alfred de Marigny for the murder of his father-in-law Sir Harry Oakes, a fingerprint, which was allegedly found on a Chinese screen next to Sir Harry's bed, was a key piece of the prosecution evidence.

During a brilliant cross-examination of Captain Barker, one of the investigating detectives on the case, the defence counsel, Godfrey Higgs, pulled no punches:

Q. I suggest that you and Captain Melchen deliberately planned to get the accused alone in order to get his fingerprints.

A. We did not.

Q. I suggest that Exhibit J did not come from that screen.

A. It did come from that screen, from the number five panel.

Q. You can show none of that scrollwork from the screen on Exhibit J, can you?

A. I cannot.

Q. This is the most outstanding case in which your expert assistance has ever been requested, is it not?

A. It has developed into that.

Q. May I suggest that your desire for personal gain and notoriety has caused you to sweep aside truth. I put it to you, sir, you have fabricated evidence! ❞

1983 Meyer Lansky
dies of cancer

HOW DID MARILYN DIE?

THE TRAGIC END OF A HOLLYWOOD SUPERSTAR SPARKS OFF YEARS OF CONTROVERSY

THE HOUSEKEEPER'S TALE Mrs Eunice Murray made strangely evasive, inconsistent statements about the time when she found Marilyn's body.

At 4.25 on the morning of August 5, 1962, the West Los Angeles police station received a telephone call: 'Marilyn Monroe is dead, she committed suicide.' About ten minutes later, on arrival at the film star's house on Fifth Helena Drive, Sergeant Jack Clemmons was led into Marilyn's bedroom where he found America's ultimate sex symbol lying naked, face downwards in bed with a sheet pulled over her body. On her bedside table, among various phials of drugs and medications, was an empty bottle of Nembutal sleeping pills.

The housekeeper, Mrs Eunice Murray, who had discovered the body, Marilyn's psychiatrist, Ralph Greenson, and her doctor, Hyman Engelberg, were present when the police arrived. The conclusion seemed clear

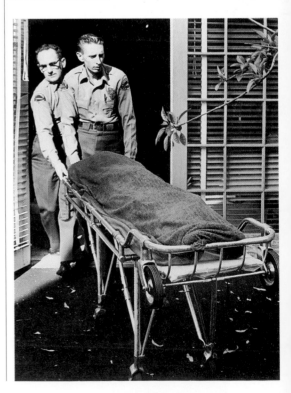

A FINAL SCENE The bedroom where Marilyn Monroe was found dead. The housekeeper, Eunice Murray, and a policeman are just visible through the doorway.

enough: the depressed actress, who had been fired by 20th Century-Fox from the filming of *Something's Got to Give*, had swallowed an overdose of sleeping pills, either in a deliberate attempt to take her own life or in a dangerous gamble with death. Marilyn had long been reliant on a psychiatrist to help her to cope with the pressures of superstardom, and was habitually taking drugs to

cope with her insomnia and nerves. Her work was suffering; the studio had fired her for persistent lateness. In *Life* magazine, the actress had spoken of her difficulties. 'Everybody is always tugging at you. They would all like sort of a chunk of you.'

The autopsy revealed that Marilyn's blood contained 8 mg of chloral hydrate (a relatively mild sedative which the film star was taking) and 4.5 mg of the stronger sleeping pill, Nembutal. Moreover, there was a much higher concentration of Nembutal – 13 mg – in the liver. These quantities greatly exceeded normal therapeutic doses, and in combination had proved lethal. There were no external signs of violence, and so the coroner's verdict was one of 'probable suicide'. On August 8, following a quiet service for relatives and friends at the Westwood Village Mortuary, the body adored by millions was laid to rest.

Only after the mourners had left were the crowds of journalists, photographers, celebrities and Hollywood hangers-on admitted to the cemetery garden. In the judgment of some close to Marilyn, the superstar had been killed by the monstrous pressures of her public legend.

The questions begin

But had quite different forces connived at her death? There were discrepancies in the official verdict. For example, no residue of pills had been found in Marilyn's stomach during the autopsy. If the actress had recently swallowed a handful of Nembutal capsules, they should have left the yellow coloured dye of their gelatine jackets in her stomach; but no such residue was present. Had she been injected with the fatal dose? If so, by whom?

Further inconsistencies surrounded the precise timing of Marilyn's death. The housekeeper, Eunice Murray, at first told the police that she had found the body 'about midnight' but later changed the time of discovery to 'about three o'clock'. Detective Sergeant Robert E. Byron, in control of the

case, found Mrs Murray particularly vague and evasive in answering questions about this critical period. In fact, from early the night before, friends of the actress had become aware that something was very wrong with her. Between 7 and 7.15 pm Marilyn had been chatting cheerfully on the phone to the son of Joe DiMaggio, the baseball star who had been her former husband.

LAST EXIT The film star's blanketed body is wheeled out on a stretcher from her home on Fifth Helena Drive.

1926 Marilyn born
Norma Jean Mortenson
(later changed to Baker)

1942 Marilyn
marries James
Dougherty

1946 Marilyn
gets her first
film contract

ON STARDOM Marilyn mistrusted her own legend. 'A sex symbol becomes a thing,' she said. 'I hate being a thing.'

But only half-an-hour later she was rung by the British actor Peter Lawford (married to President Kennedy's sister Pat) and was speaking in thick, slurred, almost inaudible tones. At the end of their conversation, with great effort, Marilyn managed to say: 'Say goodbye to Pat, say goodbye to the president, and say goodbye to yourself, because you're a nice guy.'

Lawford was seriously alarmed and rang round various friends trying to persuade them to go over to her house. It now appears that well before midnight, information had reached Milton Rudin, Marilyn's attorney, and Arthur Jacobs, her publicist, that Marilyn was dead.

What happened at Fifth Helena Drive in the four-and-a-half hours before the police were called to the scene?

Extraordinary comings and goings at Marilyn's house have been alleged, with tales of plain-clothes men who burnt tapes and

ON THE LINKS President J.F. Kennedy (third from left) golfing in Florida with his brother-in-law Peter Lawford (far right).

documents in the fireplace, and of missing phone records. Soon after her death sensational claims charged the family of President J.F. Kennedy with a politically motivated murder. Marilyn, it has been suggested, had been having an affair with the president's younger brother, Attorney-General Bobby Kennedy; Bobby made promises of marriage, and when he tried to ditch her she threatened to go public with the story so the Kennedys had Marilyn murdered to shut her up. Afterwards the house on

1954 Marries and divorces Joe DiMaggio
1956 Marries Arthur Miller
1962 Found dead

1926 Marilyn born
Norma Jean Mortenson
(later changed to Baker)

1942 Marilyn
marries James
Dougherty

1946 Marilyn
gets her first
film contract

THE BROTHERS The names of John F. Kennedy (right) and Bobby Kennedy (far right) have both been linked with Marilyn Monroe's death.

Fifth Helena Drive was thoroughly sanitised to dispose of incriminating evidence before the police arrived.

Taking another look

The story hit the headlines again in 1973 with the publication of a biography, *Marilyn*, by Norman Mailer. In his book, Mailer speculated that Robert Kennedy might have been involved in Marilyn's death; or that she might have been killed by government agents in an attempt to frame the attorney-general. The book sparked a flurry of sensational books, TV investigations, dramatisations, memoirs and magazine articles all compounding the sense of mystery with new allegations; it was said that Marilyn's home had been wire-tapped by men acting on orders from Robert Kennedy's arch enemy, union boss Jimmy Hoffa. A Mafia connection was also alleged; the CIA and the Mafia had cooperated in an attempt to overthrow the communist regime in Cuba, and 'Boss of Bosses' Sam Giancana allegedly feared that in damaging the Kennedys, Marilyn might damage a valuable relationship with the government.

In a meticulously researched biography published in 1993, author Donald Spoto dismissed such stories as fantasies which originated in smears by right-wing factions hostile to the Kennedys. He said that there was no evidence of any affair with Robert Kennedy, and that Marilyn was not especially depressed at the time of her death; on the contrary, Fox intended to reinstate her in

OFF THE SET Marilyn between scenes during the filming of *The Misfits* – written by her third husband, Arthur Miller.

ILL-FATED MOVIE Both Monroe and her co-star Clark Gable died shortly after making *The Misfits* in the Nevada desert.

'SAY GOODBYE TO THE PRESIDENT'

It has often been alleged that Robert Kennedy was involved in Marilyn's life and her death. Equally sensational claims have also been made that the actress once had an affair with Bobby's elder brother, President John F. Kennedy. These stories have more substance, for while Bobby was a devoted husband, the president had a reputation as a womaniser. It is known that Monroe and JFK met at least four times between October 1961 and May 1962, and that on Saturday, March 24, 1962, Marilyn and the president spent a night together while they were house guests of Bing Crosby at Palm Springs. They even phoned one of Marilyn's friends, Ralph Roberts, from a bedroom there. A passionate, long-term liaison has been reported by some but, according to Roberts, 'Marilyn gave me the impression that it was not a major event for either of them; it happened once, that weekend, and that was that'.

The last known occasion on which the two supposed lovers met was at a celebrated birthday gala for the president, held at Madison Square Garden in May 1962.

BIRTHDAY GREETINGS A sexy 'happy birthday' song, in front of a crowd of 20 000, was Marilyn's gift to the president.

LOVERS' TRYST? Marilyn's last meeting with JFK was at his birthday party at Madison Square Garden in New York.

needle shot, which would have caused instant death, a much higher level of barbiturate in the blood and a conspicuous bruise on the body). Instead, Greenson recommended an enema, a powerful and quite fashionable method of administering the drug.

The fatal enema was, it is alleged, administered by the housekeeper Eunice Murray – untrained as a nurse – after Greenson left. The slow absorption of the drug gave Marilyn time to take Lawford's phone call and deliver her last, slurred utterances.

If this was indeed how Marilyn died, the housekeeper – recently given notice to quit – would have had to face some awkward questions from the police, and Greenson's professional reputation would have been ruined. Perhaps they combined efforts to remove any trace of their involvement in the death of the woman who was in their care.

When Marilyn slipped into a drug-induced coma, she would have expelled the enema, soiling bed clothes and any nightwear. Here, perhaps, lies the explanation for the time lapse between Marilyn's death and discovery and the call to the police. When the police arrived at the house Eunice Murray was inexplicably washing linen and garments. 'Why, under these circumstances,' the deputy district attorney later asked, 'would a housekeeper be doing the laundry at such an hour?'

THE PSYCHIATRIST Dr Ralph Greenson with his wife. The couple were among the mourners at the movie star's funeral.

Something's Got to Give, and she was planning to marry Joe DiMaggio for a second time. She was taking control of her own life with new confidence.

How, then, to explain the mysterious time lapse between death and police discovery? And how to explain the lack of capsule residue in Marilyn's stomach? Spoto's attention focused on three characters hitherto regarded as very minor actors in the drama: the housekeeper, Eunice Murray, the psychiatrist, Ralph Greenson and the doctor, Hyman Engelberg. Greenson had stopped prescribing Nembutal for the actress and was weaning her onto chloral hydrate. Unknown to him, however, Engelberg had continued

LAST RESTING PLACE Marilyn's funeral casket stands in front of the curtain-covered crypt where she was finally laid to rest.

to prescribe Nembutal. It was a combination of these drugs that killed Marilyn. The actress had taken a powerful dose of Engelberg's prescription earlier in the day, but not all of it had been metabolised by the evening when, it is alleged, Greenson arranged for Marilyn to take the sedative chloral hydrate. There was no injection (when the district attorney reviewed the case in 1982 he rejected the possibility of lethal

THE FATE OF DORA BLOCH

WHAT HAPPENED TO THE GREY-HAIRED GRANDMOTHER WHO VANISHED AT ENTEBBE?

For sheer drama, few news stories of modern times could match the Entebbe Raid. On the night of July 3, 1976, Air France flight 139 sat on the tarmac of Entebbe airport. It had been hijacked a week earlier by Palestinian terrorists, and Uganda's pro-Palestinian government had given the aircraft sanctuary. Then out of the darkness appeared three Hercules transport planes filled with Israeli commandos on a daring mission to rescue the 105 hostages.

After a furious gun battle, involving commandos, terrorists and Ugandan soldiers, the freed hostages were in the transporter planes and heading home to Israel. The swoop was justly celebrated as a triumph for the Israelis, and for counter-terrorism worldwide.

SADLY MISSED Mrs Dora Bloch, photographed here with her granddaughter, missed the escape from Entebbe.

UNDER ESCORT 'Major' Bob Astles, Amin's adviser, in the custody of Ugandan soldiers. Did he order the death of Dora Bloch?

However, after the raid on Entebbe one of the passengers from the hijacked plane was missing – a 75-year-old grandmother named Dora Bloch, who had been on her way to her son's wedding in New York.

The Ugandan authorities revealed that Mrs Bloch had been 'released' on the day before the air raid and admitted to Mulago General Hospital in Kampala. The day after the raid, a British Embassy official visited her there. She was guarded by two plainclothes men who indicated that she would soon be taken to the Imperial Hotel in Kampala. But just one hour later, when the official returned with some food for the patient, he was denied entry. No one at the hospital could say what had happened to her, and the Ugandan authorities said only that Mrs Bloch was missing and was being searched for. They added that, from the time of the Israeli raid, Uganda had ceased to be responsible for Mrs Bloch.

On July 7 the Ugandan Ministry of Health further muddied the waters by asserting that Mrs Bloch had in fact been returned to the hijacked aircraft before the raid, a story which was obviously untrue.

Where had Dora Bloch gone? Eyewitnesses reported that the grey-haired old lady had been dragged screaming from her bed. Although it was accepted fairly quickly that she was dead, no one could say for certain until 1979, when Amin's regime was overthrown. With a new government in Kampala, investigators were at last able to piece together her fate. They discovered that four Ugandan secret policemen had come to the hospital, dragged her from her bed and bundled her screaming into a waiting Mercedes. 'I saw armed men carrying machine guns pulling her down the stairs. They were firing to frighten people out of the way,' recalled a doctor.

She was then taken to a forest and shot. In 1979, Dora Bloch's remains were recovered from an unmarked grave at a place called Nakapinyi and brought to Israel for burial.

But who was responsible for Mrs Bloch's murder? Did Amin order the killing in

NOTORIOUS AFRICAN DICTATOR The whereabouts of former Ugandan president Idi Amin are currently unknown.

revenge for the humiliation of Entebbe? According to Amin's British aide, 'Major' Bob Astles, the secret police had acted of its own accord: 'I think, in all honesty, that he was ashamed that his State Research Bureau had killed her.' One man who knows the answer is Amin himself, whose whereabouts have themselves provided an enduring mystery since his overthrow and exile.

1900   2000

1902 Dora Bloch born

1971 Coup brings Amin to power
1976 Air raid on Entebbe
1979 Amin overthrown

THE DEADLY UMBRELLA

THE FURTIVE JAB THAT ENDED THE LIFE OF BULGARIAN DISSIDENT GEORGI MARKOV

One September evening in 1978 a Bulgarian author and broadcaster working for the BBC World Service was killed on a busy street in London by a poisoned umbrella point. Georgi Markov had just finished work at the BBC and was waiting for a bus on Waterloo Bridge. Suddenly, something jabbed him sharply in the thigh from behind. As he looked round, he saw a thick-set man pick up an umbrella that had fallen to the ground. The man muttered an apology in a voice with a heavy foreign accent, jumped into a taxi and disappeared.

Back home in Clapham after dinner, Markov began to feel sick. When he was no

WORRIED MAN Markov feared for his life. He believed that his defection and his criticism of Bulgaria's communist regime made him a target for assassination.

better the next day he mentioned the umbrella episode to his wife, Annabel. 'I have a horrible feeling that this may be connected with something that happened yesterday,' he told her, and showed her the small puncture mark on his thigh. With his temperature soaring to a feverish level, Markov was rushed off to St James's Hospital in Balham. The doctors there at first took his symptoms for those of septicaemia, a blood infection, but he did not respond to treatment with antibiotics, and fell into a coma. Four days after being admitted to the south London hospital Georgi Markov died of a heart attack.

An enemy of the state

The incident might have been taken for a natural death but for Markov's own insistence that the umbrella incident had caused his fever. His past had made him suspicious.

In 1961 he had published two volumes of short stories, the success of which had resulted in his joining an elite corps of Bulgarian writers. He was a regular visitor to Mount Vitosha, where many leaders of the Zhivkov regime had villas. But Markov's skill for satire made him unpopular in the corridors of power, and in 1969 he defected to Britain. There he began working for the World Service and Radio Free Europe. In his broadcasts and writing the defector did not shrink from criticising the Bulgarian authorities.

Unlike many defectors from the East, Markov had not been assigned an 'uncle' from the British secret service to look after him, but he was a potential target for assassination. So when he died suddenly, protesting that he had been attacked, his body was examined carefully.

Several days after Markov's death a tiny metal ball made

FRONT PAGE NEWS Headlines in Britain announced that the examination of Georgi Markov's corpse had led to the discovery of a minuscule metal projectile in his leg.

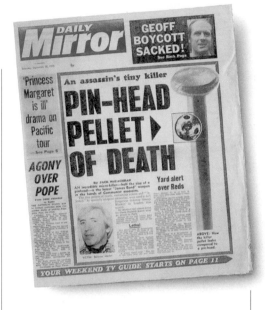

from an alloy of platinum and iridium, and no bigger than a pinhead, was found embedded in his leg. Microscopic examination revealed that two tiny holes had been precisely drilled into the pellet.

The inquest into Markov's death was held on January 2, 1979. Expert witnesses testified that the pellet found in Markov's leg had probably been filled with ricin – a poison derived from the castor-oil plant and twice as lethal as cobra venom. Experts also testified

EVERYDAY KILLER The lethal weapon which killed Markov could have been a specially adapted umbrella. The murderer would fire the fatal pellet by pulling a trigger in the handle.

that it was possible that the lethal pellet had been fired through the tip of an umbrella by a device hidden inside. In the light of the evidence the court returned a verdict of unlawful killing.

The Markov attack was not unique; Vladimir Kostov, the former head of the Bulgarian state radio and TV network, who had defected to the West in 1977, had been attacked in a similar way in Paris a few weeks before the Markov attack. As Mr Kostov emerged from the Arc de Triomphe station on the Paris Métro he was hit in the back by a pellet identical to the one used on Markov. Then in October 1978 a Bulgarian exile, Vladimir Simeonov, died in London in mysterious circumstances.

Was Zhivkov's regime in Bulgaria delivering warnings to potential defectors overseas? The Bulgarian authorities of the time denied any involvement with Markov's killing, but

OTHER VICTIMS Markov's friend Vladimir Kostov (left) was shot by a pellet identical to the one that killed Markov. Vladimir Simeonov (right) died mysteriously in London only a month after Markov.

after the overthrow of the regime in 1989 the new government accepted that the murder had been performed at the request of the old communist regime. Oleg Kalugin, a former KGB chief, has also stated that the Russian authorities furnished the Bulgarians with the necessary equipment with which to conduct the assassination.

Despite these new leads, headlines in 1991 which trumpeted the imminent arrest of the killer proved false. Precisely who killed Georgi Markov is still a mystery, and the file at Scotland Yard remains open.

THE STRANGER-THAN-FICTION WEAPONS OF SECRET ASSASSINS

The poisoned umbrella that killed Georgi Markov was just one among many ingenious weapons devised for assassination in the 20th century. During the Second World War, Britain's Special Operations Executive invented various tools for its secret agents which were worthy of 'Q' from the James Bond stories: a gas gun disguised as a fountain pen, and even an exploding cowpat for saboteurs to place in the path of oncoming tanks.

In 1954 a trained Soviet assassin who had been sent to kill the leader of a Russian exile group in Germany gave himself up instead to the man he was supposed to kill. Concealed in the battery of his car were a variety of murder weapons, including a gold cigarette case that silently fired poisoned dumdum bullets when it was squeezed at the base.

In 1961 another member of the KGB execution squad defected and brought Soviet secrets to the West. His name was Bogdan Stashynsky, and he confessed to the murders of two anticommunist exiles: Lev Rebet in 1957 and Stefan Bandera in 1959. Both appeared to have died of heart attacks, but the assassin told how he had killed them with a finger-thick metal tube, about 7 in (17 cm) long. It fired a spray of prussic acid into the victim's face, causing death when the vapour was inhaled but leaving no trace in the body. The killer protected himself by taking an antidote just before the attack and another afterwards.

DEADLY DEVICE An artist's reconstruction shows how the murder weapon may have worked.

Release catch

Tensioned spring propels the piston hammer forward when released

Piston hammer

As the piercer released the gas the pellet would have been fired

Poison pellet

Gas cylinder

Piercer

Screw-on gun barrel

POISON PELLET Two tiny holes in the pellet are believed to have contained deadly poison.

1961 Markov publishes short stories

1969 Markov defects

1975 Markov marries

1978 Markov dies

1989 End of dictatorship

THE SUSPICIOUS DEATH OF 'GOD'S BANKER'

THE BODY OF ROBERTO CALVI HUNG UNDER A BRIDGE AMID THE RUINS OF HIS FINANCIAL EMPIRE

On the evening of Saturday, June 12, 1982, Italian television's main news bulletins announced that the financier Roberto Calvi had disappeared. Calvi was the head of Italy's most important private bank – Banco Ambrosiano – and had for some time been the subject of rumour. At the time he was awaiting an appeal against a four-year prison sentence for currency offences. He had also been exposed as a member of P-2, an

GOD'S BANKER Roberto Calvi's Banco Ambrosiano had loaned millions to companies owned by the Vatican.

outlawed masonic lodge. Calvi's vanishing act was newsworthy enough; what followed astonished the world.

The following Friday, Roberto Calvi's body was discovered in London, dangling from scaffolding under Blackfriars Bridge. The corpse hung from a nylon rope which had been noosed around the neck and fastened to the scaffolding by two half-hitch knots. A false passport bearing the name Gian Roberto Calvini was found in his pockets, which were also stuffed with £7400 in cash, in a range of currencies. More than 10 lb (4.5 kg) of broken bricks were crammed in his pockets and down his trousers. They had apparently acted as weights to guarantee the financier his death.

The gruesome discovery precipitated the collapse of the already faltering Banco Ambrosiano, a financial disaster which not only shook the international banking system but also rocked the Vatican.

Banco Ambrosiano and the Vatican Bank (IOR) were intricately connected. Calvi had been, it was said, 'God's Banker'. Even the bank's balance sheet carried the words 'Thanks be to God'.

Ambrosiano had channelled hundreds of millions of dollars, loaned from banks around the world, to hollow 'front' companies in Central and South America.

The companies were rumoured to be involved in money laundering for the Mafia and were controlled by the Vatican via a holding company. But the money simply disappeared, and Banco Ambrosiano began to sink under the pressure of the loans.

There were allegations that the missing millions had been channelled into Italian political parties, into the sinister P-2 freemasons, and even into the Polish

11.17 pm

1.15 am

2.07 am

3.10 am

DUBIOUS SUICIDE The changing height of the water with the tides made a nonsense of some of the suicide theories. The plank which Calvi was assumed to have walked along would have been under water at 2 am.

trade union Solidarity (a cause close to the heart of the Pope). Calvi's struggling bank could be saved only if the Vatican agreed to repay some of the money lent to the companies. But the Vatican refused to be held responsible for the financial activities of companies simply held in its name.

Against this infinitely complex backdrop, the human drama of the financier's death posed one immediate question. Did Calvi hang himself? Or was he dropped from the bridge by unknown hands?

Had Calvi taken his own life?

From the outset the police in London treated the case as a suicide, and this was also the verdict of jurors at the inquest held in July. There was no sign of violence on Calvi's body, nor any evidence that he had been drugged. The motive seemed obvious: the financier had seen the ruin of his empire and was probably facing a four-year prison sentence. He had reportedly made a previous suicide attempt in police custody.

It was not impossible to believe that he succumbed to despair in London. But clambering across scaffolding in the middle of the night was an odd way for an overweight Italian banker who suffered from vertigo to

1920 Calvi
born in Milan

THE RECENTLY DECEASED Calvi's body, photographed minutes after he was found and cut down from his modern-day gibbet.

kill himself. Why go to Blackfriars anyway when he had enough barbiturates in his hideaway in Chelsea to kill himself privately and without the risk of pain? Calvi's family were convinced that he had been murdered, and they insisted that Calvi had not been depressed in his last days but had been frightened for his own safety and that of his family. People were threatening him, perhaps people who wanted to silence him before his appeal hearings in Italy. In order to save himself and his bank, Calvi had told his family that he was willing to 'name some names'.

The arguments of Calvi's family and complaints about the thoroughness of the first inquest had an effect; in June 1983 a second London inquest examined the case over a period of 11 days in far more detail. The suicide verdict seemed increasingly unlikely. Calvi's wristwatch, which was badly damaged by water, had stopped at around two o'clock in the morning, and at that time the Thames tides would have made the approach to the place where Calvi died extremely tricky, involving clambering over the upper part of the scaffolding. Expert witnesses testified that it was 'possible' but very difficult. How much more difficult carrying a load of bricks? However, at 2 am the water would have been at the perfect height for a small

BEHIND BARS A Calvi associate, Sicilian swindler Michele Sindona, on trial in Milan for complicity in a murder.

THE SHADOWY HAND OF THE MAFIA

Often in 20th-century mysteries of death or disappearance, research hints at a Mafia involvement. It has been discerned in cases as different as the Calvi affair, the Kennedy assassination and the murder of Sir Harry Oakes. The Syndicate's interests extend from gambling, narcotics and prostitution into the worlds of high finance, show business and big government.

The Mafia began in Sicily as a network of gangs, or 'families', hired by local landowners to protect their estates. Members began to operate protection rackets among fruit-pickers, taxi drivers and other

tradesmen, demanding regular payments to allow people to earn a living. Mafia families were bound by *omerta* (manliness), a code of honour and silence. They came to the USA as an invisible presence among the poor Sicilian immigrants who streamed across the Atlantic in the late 19th and early 20th centuries. There Mafia gangs developed interests in gambling and in labour unions and, in particular, in the bootleg liquor industry during the Prohibition years. After fierce feuding ended in a bloody purge in 1931, a new nationwide Mafia emerged, based on cooperation between mobs.

The Second World War brought an unlikely alliance with US intelligence. Sicilian gangsters and American spies shared a mutual interest in eradicating Benito Mussolini, and the Mafia cooperated with the Allies in the invasion of Italy. These links were revived in America's postwar struggle against communism – both the CIA and the Mafia wanted to see Castro ousted from Cuba (the Mafia wanted to develop gambling on the island).

Within the United States, the Mafia flourished under the name of *Cosa Nostra* (Our Thing). However, little was known about the hierarchy until 1963 when former gangster Joe Valachi (right), broke the code of silence and told all he knew. Cosa Nostra, it emerged, was run by five bosses: Vito Genovese, Carlo Gambino (above left), Giuseppe Magliocco, Joseph Bonnano and Gaetano Lucchese. Despite detailed knowledge of the organisation's structure, however, convictions remain rare.

In the United States the Mafia remains a powerful force, and in Italy its influence is a national scandal. The extent of its influence was exemplified in 1995 when former premier Giulio Andreotti was brought to trial for alleged Mafia dealings.

boat to approach the scaffolding and for a body to be strung up. The damage to Calvi's neck was insufficient for a free-fall when he dropped from the scaffold. The water must have been at a height to break his fall. More expert testimony made it seem possible that the banker might have been drugged after all, perhaps by inhalation. With the evidence mounting against suicide, the jury returned an open verdict.

In Italy in 1989 a court took things further, recording a verdict of murder. If Calvi was murdered, there is no shortage of theories as to who did it and why.

The Freemasons

Calvi had headed the financial wing of the outlawed P-2 Masonic Lodge, and it was rumoured that he was involved both with exiled Italian fascist groups and with South

1952 Married Clara Canetti

1965 Made president of Banco Ambrosiano

1975 Made chairman of Banco Ambrosiano

1982 Found hanged – first inquest

1989 Italian court returns murder verdict

1996 Gangster confesses to Calvi's murder

CALVI CONNECTIONS   Left to right: Bettino Craxi, Italian premier at the time; Archbishop Marcinkus, president of the Vatican Bank; Flavio Carboni, convicted of illegal possession of Calvi's briefcase.

American arms-trafficking through Freemasonry. There were several hints of masonic ritual about Calvi's death. A black friar is said to be the symbol of the P-2 Lodge; broken bricks (such as those found in Calvi's pockets) symbolise a discredited or failed Freemason; and the initiation of a new Mason is said to include a symbolic noose around the neck and a vow which threatens that he will be killed and left 'where the tide regularly ebbs and flows twice in 24 hours', should he break the code of silence. Had Calvi been discovered a few hours later, his body would have been soaked twice by the Thames tides.

The Vatican connection

Calvi told his lawyers that he had channelled $50 million to the Polish trade union Solidarity on behalf of the Vatican. 'If the whole thing comes out,' he said, 'it'll be enough to start the Third World War.'

Not only that, but his daughter maintained that Calvi was in London to do a deal to bail out his struggling bank and to get back at the 'priests' who he felt had let him down. *Opus Dei* (God's Work), a small right-wing Catholic organisation, is a prime candidate for such a deal, which would have had repercussions on the balance of power within the Vatican. Clara Calvi, the victim's widow, maintained in the newspaper *La*

Stampa that her husband's murder was engineered by a left-wing Catholic faction which was hostile to his connection with Opus Dei.

The Mafia theory

An odour of the Mafia lingered about Banco Ambrosiano affairs. Calvi had for many years had close dealings with the Sicilian tax lawyer Michele Sindona, who was later convicted of perjury, misappropriation of funds and murder. Sindona was also heavily implicated in money-laundering for the Mafia. He had introduced Calvi to the Vatican Bank – a lucrative connection – but when Sindona's own bank in Milan had collapsed, losing the Vatican millions of dollars, Calvi had managed to distance himself from the affair and would not help Sidona, thus making a powerful enemy.

In 1991 a reliable Sicilian supergrass under US protection testified that a prominent Mafioso living in Britain 'killed Calvi with his bare hands' and rigged up his body under the bridge. The witness, Francesco 'Mozzarella' Mannoia, said that the financier was murdered for playing fast and loose in a Mafia money-laundering operation.

The case is still wide open years later

The affair simply refused to die. One of its puzzles was the disappearance of Calvi's briefcase, from which he was normally inseparable. It was reputed to contain bunches of keys to safe-deposit boxes, as well as incriminating documents.

Incredibly, the briefcase turned up in Italy in 1986 when two Rome 'businessmen' attempted to sell documents from it to a

minor Vatican official, who reportedly was prepared to pay millions for the contents.

The courts later heard that the briefcase had appeared via Flavio Carboni, a Sardinian businessman who had acted as a 'fixer' for Calvi and had been one of the last people to see him alive in London. Carboni was convicted of illegally possessing the briefcase and was also sentenced to 15 years' jail for irregularities relating to Banco Ambrosiano's final collapse with huge debts. Those irregularities seemed endless.

In 1994 the case came sensationally alive again when the Socialist leader Bettino Craxi – a former Italian prime minister – was sentenced in his absence by a Milan court to eight-and-a-half years' imprisonment. The charges related to a sum of $7 million paid by Calvi's bank to a Swiss account controlled by Craxi. The prosecution alleged that the payment was made to reward politicians for helping Calvi's bank to obtain a loan from a state energy holding.

In 1996 newspaper headlines trumpeted the solution to the death of Roberto Calvi. Frank 'the strangler' Di Carlo, a Corleone gangster, had reportedly confessed to murdering Calvi for the Mafia. However, an arrest was never made.

Top churchmen, Socialists, Fascists, Freemasons, Mafia leaders and international arms dealers . . . all move like shadows through this affair. The collapse of the Banco Ambrosiano brought many unsavoury realities to light, but the secrets of Calvi's own death are still lost in a dark labyrinth of possibilities, and as far as the London police are concerned the case remains open.

INVISIBLE EMPIRES

THE SECRET NETWORKS AND INTERCONNECTIONS THAT RUN UNKNOWN THROUGH EVERYDAY LIFE MAY NOURISH SINISTER AIMS AND HIDDEN AGENDAS

When the body of Italian banker Roberto Calvi was found dangling from scaffolding under London's Blackfriars Bridge many investigators suspected a Masonic involvement. The secret society to which Calvi belonged is in some countries as much a part of the establishment as organised religion. Yet its aims and work are mysteries which are surrounded by tales of strange rituals. Many aspects of Calvi's death bore marks of Masonic ritual.

During the initiation rites a new recruit stands in his shirt with his left breast bared, the right sleeve rolled up past his elbow and his left trouser leg pulled up past the knee. On his left foot he wears a shoe, on his right, a slipper, so that he limps as he is led through the temple door by a hangman's rope noosed around his neck. Later he is made to swear with a dagger at his bared breast that he will not betray the secrets of the movement, on penalty of 'having my throat cut across, my tongue torn out by the root and buried in the sand of the sea at low water mark'.

Freemasonry is thought to have developed out of the guilds formed by medieval stonemasons to protect the secrets of their trade. The masons' lodge was originally their workshop and place of assembly, where news was exchanged and grievances discussed. Modern Freemasonry dates from 1717 when a Grand Lodge was established in England, and the movement subsequently spread to continental Europe and to America. Today there are thought to be about 9250 lodges around the world.

KKK TRADITION   Ku Klux Klan meetings are full of ritual drama, such as burning crosses and wearing sinister disguises.

Although its declared aims are to promote good works and spread brotherly love in the name of the 'Great Architect of the Universe', the movement has long provoked criticism from outsiders for acting as a secret interest group responsible to no one but itself.

The Fiery Cross

The same criticisms have been levelled at other sinister secret societies which wield power independent of democratic control. The Ku Klux Klan in the United States sprang up in Nashville, Tennessee, after the American Civil War, to prevent blacks from using their newly won right to vote. Cloaked and hooded Klansmen directed by a 'grand wizard', burning fiery crosses, rode out by night to lash and lynch their victims. Known as the 'Invisible Empire of the South', the movement won widespread support and reduced the Black vote, restoring White control over local government. The Klan promoted white Protestant interests in public life against Catholics, Jews and immigrants as well as Blacks, and its influence spread outside the South. A Klan involvement was suspected by some in the 1922 Lovers' Lane killing.

In 1923, 30 New York City policemen were exposed as Klansmen. During the 1950s and 1960s the Ku Klux Klan opposed the civil rights movement and, despite many prosecutions of members for acts of violence, the movement is still active in the South.

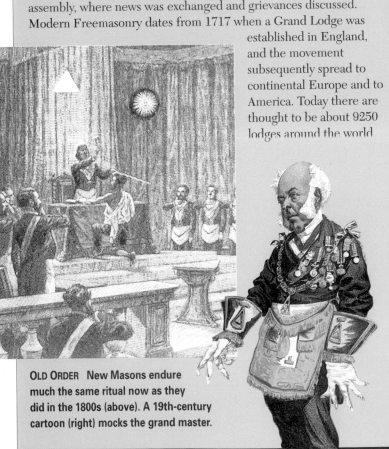

OLD ORDER   New Masons endure much the same ritual now as they did in the 1800s (above). A 19th-century cartoon (right) mocks the grand master.

THE GREGORY AFFAIR

THE MURDER OF A CHILD WHICH UNLEASHED SUSPICION AND HATE IN A VILLAGE IN THE VOSGES

On a chill October afternoon in 1984, the body of four-year-old Gregory Villemin, clad in a blue anorak, was fished out of the fast-flowing Vologne river in the Vosges region of eastern France. His hands and feet were tightly bound with twine.

It was the beginning of a nightmare that would drag on for almost a decade, plunging the Villemin family into a vortex of suspicion and hatred.

Gregory was the only child of Jean-Marie and Christine Villemin, part of an extended family with deep roots in the isolated Vologne valley. Jean-Marie was the foreman in a local car plant; his wife worked in a factory. They were comfortably off by local standards and lived in Lépanges, a few miles from where their son's body was discovered.

On the day of Gregory's death, an anonymous letter was sent to his parents from the village post office. Written in clumsy capitals, it exulted: 'Now look where you are with all your lolly. The chief's son is dead and I have my revenge. May you die of sorrow too.' That was the last known message from Le Corbeau – The Crow – a mysterious figure who had plagued the entire Villemin clan for several years with poison-pen letters and malicious telephone calls.

Jean-Marie and his wife particularly had suffered from the attentions of The Crow, who had bombarded them with abusive phone calls for years – in a voice that was so distorted with rage that it could not even be identified as that of a man or a woman.

The Crow was an obvious, but anonymous, suspect. The police set about trying to identify him or her. The post-mortem had found no traces of a struggle on

Gregory's body, and the low level of adrenaline in his blood implied that he might have known his murderer well enough not to panic even when he was tied up.

After the funeral, experts examined handwriting samples from 130 members of the Villemin family. As a result they named Jean-

REVENGE When Gregory Villemin was recovered from the river Vologne (above), his parents received an anonymous, gloating letter (left).

Marie's cousin, Bernard Laroche, as The Crow. The news stunned the village of Lépanges. Bernard Laroche was a respected, easy-going man and devoted father. At first Jean-Marie refused to believe

it: 'Not Bernard, we've never fallen out and he has everything I've got.'

But the police also possessed a damning statement from Laroche's sister-in-law, a 15-year-old girl called Muriel, who claimed she had been with Laroche when he had abducted Gregory and driven to the banks of the Vologne. Within 48 hours Muriel had retracted her testimony, claiming she had lied under fierce police pressure, but Laroche was charged with the murder. He was released two months later due to lack of evidence.

A mother falls under suspicion

Fresh leaks to the press claimed that handwriting experts now believed Christine Villemin was The Crow. Her workmates claimed to have seen her posting a letter around the time of the murder from the same post box used to post The Crow's gloating letter.

The examining magistrate handling the investigation interrogated Christine in hospital, where she had been admitted with a suspected miscarriage. She protested her innocence with a quiet dignity that impressed impartial observers.

Jean-Marie found their ordeal harder to bear. In late March 1985 he heard a radio bulletin claiming that Laroche had accused Christine of murdering Gregory because she felt herself an outsider and hated the Villemin clan. The report proved to be totally baseless, but something in Jean-Marie snapped. He went straight to his cousin's home, armed with a hunting rifle, and killed Bernard Laroche in front of his pregnant wife and little boy. Later Jean-Marie told Christine: 'I did it for you.'

Christine continued to be branded in the press as 'the monstrous murderer of her own child'. Then in July 1985, following the discovery of twine identical to that used to bind Gregory in the family home, she was formally charged with Gregory's murder.

As her lawyers looked into the case it became clear that there had been serious

GRIEF FOR GREGORY The whole clan came together for the funeral. Suspicion and hate shattered close bonds in the years that followed Gregory's death.

have drowned in the bath at home had been botched, and The Crow's last letter was almost obliterated by detectives looking for fingerprints.

By now, both the Villemins were buckling under the strain. Late in December 1986, a week after being committed for trial, Christine tried to commit suicide. Twelve months later, with little progress having been made in either of their cases, a court provisionally freed Jean-Marie to join his tormented wife.

Three more years passed in repeated questioning of the Villemins and other witnesses and elaborate 'reconstructions' of the murder. A magistrate newly appointed to the case told *Detective* magazine that he was leaning towards Laroche's guilt. Christine finally appeared in court in June 1992, visibly aged and bowed down by her ordeal. In his final address, the chief prosecutor applied for the charge against her to be dropped for lack of evidence and the case to be closed: 'It has not been possible to discover who killed the child.'

That judgment was confirmed the following February by the president of the Dijon appeal court, who found that every investigation of Christine Villemin left the inescapable conclusion that she was innocent of the murder of her child. The president concluded that 'In the circumstances, the involvement of a third party has to be considered' – a verdict that pointed the finger at Bernard Laroche and his sister-in-law.

KILLING COUSINS A police reconstruction of the murder of Bernard Laroche.

In November 1993, it was Jean-Marie's turn to stand trial. Lawyers for Bernard Laroche's family mounted a venomous attack on Christine's character, depicting her as an amoral slut who had conceived Gregory with a lover and persecuted her husband's family as The Crow. Christine bravely asked to join Jean-Marie in the dock and gave such moving evidence of their love for each other and their first-born child Gregory that many onlookers were in tears.

The final trial

A month later, Jean-Marie was sentenced to four years in prison for killing Bernard Laroche. But having served almost as long while awaiting trial, he was conditionally released within a few days. Reunited with Christine and their two children Julien and Emelyne, who were born after Gregory's death, the tormented couple departed for a secret destination far from Lépanges.

In the village they left behind, the climate of bitterness and suspicion created by 'l'affaire du petit Gregory' still festers. The feuds remain raw and unresolved. In the bleak judgment of Jean-Marie's younger brother, Gilbert: 'We'll think about this until our death, because the mystery will always be there . . . I know that one day there will be another killing.'

errors in the investigation of Gregory's death; forensic tests to establish whether – as Lépanges' rumour mill suggested – he might

FAMILY AFFAIR Laroche and his sister-in-law Muriel, whose testimony implicated him in the murder of his cousin's son Gregory.

1950 ▬▬▬ ▬ ▬ ▬ 2000

1984 Gregory murdered
1985 Christine charged
with murder

1993 Christine found not guilty
Jean-Marie convicted of
Laroche's murder

BRUTAL MURDER AT THE GORILLA CENTRE

WHO KILLED DIAN FOSSEY IN HER REMOTE CABIN HIGH IN THE MOUNTAINS OF RWANDA?

The republic of Rwanda is the smallest and possibly the most inaccessible country in Africa. It lies buried in the heart of this vast continent, encircled by high volcanic mountains. Here, in December 1985, an American woman called Dian Fossey was apparently hacked to death in a deeply puzzling murder case. Dian Fossey was a scientist known worldwide for her work with the rare mountain gorillas of Rwanda's damp, green highlands. She was also, by temperament, a difficult woman: tough, sometimes arrogant, and very much a loner. Dian was the focus of a worldwide conservation effort to preserve the mountain gorilla and lived in the research centre of Karisoke high amid the Virunga mountains. And it was here that her body was found; she had been brutally murdered in her cabin.

A fellow American researcher named Wayne McGuire was charged with the crime. He was alleged to have killed Dian to steal her research notes and so complete his own thesis. In this he was said to have been aided by a Rwandan tracker called Emmanuel Rwelekana. The case against them was based on evidence supplied by a Paris police laboratory. Hair found in the murder victim's hands was Caucasian, but not Fossey's own. Blood matching Fossey's was found on Rwelekana's shoes.

An escape and a suspicious death

However, very few members of Rwanda's scientific community believed the official version of events. The idea that McGuire killed Dian for her research notes seemed absurd. In fact, the American was allowed to escape the country and went on to pursue his studies at an American university. That the Rwandan authorities seem to have made little effort to stop him leaving and even less to extradite him is suspicious.

The tracker Rwelekana was never brought to trial either – he was found hanged in his prison cell under suspicious circumstances. Although he was allegedly found hanged with his own shirt, the autopsy stated that the cause of death was a broken neck – a feature more common to executions than suicides – and records of his interrogation indicate that he maintained his innocence with dignity throughout, despite being tortured for information. He could only explain the Caucasian-type hair found in Dian's fist, and the blood on his own shoes, by saying that someone was trying to frame him.

Journalist Nick Gordon, who made a detailed study of the Fossey case, exposed a number of anomalies. For example, Dian Fossey was supposed to have been hacked to death with a native panga, or hatchet.

FOREST COMPANIONS At home among the gorillas, Dian Fossey experienced greater problems in human company.

THE SCIENTIST After fifteen years at Karisoke, Dian Fossey was a respected expert on the world's largest living ape.

MIDDLE OF NOWHERE A light in Dian's cabin at twilight. The remote Karisoke camp is habitually shrouded in heavy mist.

Blows from a panga would have left blood spattered everywhere, and the blood in the hut was concentrated on the floor around the body. There was a strong suspicion that

GORILLA GRAVEYARD Dian visits the graves of victims of Rwanda's gorilla poachers. She was buried here among her friends.

she had been strangled first, then hit with a panga after she was dead. It was odd that a panel from the side of her hut had been broken down, apparently for the murderer to gain access. McGuire had keys to the building and would not have needed to make so noisy an entrance. If anyone had broken in in this way, Fossey would have had time to get her gun and defend herself. Had the panel been removed to fake a violent entrance?

Nick Gordon's investigation led him to conclude that certain prominent Rwandans were seriously implicated in both the murder and a subsequent cover-up.

Making powerful enemies

In Rwanda Dian Fossey had come upon evidence of gorilla poaching on a large scale and had campaigned vigorously to stop the barbaric trade. The gorillas that she worked with were highly prized by zoos around the world, and a healthy young specimen might fetch as much as $32 000 on the illegal market. The heads, hands and feet of gorillas are valued as souvenirs and trophies. Dian had

confronted local poachers many times and was not afraid to use force to protect the gorillas on the mountain. She had also compiled a report naming almost 100 poachers and describing their operations.

Had her investigations led her to know more than was good for her about the illegal traffic in gorillas? Nick Gordon suggests that

CONVICTED The graduate student Wayne McGuire was convicted by a Rwandan court, in his absence, of Fossey's murder.

a highly placed Rwandan named Zed was responsible for Dian Fossey's death. Zed was the brother-in-law of the Rwandan president and was involved with his sister, Agathe, the president's wife, in a lucrative gorilla business. Perhaps the murder was set up to look like the work of local poachers, but the plan misfired when it was discovered that the intruders had stolen no valuables – only Dian's notes. The thieves were looking for incriminating documents relating to the gorilla traffic. The story about McGuire and the theft of the research notes was quickly concocted as a cover-up.

There was certainly one cover-up. A feeling was widespread among scientists working in Rwanda that to re-open the Fossey case and provoke hostility from the Rwandan authorities would damage the efforts of conservationists in the country. And so no one created a fuss, not even the US State Department, which failed to institute an enquiry into Fossey's death. A mist was quietly allowed to descend over the whole affair, as impenetrable as the mists which habitually fall upon the lush Virunga mountains where Dian Fossey lived and died.

1963 Dian Fossey first visits Africa

1967 Dian returns to Africa

1985 Dian Fossey murdered
1986 McGuire and Rwelekana arrested

A FULLY DRESSED POLITICIAN IN THE BATH

A POTENT COCKTAIL OF DRUGS KILLED UWE BARSCHEL, BUT WAS IT SUICIDE OR MURDER?

Uwe Barschel was a German politician whose death could have been scripted by Agatha Christie. The scene was the luxurious Beau Rivage Hotel on the lake front in Geneva, Switzerland. At midday on Sunday, October 11, 1987, reporters from *Stern* magazine arrived at the hotel for an interview with Mr Barschel about his involvement in Germany's biggest political scandal since the Second World War. The reporters found the disgraced politician reclining in his bath, fully clothed and dead.

The bath was filled with water, but the occupant had not drowned. There were no signs of violence, either in the room or on the dead man's body – was it suicide? Within 24 hours of his death, Barschel's widow, Freya, and his brother, Eike, electrified a Geneva news conference when they announced their belief that Barschel

DATE WITH DEATH *Stern* reporters arranged to meet Uwe Barschel at the Beau Rivage Hotel (right) to get the inside story on a political scandal. Instead they got a scoop – Barschel was dead in the bath (far right).

had been murdered for political reasons after meeting an informant who had claimed to have evidence that could clear his name. The pair claimed that Barschel had phoned them in a nervous state and told them: 'For the first time in my life I am afraid.' A day later, Eike said that his brother might have been murdered by 'terrorists' who used the informant as a decoy.

A month before his death Barschel, Christian Democrat and former premier of the northern German state of Schleswig-Holstein, had been forced to resign following allegations that he had masterminded a 'dirty tricks' campaign against his rival –

HAPPY COUPLE Barschel and his wife Freya, who remains convinced that he was murdered.

Bjorn Engholm, of the Social Democrats (SPD). On the eve of state elections Reiner Pfeiffer, a former Barschel aide, had revealed that he, under the direction of Barschel, had tried to smear Engholm, a young politician with a reputation for high moral standards. Pfeiffer told of paying detectives to spy on Engholm, writing an anonymous letter accusing him of tax fraud, and planting a fake bug in Barschel's phone so that it could be blamed on the SPD. The voters turned against Barschel and brought the SPD to power. He was to have testified before a parliamentary enquiry into the scandal on the day after his death: October 12, 1987.

The Geneva police began a painstaking reconstruction of Barschel's final days. After resigning on September 25, Barschel had slipped away to the Canary Islands with his wife. While on vacation he received a call from a stranger calling himself Robert (or Rudolf) Roloff who claimed to have proof that Barschel's accuser, Pfeiffer, had been secretly working for the Social Democrats. Roloff offered to meet Barschel at Geneva Airport.

On Thursday, October 8, Barschel telexed his party leaders saying that he hoped to obtain information to clear his name. That Saturday, in a call from Geneva, he is said to have sounded euphoric. He also called his brother to say he had met Roloff, who had promised to hand over a photograph incriminating Pfeiffer as an SPD agent. But the police investigation reached a dead end when Roloff could not be traced.

An autopsy showed that Barschel had died after ingesting a lethal cocktail of five different types of drug. Although no empty pill bottles were found in the hotel suite, in the absence of any evidence to the contrary the Swiss authorities concluded that Uwe Barschel had committed suicide.

Barschel's family persisted with their murder claims and demanded a second autopsy, bolstered by allegations that he might have been killed by a South African 'hit squad' to cover up an illicit arms deal. The state finance minister admitted that South Africa had illegally purchased blueprints for military submarines from a state shipyard in Schleswig-Holstein. 'It is impossible to imagine that Barschel did not know,' an intelligence source said. 'The suspicion is that he was in a position to accuse others.'

Freya Barschel hired her own investigator, who discovered that Barschel had made many lone trips to East Germany, meeting

DOUBLE AGENT? Reiner Pfeiffer, who blew the whistle on 'dirty tricks' by his Christian Democrat boss, was working for the SPD at the same time.

women suspected of being secret agents. He had also reportedly had contacts with Mossad, the Israeli secret service. The family maintained that he had been working closely with the West German secret service (the BND), and Freya Barschel believed that 'Roloff' was an East German secret agent. The theory that Barschel was murdered by West German agents provided the basis for a feature film released in Germany in 1994.

Then Victor Ostrovsky, a former Israeli intelligence agent, wrote a book claiming that Israeli agents killed Uwe Barschel because he knew too much about a secret arms trade between Israel and Iran, being conducted through German middlemen.

In December 1994 the Germans reopened their investigations into the Barschel case after new tests showed that some of the drugs in his stomach had got there when he was already dead. This suggested that he had been fed the poison to fake suicide.

New information was now available from East German intelligence files, including

REVELATION Freya and Eike Barschel announced at a press conference that Uwe Barschel had been murdered.

CIA communications. The CIA cables referred to a person whom they code-named 'Perch', which is 'Barsch' in German. A cryptic message of October 9, 1987, reported: 'Jerry took Perch to temple, met with Lokal and Rabbi at 21:30. Perch unyielding. Refuses co op.'

Hours before Barschel's body was found there had apparently been a meeting in Geneva of Iranian arms dealers and officials, who may have included Ahmed Khomeini, son of Iran's late spiritual leader Ayatollah Khomeini. German investigators had been aware for two years of an informant's claim that on the day of his death Barschel had met Ahmed Khomeini as well as Israeli, German and other agents to talk about weapon deliveries. Perhaps Barschel had refused to give in to certain demands and was then a marked man.

It now seems certain that a third party was involved in Barschel's death, but the whole affair is such a web of deceit that German investigators hold out little hope of ever knowing the truth about Uwe Barschel.

MYSTERIOUS DROWNING OF A TROUBLED TYCOON

ROBERT MAXWELL'S BODY WAS FOUND FLOATING IN THE ATLANTIC OCEAN NEAR TENERIFE

He was one of Britain's most flamboyant tycoons: a billionaire publisher, newspaper proprietor and friend of the rich and famous. Robert Maxwell's charisma was matched by a reputation as a bully and cheat. When his 22-stone corpse was winched from the sea by helicopter in 1991 the shock waves rippled around the world for years afterwards. Maxwell rose to become a figure of national importance in July 1984 when he bought Mirror Group Newspapers Ltd for £113.4 million. Through a ruthless modernisation programme 'Cap'n Bob', as he was dubbed, made the company highly successful. He also headed several notable charities and indulged his love of football by buying his local club, Oxford United.

But the tycoon overreached himself in his desire to create a global communications empire through purchases which included the *New York Daily News*. Colossal debts

ALL ABOARD Maxwell looking every inch the billionaire aboard his luxury boat, the *Lady Ghislaine*, at Cannes in April 1987.

CAP'N BOB Maxwell on the football terraces with pop star Elton John and (below) with a copy of one of his newspapers.

began to accumulate. Meanwhile a curious story began to circulate in the press, alleging that Maxwell was an agent of Mossad – the Israeli intelligence service. It had a damaging effect on the already tumbling value of Maxwell company shares.

In the autumn of 1991 the ruin of his business empire threatened, and Robert Maxwell flew south for a break on his boat, the *Lady Ghislaine*.

He spent Sunday, November 4, swimming and taking business phone calls. That night Maxwell dined in Santa Cruz, Tenerife, before setting out to sea again. He was still awake at 4.25 am; a crew member saw him, dressed in his nightshirt on the stern deck, and 20 minutes later he rang to ask the bridge for the air conditioning to be turned down. But the next morning, though the ship was searched, and searched again, Robert Maxwell had vanished.

A body is found in the Atlantic

His family were informed, and a satellite distress signal was put out. At 5.55 pm a body was sighted in the sea to the east of Tenerife, and within the hour a helicopter had located Robert Maxwell's weighty corpse, floating naked, face-up in water. How had he died?

Was it an accident, suicide or murder?

The verdict of the autopsy carried out on Gran Canaria stated that Maxwell had died of a coronary thrombosis or heart attack. But it was not clear whether the tycoon had first succumbed and then fallen into the water, or fallen first and had a heart attack in the sea.

Then in January 1992 the French magazine *Paris Match* published the verdict of a second post mortem conducted in Israel. A video recording of this examination appeared to reveal bruising on Maxwell's face and body. Two French forensic experts who studied the video concluded that the tycoon had received several heavy blows before his death, which had fractured his nose and torn his ear. British pathologists, however, dismissed all talk of foul play.

The question was of critical importance because Maxwell's

SUNK WITHOUT TRACE Robert Maxwell seemed to have everything – family, fame and fortune. But his rags-to-riches fairytale ended in tears.

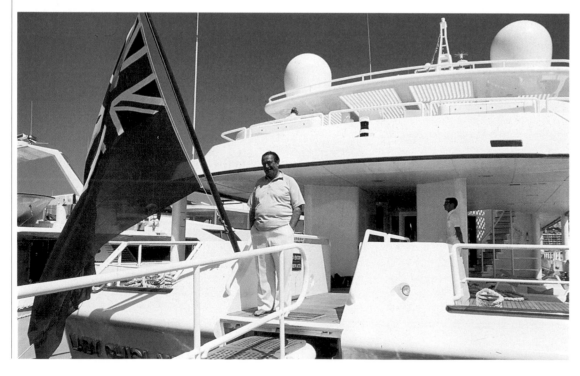

1923 Maxwell
born in
Czechoslovakia

1945 Maxwell
awarded MC during
Second World War

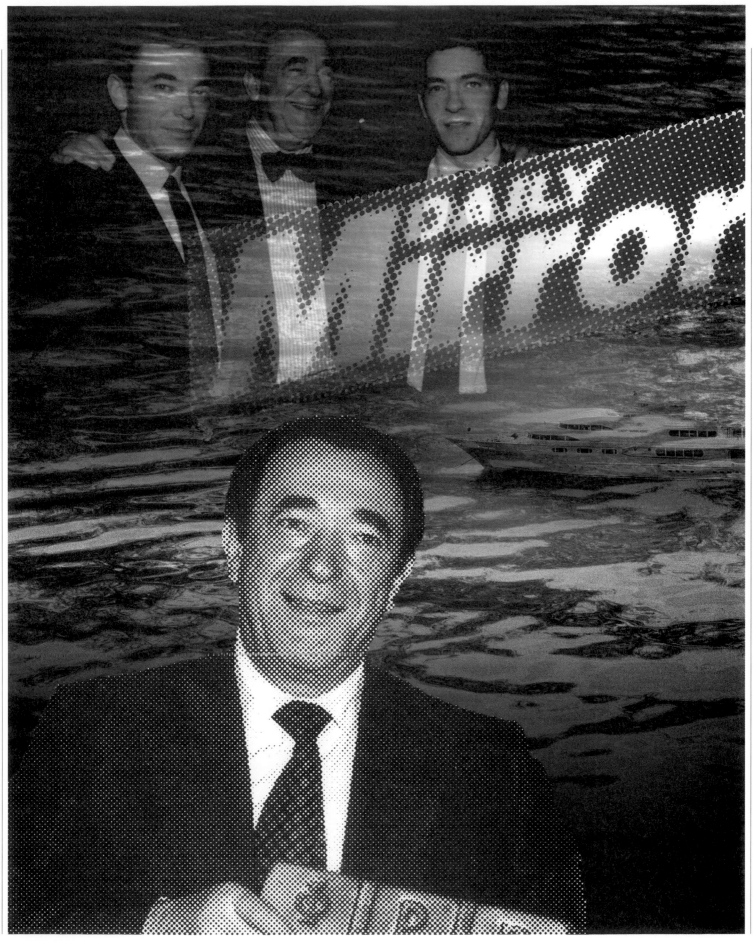

1984 Maxwell
buys Mirror
Group

1989 Maxwell
found dead in the
sea near Tenerife

1994 Trial of
Maxwell's sons
begins

life was insured for £20 million, and the insurance companies refused to pay out without evidence that his death at sea was either accidental or murder. The policies did not apply in the case of death by natural causes or suicide.

Dr Iain West, a leading pathologist was called in to investigate the case for the insurers. He believed it more likely that Maxwell had died by drowning than of a heart attack. This meant that the four possibilities now were:

Accident: Maxwell might have had a dizzy spell, slipped and fallen into the sea where he drowned. However, it was a calm night and there was a railing round the deck.

Heart attack: Maxwell was under severe stress, hugely overweight and suffered from a lung complaint. However, it is likely that after a seizure he would have fallen to the deck, not into the water.

Suicide: Dr West identified injuries to Maxwell's left hand and a tearing of the left shoulder muscles. This, said Dr West, was a common pattern of injury among some people who kill themselves by jumping from high places. They 'will gradually ease themselves over the edge and hold on for a time with one or both hands before letting go'. The scale of the disaster facing Maxwell's empire should not be underestimated;

£400 million were missing from pension funds. On his return to London he might have faced imprisonment.

Maxwell had been uncharacteristically indecisive before his death, first wanting his sons to fly to him to discuss business matters, then countermanding the order to give himself more time to think. Did he conclude that there was no way out? On the last day he had called for his private jet to circle round the yacht as if in a last proud flypast. He had locked his stateroom on the yacht before venturing onto the deck for the last time. Why lock the door if he was only going out for a breath of air?

The final possibility

Dr West did not dismiss the possibility of murder – he simply found no evidence either for or against it. The injuries on the body could be explained by it striking either the ship or floating objects in the water.

Maxwell had no shortage of enemies. No suspicions attached to the crew, but it would not be impossible for a hit team to stalk the undefended yacht by night. Any powerful victim of his business malpractices would

THE END Though Robert Maxwell lived in Britain, his funeral was held in Israel at the Mount of Olives in Jerusalem.

have had the means and motive. Maxwell's interests included arms dealing, and if he were an agent of Mossad his weapons traffic in the Middle East could have made him a target for Arab assassins.

There are other shadowy possibilities. Since his death it has emerged that Maxwell had been investigated several times by the FBI on suspicion of spying for the Soviet Union. The files were censored so that it is impossible to say whether conclusive evidence was found against the tycoon, but this contributes yet another dimension to the mystery of Maxwell's death.

AFTERMATH In 1994, three years after their father's death, Maxwell's sons Kevin (left) and Ian (right) were tried for conspiracy to defraud.

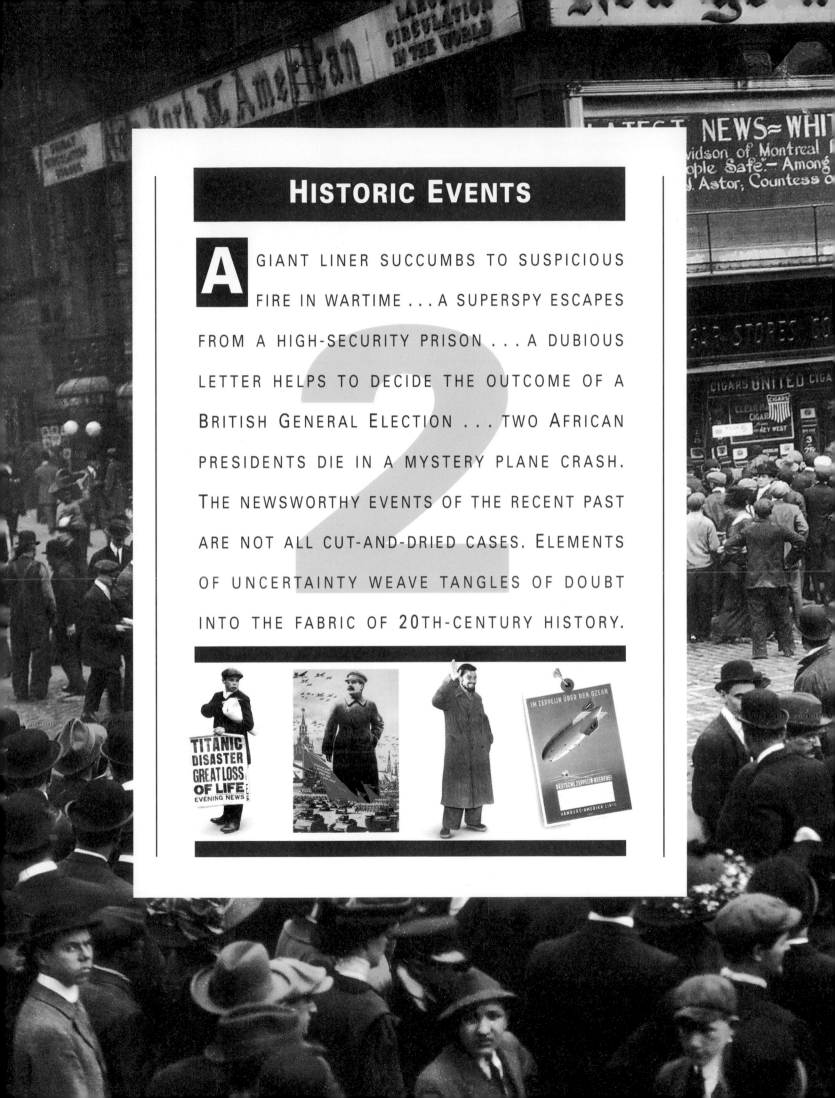

HISTORIC EVENTS

A GIANT LINER SUCCUMBS TO SUSPICIOUS FIRE IN WARTIME...A SUPERSPY ESCAPES FROM A HIGH-SECURITY PRISON...A DUBIOUS LETTER HELPS TO DECIDE THE OUTCOME OF A BRITISH GENERAL ELECTION...TWO AFRICAN PRESIDENTS DIE IN A MYSTERY PLANE CRASH. THE NEWSWORTHY EVENTS OF THE RECENT PAST ARE NOT ALL CUT-AND-DRIED CASES. ELEMENTS OF UNCERTAINTY WEAVE TANGLES OF DOUBT INTO THE FABRIC OF 20TH-CENTURY HISTORY.

SIBERIA'S COSMIC CATASTROPHE

THE FIREBALL WHICH BLASTED A HOLE IN THE FORESTS OF SIBERIA REMAINS A MYSTERY TODAY

In 1908, while the tsar still ruled over a Russia seething with revolutionary unrest, a disturbance of a wholly different kind rocked northern Siberia. In the remote Tunguska Basin, a blast estimated to be equal in energy to the detonation of 30 million tons of high explosive devastated the inaccessible forests. The fireball which appeared suddenly in the sky materialised not long after dawn on June 30, with a monstrous flash and bang that caused villagers as far as 200 miles (320 km) away to run in terror through the streets, believing the world's end to be nigh. Some inhabitants of the sparsely populated region were badly burnt or hurled through the air by the shock waves. Within a radius of some 40 miles (64 km), forests were laid waste and herds of charred reindeer lay among the uprooted trees.

Although the facts were reported at the time, the region was so bleak and remote that the actual site of the mystery blast remained uninvestigated by scientists for many years. Only in 1927 did a Soviet research team arrive at the scene, and its members were mystified by what they saw. As they approached the centre of the oval-shaped blast area, the investigators expected to discover evidence of a meteorite collision. But they found no hunks of meteoritic rock. Whatever had exploded at Tunguska had vanished like a bomb, instead of breaking into fragments as meteors do. Nor was there a central crater; the trees at the heart of the blast area were relatively undamaged.

Extraterrestrial activity

What happened at Tunguska has fascinated both scientists and students of the paranormal. According to some reports, the soil in the devastated area was highly radioactive, and in 1946 a Russian author, Alexander Kazantsev, proposed in a science-fiction story that the disaster resulted from a nuclear explosion in an atomic-powered alien spacecraft flying overhead. This fanciful theory has lingered on among UFO aficionados, although it is wholly unsupported by any evidence. In the 1970s, two British physicists, A.A. Jackson and M.P. Ryan, suggested in the science journal *Nature* that a mini black hole, no bigger than an atom, entered the Earth's atmosphere. Colliding explosively at Tunguska, it may have passed through the planet and emerged on the other side, in the North Atlantic (although there is no evidence of a corresponding explosion here). Objects known as 'anti-matter meteorites', originating beyond the Milky Way, have also been suggested as culprits.

A more orthodox theory – and the current favourite among scientists – proposes that the disaster was caused by a comet exploding overhead. Consisting of ice and dust, with a luminous, trailing gas cloud, a comet would have left no meteoric fragments after detonating. However, because a comet is normally seen coming from some distance away, and because it is not certain that an exploding comet would change radiation levels, the Tunguska event provokes continued debate.

WRECKED FORESTS The devastation at Tunguska testifies to the awesome power of the mystery blast. Leonid Kulik (above right) investigated the impact site.

WITNESS TO DISASTER Ilya Potapovich, of the local Tungus people, observed the effects of the explosion and, in 1927, guided Kulik's team into the blast region.

THE RIDDLE OF THE MONEY PIT TREASURE TROVE

DESPITE FORTUNES SPENT ON EXCAVATION, THE MONEY PIT HAS YET TO YIELD A SINGLE DOUBLOON

In a prospectus issued in 1909, New York engineer Henry Bowdoin asserted that treasure estimated at over $10 million was buried on Oak Island off Nova Scotia, probably by pirates, and that by using modern equipment it would be 'easy, ridiculously easy' to retrieve it. To attract potential investors, Bowdoin invented the figure of $10 million – but the Oak Island enigma had a very real historical pedigree, and its allure was sufficient to attract the future president Franklin D. Roosevelt among other backers. However, Bowdoin was to drill 26 boreholes

TREASURE HUNTERS Dan Blankenship, fortune seeker, and M.R. Chappell, Oak Island's owner, survey maps of the site.

around the island without finding anything. And his successors have not had much more luck in what has proved to be one of the most enduring mysteries of the 20th century.

Booby-trapped booty?

The story began in 1795, when three local farm boys exploring the uninhabited island discovered a depression in the ground, a few yards in diameter, at the foot of an old oak tree. Thinking that someone might have buried something there, they fetched tools and helpers from the mainland, and discovered a man-made shaft sealed at intervals with oak-log platforms. About 30 ft (9 m) down, the youths abandoned their excavations, but early in the following century a syndicate of local businessmen took up the quest. The searchers got 90 ft (27 m) down, through further layers of log platforms, and reached a stone slab covered with cryptic symbols which were later decoded to reveal the message: 'Ten feet below, two million pounds are buried.'

However, when attempts were made to reach the treasure itself, the shaft flooded with seawater – and the same calamity occurred when searchers angled a second shaft towards the base. It appeared that whoever made the Money Pit (as it was dubbed) had also booby-trapped it with flood tunnels dug from the ocean's edge.

Oak Island's fame spread with these and all subsequent attempts to unlock its secrets. In the 20th century new attempts were made on the treasure with heavy bulldozers, rotary drills, turbine pumps and crawler cranes. The original shaft was so damaged by flooding, digging and cave-ins that it became a huge, maimed crater, and both flood tunnels were destroyed. Meanwhile, hundreds of new shafts and boreholes pitted the 128 acre (52 ha) island, for the belief spread that the Money Pit itself might simply have been a decoy on an island honeycombed with interlocking tunnels. In 1965 a causeway was built to the island, and in the 1980s two separate visitor centres were set up by rival treasure companies.

The irony is that, despite its name, the Money Pit has to date disgorged not a single penny. Some sceptics have claimed that the labyrinth of tunnels in fact consists of sink-holes naturally formed in limestone and filled up by tide-borne debris;

BOX OF TRICKS?
This wooden box is one of the tantalising clues that has been dug up on Oak Island.

the rest, they say, can be explained by self-delusion and the wilful fakery of such objects as the hieroglyphic stone slab.

But the quest continues to the present day. In 1995 newspapers published photographs taken in one 235 ft (70 m) deep borehole. Treasure-seeker Dan Blankenship lowered a video camera into the murky abyss and found what he believes to be clear evi-

WHO BUILT THE MONEY PIT?

Serious researchers have dismissed the idea that the Money Pit could have been the work of pirates. For, although Carbon-14 dating of its timbers has suggested that it might have been built during the 16th century, it would have required a more disciplined workforce and more advanced engineering skills than buccaneers could have mustered. Other equally improbable theories have suggested that it was built to conceal Marie Antoinette's jewels or even a cache of Shakespeare's plays.

dence of at least two chests at the bottom of the hole. Meanwhile, plans were launched by the Oak Island Exploration Company to fund an investigation to solve the mystery 'through the application of scientific analysis and historical research'. Experts have already been brought in from the Woods Hole Oceanographic Institute – the respected body that located the *Titanic* – to help resolve this most tantalising of riddles.

MYSTERIES OF THE *TITANIC*

HI-TECH EQUIPMENT CONTINUES TO UNCOVER THE SECRETS OF A GREAT SHIP'S WATERY GRAVE

God Himself could not sink this ship', a crew member is reported to have said of the liner *Titanic*. Pride of the White Star fleet, she was the largest ship afloat and was equipped with luxurious fittings that ranged from elevators to a swimming pool, a squash court, a gymnasium with the latest exercise equipment from Germany, and a French 'sidewalk café'. Yet in the early hours of April 15, 1912, the great ship struck an iceberg in the Atlantic south of Newfoundland, and not even her specially constructed steel hull could save her from disaster. The *Titanic* went down with the loss of more than 1500 lives.

Several mysteries surrounded her grim

FLYING THE FLAG The *Titanic* was the pride of the White Star fleet.

fate, and some were not solved until after September 1, 1985, when world headlines proclaimed that the wreck of the *Titanic* had been found. On that morning, using deep-sea sonar search aids, Dr Robert D. Ballard and a joint French-American team located the lost ship on the floor of the Atlantic. The massive, rusted hull lay 2½ miles (4 km) down on the ocean bed, and in the summer of 1986 Ballard's team went down in a three-man submarine named *Alvin* to explore the ghostly wreck. Landing on the deck of the great liner, Ballard obtained close-up photos by sending out a robot camera named Jason Junior as a 'swimming eyeball' to explore the Grand Staircase and the state rooms. From the depths of the ocean came photographs of the giant liner's silverware and of glass chandeliers that still hung in place. In ten further descents, Ballard and his team explored much of the ship and the debris field around her broken hull.

How had the iceberg caused such damage?

SAD SOUVENIR A postcard commemorates the tragedy which claimed more than 1500 lives.

For safety, the *Titanic*'s hull had been constructed in 16 watertight compartments; survivors of the disaster, who had seen where the water entered the ship, reported that the damage to the hull extended from the first to the fifth of these sections.

The ship goes down

Many historians believed that the impact of the ice must have torn a long gash in the hull. However, Ballard's investigation showed this to be unlikely. Although much of the damaged area was buried in the mud, bits that could be seen revealed hull plates knocked apart intermittently at their seams.

1912 The *Titanic* is struck by an iceberg and sinks. An inquiry is launched

There was no single ice wound. What had happened was that the ship's starboard bow plates had buckled under the impact of the collision with the iceberg, the rivets had popped from their sockets, and water had rushed in through cracks between plates no more than a few inches wide.

Again, conventional views about the disaster held that, flooded at the prow, the great ship nosed down and sank headfirst and intact into the cold Atlantic. Indeed, two inquiries in 1912 concluded that the ship went down in one piece. Some eyewitnesses had reported, however, that the ship had in fact broken in two: the bow plunged while the stern briefly righted itself before turning almost vertical and then sinking at speed. These witnesses were proved right by Ballard's findings. The hull was found snapped in two on the ocean floor, the segments 1970 ft (600 m) apart and pointing in different directions. Their position clearly indicated that the liner had broken apart at or near the surface.

Yet again, many historians had assumed that when the bow reached a certain angle,

DOOMED COLOSSUS Only 705 people survived the *Titanic* sinking. Afterwards, new laws demanded that liners should have one space on a lifeboat for each passenger.

the boilers broke loose from their fittings and crashed headlong through the hull, hastening the descent. Ballard's findings suggested that this was highly unlikely.

Based on a careful study of the evidence, it is now possible to reconstruct with some certainty how the liner, flooding at the prow, began to lurch downwards. As the stern rose high out of the water, the hull snapped under the intolerable strain of the tilt and the two segments sank independently of one another, spilling a wealth of debris from the shattered midsection. Finds have included tons of coal from the breached boiler rooms, thousands of bottles of wine and champagne, kitchen utensils, light fixtures, bathtubs, chamber pots and silver serving trays.

LATEST NEWS A London newsboy gives details of the disaster.

The empty safe

Are there greater riches to be recovered? In 1980, five years before Ballard located the liner, Hollywood had produced a film called *Raise the Titanic*, in which assorted treasure-seekers tried to recover rare minerals from the wreck. The theme echoed a widespread belief that – given the wealth of many passengers – fortunes in gold and jewellery await discovery on the ocean bed. For Ballard, a moment of great excitement occurred when his headlights picked out a ship's safe. However, when *Alvin*'s robot arm lifted the box, the investigators saw that the box's bottom was missing – and there was no sign of any contents on the ocean floor. It appeared to be a safe from the second-class purser's office and had perhaps never held anything of great value.

Still, it is known that some items of exceptional value were carried on the *Titanic*, among them a gold-covered copy of the *Ruba'iyat of Omar Khayyam* which had more than 1000 precious stones studding its binding. Perhaps further research will reveal treasures. But for future investigators the problem is not only a technological one; it has moral and legal dimensions. The *Titanic*

UNDERSEA IMAGES In 1985 a joint French-American team located and photographed the wreck 2½ miles (4 km) below the surface of the Atlantic.

BREAK-UP Investigators believe that the hull snapped in two before the great ship plunged deep underwater.

is a graveyard. Attempts have been made by the United States government to declare the wreck an international memorial and to leave it unmolested by treasure-seekers, but international expeditions continue to this fascinating submarine museum.

1980 Hollywood's
Raise the Titanic

1985 Wreck of the *Titanic* discovered
1986 *Alvin* explores the wreck

1996 Attempt was made to raise a section of the *Titanic*

WAS MATA HARI GUILTY?

HOW THE FATE OF AN EXOTIC DANCER CAPTURED THE IMAGINATION OF A WORLD AT WAR

Oriental mystique, intrigue and sexual allure . . . all were united in the figure of Mata Hari, history's very archetype of the glamorous female spy. Arrested by the French during the First World War, the exotic

EXOTIC ALLURE Dutch-born Mata Hari cultivated one legend that she was a half-caste Javanese and another that she was the daughter of an Indian temple dancer.

dancer was tried for espionage and died in front of a firing squad in 1917. But a certain unease about her case lingered on. In 1925, an article published in France stated doubts as to her guilt. Was Europe's most famous courtesan really a German agent?

Born Margaret Geertruida Zelle in Holland in 1876, she married disastrously – a Dutchman of Scottish extraction named Rudolph MacLeod. He was a violent drunk, and the marriage only lasted 11 years. But

while living with him in Java she had become fascinated by the local dancing girls and their erotic arts. When she returned to Europe, she took the name of Mata Hari ('Eye of the Day', or 'Dawn', in Malay) and appeared in Paris in 1905 as a 'temple dancer', purportedly trained by Hindu priests in either Java or southern India, and dedicated to the god Siva. Her dances, she said, demanded nudity.

Scoring an instantaneous hit by dancing naked but for a few bangles, Mata Hari became a famous courtesan whose reputation spread to all the capitals of Europe. Princes, dukes, ministers and generals paid court to her, and she commanded immense fees for her favours. In 1914, when war broke out, she happened to be in Berlin where she was seen by French agents in the company, or so they said, of the chief of police. This was not especially sinister. The policeman was an old friend who had first made her acquaintance when investigating a complaint about her naked dancing and who had found ways to help her get around the law.

Code name H21

French prosecutors were later to claim that by this time Mata Hari was already a German spy with the operational number of H21 (H being short for Holland, where she lived for a few months in 1915). By the time she returned to France towards the end of 1915, she was shadowed everywhere: not only in Paris but also on visits to other European cities. However, for another year, Allied counter-intelligence services could find no grounds for arresting her. It was true that she had many male friends in diplomatic circles, including neutral Dutch, Swedish and Spanish attachés through whom she could pass information to the Germans. But there was no proof that she did so. The plain fact was that the courtesan had male friends in many important circles.

Threatened in 1916 with deportation from France, Mata Hari vehemently protested that she had never spied for the Kaiser – but that if the French wanted to employ her, she knew many high-ranking Germans from whom valuable information might be gleaned. Captain Georges Ladoux of the Deuxième Bureau, the French intelligence service, pretended to believe her, and together they discussed an assignment in which she would travel to German-occupied

THE COURTESAN Mata Hari made no secret of her profession. '30 000 marks was the fee for my services', she admitted at her trial.

1901 Mata Hari returns from the East to Amsterdam

1914 Dances in Berlin

1917 Mata Hari arrested in February, sentenced in July and executed in October.

PRIM POSE The artiste appears modest enough in this photograph – but her dances, Mata Hari claimed, required nudity.

Belgium and seduce the German Crown Prince in return for a reward of a million francs. Mata Hari never made it to Belgium that year, but on a journey to The Hague via Spain and England she was detained when the ship on which she was travelling docked at Falmouth in November 1916. The exotic

FIRING SQUAD Sentenced to death on July 25, 1917, Mata Hari faced her executioners with silent courage.

dancer was taken to Scotland Yard in London, where she was questioned by Sir Basil Thomson, chief of Special Branch. To him Mata Hari admitted being a spy, but said that she was working for French intelligence. Sceptically, Sir Basil replied: 'Madame, if you will accept the advice of one nearly twice your age, give up what you have been doing.'

'Traitress, never!'

From London, Mata Hari moved to Madrid where she seduced the German military attaché, Major Arnold Kalle. He gave her a few worthless pieces of tittle tattle and disinformation, which she hoped to pass on to her new spy-master in Paris. On her return to Paris on January 3, 1917, Mata Hari intended to collect a reward from Ladoux, but instead she was arrested at the Elysée Palace Hotel by the French police on February 13, 1917. During her interrogation and subsequent trial she was questioned closely about the 3500 pesetas she had received from Kalle. The prosecution alleged that it came from German Intelligence. Mata Hari, on the other hand, claimed that it was her fee as Major Kalle's mistress.

'Harlot yes – but traitress, never!' was Mata Hari's bold line of defence at her court martial, held in camera, in July. The money given to her by high-ranking Germans were payments for nights of love, she claimed. And

INTERPOL Sir Basil Thomson from Scotland Yard interrogated Mata Hari in 1916.

> ### THE MATA HARI FILE
>
> In 1915, the Italian Secret Service telegraphed officials in Paris to warn that Mata Hari was returning to France – thereafter she was shadowed everywhere as a suspected spy:
>
> 'While examining the passenger list of a Japanese vessel at Naples we have recognised the name of a theatrical celebrity from Marseilles named Mata Hari, the famous Hindu dancer, who purports to reveal secret Hindu dances which demand nudity. She has, it seems, renounced her claim to Indian birth and become Berlinoise. She speaks German with a slight Eastern accent.'

for every German that the prosecution named, she countered with an exalted Frenchman. Jules Cambon, the secretary general of the French Ministry of Foreign Affairs, had been one of her lovers and was even called as a witness for the defence.

'I am not French', declared the courtesan, 'so what is to prevent my having friends of any nationality I choose?' After several heated exchanges, Mata Hari delivered a final statement: 'Please note that I am not French, and that I reserve the right to cultivate any relations that may please me. The war is not a sufficient reason to stop me from being a cosmopolitan. I am a neutral, but my sympathies are for France. If that does not satisfy you, do as you will.'

The prosecution case rested on little more than suspicion. It may well be that Mata Hari did dabble in espionage, but whether she was a genuine secret agent, code-named and committed to the German cause, remains much more doubtful. What is certain is that she was unlucky to have been apprehended at a time of national unrest, when France was facing mutinies at the front and fears of subversion at home. In this climate, despite a desperate fight by her lawyers for a reprieve, Mata Hari's fate was sealed. Found guilty and sentenced to death, she was taken to the barracks at Vincennes early in the morning of October 15, 1917. There, she placed herself against a stake where a cord was knotted around her waist. Mata Hari comported herself with great courage as the firing squad assembled, and refused the bandage for her eyes.

THE FATE OF THE TSAR'S FAMILY

DID ANY OF THE ROMANOVS ESCAPE ALIVE FROM THE FIRING SQUAD AT EKATERINBURG?

The Romanov dynasty which had ruled Russia for more than four centuries ended in a brutal massacre after the Revolution of 1917. Following the Bolshevik seizure of power in October that year, Tsar Nicholas II and his family were moved with a small number of courtiers to the town of Ekaterinburg in Siberia. On July 16, 1918, at the house there of a wealthy merchant called N.N. Ipatiev, Nicholas, his wife Alexandra and their son and four daughters were reportedly herded into a room and raked

FAMILY PORTRAIT Tsar Nicholas and the Empress Alexandra with their son and four daughters grouped around them.

INFORMAL GATHERING The tsar's daughters Olga, Tatiana, Marie and Anastasia take a stroll in the forest on a search for wild mushrooms.

with bullets by their guards. Those who did not die at once were finished off by blows with rifle butts and bayonets.

The Romanovs met their gruesome end at a time when civil war was still raging between Tsarist and Bolshevik armies in Russia. Not long after the massacre Ekaterinburg fell to counterrevolutionary forces, and Tsarist investigators explored the site to try to determine precisely what had happened to the royal family. They concluded that, after the killings, the corpses were hauled off to a secluded pine forest where they were dismembered, soaked in petrol and burnt. Sulphuric acid was poured on the remains, which were dropped down a deep shaft at the nearby Four Brothers Mine. From the pit, the investigators recovered a handful of charred bones and one

severed finger, along with bits of clothing, an emerald cross, women's corset stiffeners, diamond-studded shoe buckles, a doctor's false teeth and glasses, and more. The jewellery was easily identified as that of the Romanov women, and the searchers also found brass buttons with coats of arms that had belonged to Nicholas and his haemophiliac son Alexis.

A train with the blinds down

However, certain puzzles have continued to surround the Ekaterinburg findings. For one thing, the few human remains discovered at the mine did not suggest that the whole family and their servants – 11 people – had been disposed of there. Bodies do not simply turn to ash when burned in petrol and soaked in acid. Where were the rest of the skeletons?

For a long time, serious researchers were convinced that some members of the royal family, at least, had escaped death because they were needed as bargaining counters in secret talks between the Bolsheviks and the German government. Alexandra was a relation of the German Kaiser and, so they argued, she and her children were to be exchanged for certain revolutionaries and then imprisoned in Germany. These clandestine negotiations are well documented. As late as September 10, 1918 – long after the supposed massacre

1900

1901 Birth of Anastasia, the tsar's fourth daughter

1904 Birth of Alexis

1914 Germany declares war on Russia

1917 The Bolsheviks seize power

1918 Execution of the tsar's family

1950

THE CAPTIVES Interned by the Bolsheviks, the tsar and his family soak up the sunshine on the rooftop of a Siberian greenhouse.

– the German consul in Moscow reported: 'I talked with Radek [a Bolshevik leader] again today about releasing the Empress and her children.' In October, Sir Charles Eliot, the British High Commissioner in Siberia, reported the rumour that: 'On 17 July a train with the blinds down left Ekaterinburg for an unknown destination, and it is believed that the surviving members of the imperial family were in it.'

Spice was added to the possibility of escape by the fact that if any of the tsar's family did survive, they might inherit fabulous riches. At the time of the Revolution, the Romanovs' wealth was estimated at an incredible $9000 million – the present-day equivalent of £30 billion. How much of this was saved from Bolshevik hands was a mystery in itself, but rumours were rife of huge gold shipments out of St Petersburg during the Tsarist regime's last days. Fortunes were reputedly hidden away in private accounts at banks in London, Paris, Berlin and New York. And with such an inheritance, there was no shortage of pretenders to the tsar's estate. Over the decades

that followed the Revolution, scores of treasure-seekers, fantasists and downright maniacs came forward, asserting that they were royal survivors of the Ipatiev house massacre.

Anna Anderson and others

The most famous claimant was a woman called 'Anna Anderson' who was rescued in 1920 from a suicidal drowning attempt in a Berlin canal. After a long period in hospital when she was reluctant to say anything about her past, she claimed to be the Grand Duchess Anastasia, the tsar's youngest daughter. She had, she said, been spared death at Ekaterinburg and sent off by train with her mother and sisters to another place of imprisonment. In the course of three escape attempts, she said, she was beaten and raped. Eventually, she got free and travelled incognito, with help from a Russian soldier, in a farm cart to Bucharest.

Some of the relatives, friends and staff of the Russian royal family, brought to meet 'Anastasia', became convinced of her authenticity,

including the Grand Duke Andrew, the tsar's cousin. Others were more dubious; Prince Felix Yusupov called her 'an adventuress, a sick hysteric, and frightful play-actress'. Anna was the subject of a famous play, Ingrid Bergman and Lilli Palmer movies, a Lynn Seymour ballet, several books, countless newspaper articles and a 32-year-long lawsuit in

Germany. She died in February 1984 with historians no more certain of her identity than they had been 60 years earlier.

Many other claimants appeared. It has been said that in Siberia after the massacre, every town had its clutch of grand duchesses and sons of the tsar – all of them obvious frauds. Among the female hopefuls, pretenders to be Anastasia have been the most numerous, although there were others who claimed to be her sisters Olga, Tatiana or Marie. Nor was there a shortage of men asserting themselves to be the Grand Duke Alexis, the Tsar's only son. One of these was Colonel Michael Goleniewski, a Polish Army Intelligence officer who defected to the United States in 1960 after feeding the American CIA with microfilm secrets for two years. Not long after his defection had hit the headlines, Goleniewski began to make public claims to be Alexis. His story was astonishing – that the whole family had been smuggled out of Ekaterinburg. In Goleniewski's account, Tsar Nicholas lived on until May 1952, when he died incognito in Poznan in Poland and was buried in the cemetery of Wolsztyn.

The secret grave

The claims of many Romanov pretenders were shattered by dramatic developments in 1989. In that year, with the *glasnost* spirit of free enquiry spreading in the Soviet Union,

SLAUGHTER HOUSE The building in Ekaterinburg where the Romanovs met their end belonged to a successful merchant called Ipatiev. Below: the room where the family were raked with bullets by their captors.

1960 Goleniewski defects and later claims to be Alexis

1984 Death of 'Anna Anderson', who had claimed to be Anastasia

1992 Remains sent for DNA testing

BURIAL SITE It was at this spot, in the birch swamp outside Ekaterinburg, that the remains of several Romanov family members were located in 1989.

investigators announced that they had found skeletons of the Russian royal family in a birch swamp 12 miles (19 km) outside Ekaterinburg. The location had been revealed in notes left by Jacob Yurovsky, the commander of the Bolshevik execution squad at the Ipatiev house.

The case is reopened

On the orders of the Russian president, Boris Yeltsin, an official investigation of the burial site was later carried out. The grave yielded nine skeletons, and in September 1992 remains were sent to British forensic science laboratories at Aldermaston in Berkshire for DNA testing. Meanwhile, blood samples were taken from relatives of

the Russian royal family who included Prince Philip, Duke of Edinburgh (a direct maternal descendant of Alexandra's sister). A year later, it was officially announced that the mystery of the Romanovs was just about solved. Combining historical evidence with the DNA results, it was possible to identify the nine bodies in the grave as those of Tsar Nicholas II, the Empress Alexandra, three of their daughters, Dr Botkin (the family physician), a footman, maid and cook.

Fascinatingly, two figures remain unaccounted for. Remains of the tsar's son, Alexis, were not present in the grave and one of the Romanov daughters was missing (although experts disagree as to whether this is Marie or Anastasia). Were their lives spared? Or were they butchered like the others and buried elsewhere for reasons now forgotten? The answer continues to baffle, though the evidence from the birch swamp grave has debunked the claims of many a pretender to the identity of the Grand Duchess Olga or Tatiana. It also makes nonsense of Goleniewski's claim that

MYSTERY WOMAN A woman known as 'Anna Anderson', photographed (left) in 1928 and (right) in 1955, claimed to be the tsar's daughter Anastasia.

the tsar died in Poznan in 1952. As for the fascinating Anna Anderson, historians are now satisfied that she was in fact a Polish peasant called Franziska Schanzkjowska who had endured the very real ordeals of rape,

---

THE FINAL HOURS

Pavel Medvedev was commander of the guard keeping watch on the royal family at the Ipatiev house. In 1919 he was interrogated in Ekaterinburg on charges of conspiracy and murder. This is his evidence:

'I, Pavel Spiridonovich Medvedev, 31 years of age, am Orthodox, literate, have never been charged with breaking the law, am of peasant origin . . . I took up duty the night of 16 July, and around 8 o'clock the same evening, Commander Yurovsky ordered me to confiscate all the Nagant revolvers in the detachment, and to bring them to him. I took revolvers from those at their posts and from some others, a total of twelve revolvers, and brought them to the commandant's office. Then Yurovsky said to me "Today we'll have to shoot everybody. Warn the detachment so they won't worry if they hear shots." I guessed that Yurovsky was talking about the shooting of the entire royal family and the doctor and servants who lived with them . . . Around 2 o'clock in the morning the tsar, tsaritsa, four royal daughters, the maid, doctor, cook, and footman came out of their rooms. The tsar carried the heir in his arms. The sovereign and heir were dressed in soldiers' shirts and caps. Her Majesty and the daughters were in dresses with no outerwear and uncovered heads . . . None of the members of the imperial family asked anybody any questions in my presence. There were no tears, no sobbing, either. Having descended the stairs leading from the second entrance hall to the lower floor, we went into the courtyard and from there through a second door (counting from the gates) into the inner lodgings of the lower floor. Yurovsky showed the way. They were brought into the corner room on the lower floor adjacent to the sealed storage room. Yurovsky ordered that chairs be brought . . . It seems that all of them suspected the fate that was about to befall them, but no one made a single sound. Simultaneously, eleven people walked into the same room ... Yurovsky sent me out, saying "Go to the street, to see whether anybody's there and whether the shots will be heard." I walked out into the courtyard enclosed by a tall fence, and I heard the sound of shots before I had reached the street. I immediately returned to the house.'

---

pregnancy and suicidal breakdown – but was not Anastasia.

Much has now become clearer. But the fate of the two missing Romanovs remains unknown, and until it is settled the memory of the tsar's family is unlikely to rest in peace.

THE ZINOVIEV LETTER

DID A FORGED LETTER CHANGE THE COURSE OF 20TH-CENTURY BRITISH POLITICS?

RED PLOT AGAINST BRITAIN.

SENSATIONAL EXPOSURE.

RUSSIAN INSTRUCTIONS SENT TO THE BRITISH COMMUNIST PARTY.

ARMED REVOLUTION.

ORDERS FOR TAMPERING WITH ARMY & NAVY.

SENSATIONAL documents were issued from the Foreign Office last evening, exposing a Russian Communist plot against Great Britain, and announcing a strong protest which our Government has made to the Soviet.

One of these documents is a letter which has been addressed to the Central Committee of the British Communist Party from the Executive Committee of the Communist International, over the signature of Zinoviev, its president. This letter is dated Sept. 15 last, and it contains detailed instructions to British subjects to work for the violent overthrow of existing institutions in this country, and for the subversion of the British armed forces as a means to that end.

The other document is the British protest, sent by the Foreign Office to Rakovski, the Russian Chargé d'Affaires in London. In it the Government declare they "cannot allow this propaganda," and stigmatise it as a direct violation of the agreement concluded on August 8 last.

BRITISH GOVERNMENT'S CHALLENGE TO SOVIET.

EARTHQUAKE AT BIRMINGHAM.
City Surprised by a Sudden Jolt.
BUILDINGS TREMBLE VIOLENTLY.

In January 1924, after a snap general election, James Ramsay MacDonald led the Labour Party to power in Britain. For the first time in history the country had a socialist government, a fact which provoked uproar among the upper classes who still regarded government by working men with a mixture of snobbish amusement and real alarm. However, MacDonald was in no position to initiate a social revolution; his was a shaky minority government which depended on the goodwill of the Liberals. And when that failed, the new Labour prime minister was forced to call another election, scheduled for October 29.

Just four days before polling day, a letter published in the daily newspapers caused a political earthquake. The letter purported to be from Grigori Zinoviev, the Soviet chairman of the Communist International. Marked 'Very Secret' it was addressed to the central committee of the British Communist Party, and it told them how to control the Labour Party and thereby start a revolution.

A CALL FOR INSURRECTION

Whether the Zinoviev Letter was genuine or a forgery, middle-class Britons voted Conservative in the 1924 election, frightened by its appeal for revolution:

'The establishment of close contact between the British and Russian proletariat, the exchange of delegations and workers, etc., will make it possible for us to extend and develop the propaganda of ideas of Leninism in England and the Colonies. Armed warfare must be preceded by a struggle against the inclinations to compromise which are embedded among the majority of British workmen, against the ideas of evolution and peaceful extermination of capitalism. Only then will it be possible to count upon complete success of an armed insurrection ... It is evident that agitation-propaganda work in the army is weak, in the navy a very little better ... it would be desirable to have cells in all the units of the troops, particularly those quartered in the large centres of the country, and also among factories working on munitions and at military store depots.'

THE STORY BREAKS British Prime Minister Ramsay MacDonald (above) and Foreign Secretary Austen Chamberlain (right) were shocked by reports of a communist plot to subvert parliamentary democracy.

It called for an armed struggle against capitalism and for seditious propaganda among the forces, too.

Conspiracy theory

When published in the press, the letter was accompanied by the text of a strong Foreign Office protest to Russia. And the scare which resulted prompted a Tory landslide on polling day: the Conservatives romped home with 419 seats in the new parliament compared with 258 in the last. Interestingly, these seats were won not so much from Labour (whose vote actually went up), but from worried Liberals who defected in droves to the Conservatives. The election proved to be a historic one, for the collapse of the Liberal vote helped to sharpen what was to become an increasingly two-party polarisation in British politics.

Was the letter authentic? In Russia, Grigori Zinoviev immediately denounced it as a hoax, and the Soviet Government demanded an apology for the charges of propaganda activity laid against it. In Britain,

STIRRING REVOLUTION Zinoviev, the Comintern leader, was at the heart of the 1924 furore.

the bulk of the Labour Party was also convinced of a forgery. But the Conservatives were just as sure that the letter was authentic. On November 19, a British Cabinet committee declared it to be genuine, and two days later the Foreign Secretary, Austen Chamberlain, put an end to ongoing Anglo-Soviet treaty negotiations. Chamberlain refused to disclose much about the source of government information, since 'it is of the essence of a Secret Service that it must be secret'. However, the government claimed that the original letter had reached England by a route that could be traced all the way back to Leningrad.

The original was not available for study. In the official story, the Zinoviev Letter had been received by members of the British Communist Party and destroyed by them. So the version published was a translation of a copy which reached the Foreign Office, Conservative Central Office and the *Daily Mail* (the first newspaper to possess the text) through the Secret Service. Though this does not in itself prove forgery, many historians incline to the view that it was a fake, produced by Russian emigrés in Berlin. If so, it stands among the most politically influential hoaxes of all time.

THE CRASH OF THE HINDENBURG

WHY DID AN AIRSHIP THAT HAD BECOME SUCH A SYMBOL OF HITLER'S NEW GERMANY EXPLODE?

It is one of the most moving commentaries in the archives of recorded sound. The date was May 6, 1937, and radio journalist Herbert Morrison was reporting for WLS Chicago on the arrival in New Jersey of the giant German airship *Hindenburg*. The great Zeppelin with 97 people on board had been circling Lakehurst naval base for some time, waiting for storm clouds to pass, but at last it moved towards the mooring mast. 'Here it comes, ladies and gentlemen, and what a sight it is, a thrilling one, a marvellous sight', Morrison told his listeners before suddenly breaking into an anguished scream. 'Oh, oh, oh . . . It's burst into flames! . . . Get out of my way please, oh my this is terrible . . .'

The rear of the ship had exploded in a mass of incandescence and begun to sink groundwards, while passengers and crew jumped for their lives, screaming so loudly that they

SAILING THE SKIES Before the crash, Zeppelins epitomised luxurious air travel.

were heard by spectators on the ground. Herb Morrison broke down in tears, and a newsreel photographer muttered 'Oh my God, oh my God' over and over as he tracked the flaring ship's descent. In just 32 seconds the whole flaming ball of hydrogen had completely burnt out, leaving only the twisted metal frame and a charred remnant of the swastika-emblazoned tailfin. Altogether, 20 crew members, 15 passengers and one member of the ground staff died.

End of an era

What had caused the catastrophe? The great airship carried nearly 7 million cu ft (198 100 m³) of hydrogen, a highly inflammable gas with obvious hazards. Nonetheless, safety precautions on the *Hindenburg* were stringent, and the airship had already made many perfectly safe trips back and forth across the Atlantic. The best guess of baffled inquiry officials was that the hydrogen had been ignited after the thunderstorm by a freak discharge of static electricity known as St Elmo's Fire. However, some of the ground staff believed that one of the *Hindenburg*'s engines was sparking badly, and that this might have ignited the gas.

Sabotage has also been suggested as a possible cause. The luxury airship was a prestige product of Hitler's Germany, and as such a prime target for enemies of Nazism. Crew members had heard a bang like gunfire just before the ship burst into flames, and some of them suspected deliberate destruction. In his book about the disaster, published in 1972, Michael Mooney made the

FLY PAST At about 3 pm on the day of the crash, the *Hindenburg* passed over Manhattan en route for the Lakehurst landing ground. Far left: a luggage label.

specific claim that the airship was sabotaged by crew member Eric Spehl. The 25-year-old German rigger had, it is alleged, placed an incendiary bomb on board as an act of anti-Nazi terrorism. This was due to explode after the ship had landed, but Spehl's plan went awry because of the delay caused by the storm. Mooney further claimed that German and American officials agreed to a cover-up to avoid an international incident.

True or not, the *Hindenburg* disaster had the historic consequence of putting an end

DISASTER STRIKES The giant dirigible crashes in flames following an explosion that occurred just as the airship was about to be moored to her mast.

to the age of airships. Powered balloons had, until then, been thought more suitable for passenger transport than winged aircraft, being more spacious and virtually silent. In the wake of the mystery crash, public feeling turned against them and aeroplanes became the preferred form of passenger flight.

1950 ▮▮▮▮▮▮▮▮ 2000

1972 Michael Mooney
publishes *The Hindenburg*

THE NORMANDIE DISASTER

WAS IT SABOTAGE OR SIMPLY AN ACCIDENT THAT CAUSED THE FIRE THAT SANK THE PRIDE OF FRANCE?

The majestic *Normandie* was the pride of France's passenger fleet during the 1930s. The largest of the inter-war Atlantic liners, weighing 83 000 tons, she could carry 2170 passengers. And the great ship was fast, too: she travelled at a mean speed of 31.2 knots (57.7 km/h), which won her the Blue Riband award for the quickest Atlantic crossing by a recognised shipping route.

When France fell to the Germans in 1940, the *Normandie* was in New York harbour where she was placed under restraint by the US authorities. After Pearl Harbor, when the USA entered the Second World War, she was expropriated by the US Maritime Commission for conversion into a troopship. The plan was to relaunch her as the USS *Lafayette*, and more than 3000 workmen began the task of refitting her.

On February 9, 1942, a catastrophic fire

OUT OF ACTION The flame-charred hull of the *Normandie* lies on its side at the Hudson River Pier in New York, presenting the US Navy with a mighty salvage job.

engulfed one of the lower decks. For 12 hours the flames roared, and while the asphyxiating fumes and smoke blackened parts of New York City the liner capsized at her pier to sink into the harbour mud, with her funnels poking above the water.

A subsequent investigation concluded that an acetylene torch had ignited a pile of

UNDER RESTRAINT The French passenger liner SS *Normandie*, at the pier in New York, was due for refitting for troop transport when the disaster occurred.

kapok – the waterproof cotton-like stuffing used to fill life jackets. But the timing of the disaster was suspicious. The accident occurred just one day after the *Normandie* had been turned over to the US Navy. Why did the fire spread so quickly? Why

did it take so long for the New York fire service to be alerted? And why were the ship's hose fittings being changed at the moment the blaze broke out? Some blamed sabotage, either by Germany or by French Nazi-sympathisers, for the loss of the vessel, and the controversy endures to this day.

1900   2000

1932 The *Normandie* is launched at the Saint-Nazaire shipyard in France
1940 France falls to the Germans
1942 The *Normandie* sinks in New York harbour

THE KATYN GRAVES

**THE FATE OF 15 000 POLISH SOLDIERS HAS
REMAINED A MYSTERY UNTIL THE LAST FEW YEARS**

On April 13, 1943, Berlin radio announced that the bodies of some 10 000 Polish officers had been unearthed from seven mass graves in a forest at Katyn, near the Russian city of Smolensk which was occupied during the German advance. The figure was an exaggeration – in reality, the dead numbered about 4500. But the discovery bore witness to what was undoubtedly one of the worst atrocities of the 20th century. All the signs pointed to a massacre: the officers, hands bound, had mostly been shot in the back of the head. The Nazis blamed the Russians for it, and the Polish government-

**COLD-BLOODED SLAUGHTER Mass graves
uncovered in the Katyn forest in 1943
contained the bodies of 4500 Polish soldiers.**

in-exile broke off diplomatic relations with the Soviet Union. In 1944, when the Red Army recaptured Katyn, the Russians countered with the claim that the Nazis had been responsible for the atrocity.

Gunshots were heard

With Europe still gripped by war there was no way of proving anyone culpable, but the evidence suggested that Stalin was the guilty party. In 1939, the Red Army had occupied part of Poland and transported some 15 000 Polish officers and intellectuals from their sector back to three labour camps in Soviet-occupied territory. Most of these men remained in the camps until April 1940 when they mysteriously disappeared. It was reported that 4500 prisoners from the camp at Kozielsk were shipped by cattle train to Katyn. Day after

**UNEASY ALLIANCE Stalin
greets von Ribbentrop during
the 1939 Nazi-Soviet pact.
Both sides later blamed the
other for the Katyn massacre.**

day in the early months of 1940, local peasants saw men spilling out of the wagons and being driven into the woods. Soviet troops with picks and spades were also seen, and gunshots were heard. It is believed that the victims were lined up in rows while the Russians shot them one by one before rolling them into a pit.

In 1990 the Soviet Union admitted responsibility for the massacre of all 15 000 Poles; according to a news bulletin, the killings were 'one of the greatest crimes of Stalinism'. But although this ended speculation about one of the great unsolved crimes of modern times, it failed to locate the whereabouts of the remaining bodies. Are there other mass graves waiting to be found?

1939 15 000 Polish men transported to Soviet-held territory
1943 The Germans announce discovery
of the mass graves

1985 Gorbachev becomes
leader of the Soviet Union
1990 Soviets admit
to Katyn massacre

HOW DID HITLER DIE?

RECENTLY RELEASED ARCHIVES SOLVE SOME OF THE PROBLEMS SURROUNDING HITLER'S FINAL HOURS

On the evening of May 1, 1945, Hamburg Radio announced the death of Hitler who had, it was said, fallen that afternoon fighting 'at the head of his troops'. Like much of the information that issued from Germany's wartime propaganda machine, this was, in fact, a lie. At the close of the war in Europe, as the Allies advanced through the bombed-out rubble of the Reich, the Führer was not at the Front but in a Berlin bunker, ranting about the betrayals that had brought him down.

In that bunker, the history books now record, he killed himself. But throughout the summer of 1945, rumours circulated that the Nazi leader was still alive: he had found refuge at Innsbruck, or in a moated Westphalian castle. He was sighted living as a shepherd in the Swiss Alps, as a recluse in a cave near Italy's Lake Garda, and as a casino croupier at Evian in France. Hitler was living in purpose-built underground quarters at a German-owned hacienda in Argentina,

INSIDE THE BUNKER

As the Allies approached Berlin in 1945, life in Hitler's bunker became increasingly fraught. The bunker was built on two levels, connected by a spiral staircase. On the upper level were the servants' quarters and the dining area, and on the lower level 18 rooms including the map room, a conference area, the generator, toilets and the bedrooms of Eva Braun, Goebbels and Hitler himself. The ceilings were low, the corridors narrow and conditions cramped. Condensation dripped from the walls, and, as Hitler became increasingly nervous, the body odour for which he was well known got worse.

with a stone-walled entrance operated by photo-electric cells ...

In September 1945, an official inquiry into Hitler's death was set up by the British to establish the truth. It was led by Hugh Trevor-Roper, a young army major who was also an historian by training. Having tracked down witnesses from the Führer's last days, he concluded that Hitler had committed suicide in the Berlin bunker – a suite of rooms 50 ft (15 m) beneath the gardens of the

Reich Chancellery. At about 3.30 pm on April 30, 1945, the Nazi leader had put a pistol in his mouth and pulled the trigger. Eva Braun, his mistress whom he had married the day before, had taken a cyanide capsule and died with him. Trevor-Roper's report, published in 1947 as *The Last Days of Hitler*, became the classic work on the subject.

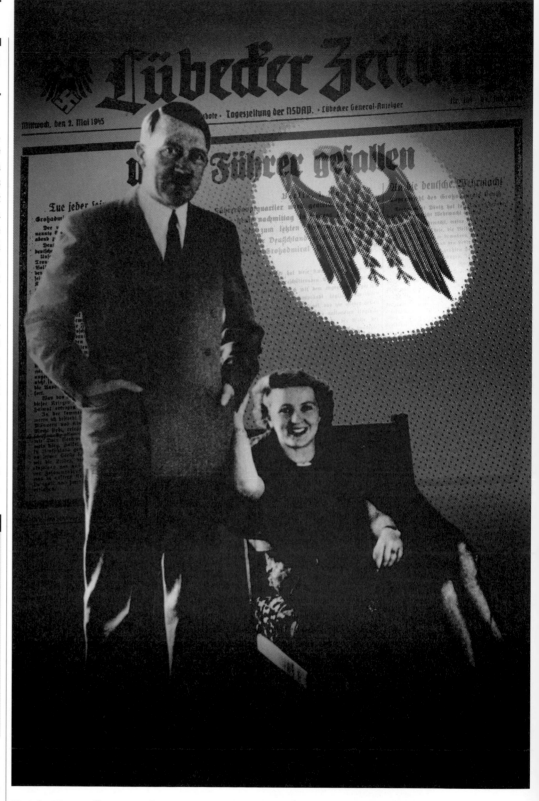

MASTER OF LIES A newspaper falsely proclaims Hitler's death in battle: Hitler and Eva Braun probably committed suicide.

But the all-important question of Hitler's remains was still an unresolved mystery. According to the reports, the corpses of Hitler and Eva were taken up to the

WAR'S END Investigators in 1945 found fragments of Hitler's clothing among Eva Braun's possessions, and explored the wreckage of the Berlin bunker (below).

The attitude of the Soviet authorities compounded the mystery. The Russians were the first to reach Berlin, and were known to have dug up a number of bodies in the Reich Chancellery garden. Among the remains were said to have been Hitler's teeth – identified by a woman who was assistant to the Führer's dentist – but for more than 20 years, the Soviets refused to comment on any such finds. Then, in 1968, a book written by a Russian journalist called Lev Bezymenski described how in 1945 Soviet troops had recovered the charred bodies of Hitler and Eva Braun from a bomb crater in the Reich Chancellery garden. Doctors, he claimed, had identified them by their dental work and carried out autopsies. The smell of bitter almonds emanated from their bodies, indicating poisoning by cyanide.

Recent revelations

More sensational revelations were yet to come. In 1992, in the new climate of freedom in Russia, a researcher named Ada Petrova was given access to six secret files on Hitler's death, which had been hidden in the KGB archives. These revealed that, at the war's end, the Russians had taken extraordinary

Chancellery garden, doused with petrol and set alight so that they should burn, as the Führer had ordered, 'until nothing remained'. However, Trevor-Roper himself acknowledged that although a petrol fire might char the bodies beyond recognition, the bones would have withstood the heat. Hitler's bones have never been found. What had happened?

Some continued to doubt whether the Führer was dead at all: Hitler sightings continued for decades after the report was published, and as late as 1992 a Canadian newspaper reported the death of the Führer in Latin America. Even among those who accepted the idea of a suicide in the bunker there was controversy. Did Hitler really shoot himself, in soldierly fashion? Or did he take poison – an act perceived to be a coward's way out? There were some discrepancies in the reports and, with no remains available for analysis, these questions remained open to debate.

pains to find out precisely what had happened to the Nazi leader. Some 800 people were interrogated, and 70 were brought back to Russia for long-term questioning, along with a mass of material from the bunker. Stalin, it is known, had been sceptical about Hitler's death and wanted to be absolutely certain that the Führer had not escaped. Among the material in the Soviet archives were Hitler's uniforms, his photograph album and 42 watercolours by the Nazi leader. There were also pictures from the Chancellery of a man bearing a striking resemblance to Hitler, who seemed to have been shot through the forehead. This was not Hitler himself but his double – a man named Gustav Weler who was employed in the Chancellery and occasionally wheeled out in suitable costume to stand in for the Nazi supremo. He either shot himself, or was shot, in the last days

NEW FINDS Hitler's fire-scorched uniform (with his name sewn on the inside of the armband) and a sketchbook, containing 42 watercolours painted by the Führer, were among the relics which came to light in the 1990s, when the KGB archives were opened up.

1968 Bezymenski claims that the Soviet authorities had, in 1945, secretly investigated Hitler's death

1992 Ada Petrova is given access to secret Soviet files

MACABRE RELICS   Using dental records, researchers believe that they have identified fragments of Hitler's lower jaw (right) and upper jaw (far right). A bullet-hole is clearly visible in a piece of his skull (below).

AFTER THE FALL   Soviet ministers and officials visit what was left of Hitler's Bunker in May 1945.

before the fall of Berlin. When the Russians first came upon his corpse they mistook him for the Führer himself.

Crucial among the finds in the Soviet archives were fragments of what was alleged to be Hitler's skull, burnt at the edges, with the exit wound of a bullet hole clearly visible in one of them. This astonishing relic indicated that the Führer had, indeed, shot himself. Piecing together the evidence, researchers proposed a theory in which the Nazi leader had taken poison *and* shot himself, placing a cyanide capsule in his mouth before firing a pistol through the underside of his chin.

Some critics have doubted the authenticity of the finds, suggesting that the forensic evidence was faked, perhaps by Soviet bureaucrats who were under considerable pressure to convince a deeply suspicious Stalin that his old rival really was dead. Why, if the finds were genuine, did the Russians not make them public sooner? The answer may lie in their discovery that Hitler did shoot himself; Stalin would have preferred a coward's death for the Nazi leader. Besides, the Soviet secret services were notoriously secretive about everything. Who knows whose interests the silence best served?

Forensic evidence

In 1995, an independent Russian expert, Professor Viktor Zyagin from the Federal Centre of Medical Forensic Examination, declared himself 80 per cent certain that the skull was Hitler's. He even deduced, from the colour of the pieces of skull, that its owner had been a vegetarian – as Hitler was. But the story need not end there: an absolute confirmation could still come from DNA fingerprinting. Some relatives of Hitler are still alive, and tests on them could be matched against analysis of the skull bones to see whether genetic material is common to both. One way or another, such an investigation could help to answer one of the most enduring mysteries of modern history.

DETECTION AND DNA

Is the 'Hitler skull' in Moscow truly a relic of Germany's wartime Nazi leader? A DNA analysis could help to resolve this problem, just as it has helped to clear up mysteries surrounding the last Russian Tsar's family, and many criminal cases besides. Genetic fingerprinting has revolutionised forensic science in the late 20th century. The technique derived in the 1980s from research into DNA, an acid in the nucleus of every living cell which carries genetic information. This determines a person's individual characteristics, such as the colour of hair and eyes, and the structure is different in everybody (except identical twins). As a result, a person's DNA profile is as distinctive as his or her fingerprint.

To obtain a specimen, scientists work from a tiny sample containing some human cells: a spot of blood, for example, or a single hair. To produce a visual record, the genetic information is translated into a series of bars on an X-Ray film; the result resembles the bar code printed on a consumer product. There is enough cellular material in human saliva to take a reading from a cigarette butt left at the scene of a crime, or an envelope licked by a blackmailer.

The technique can be employed in paternity disputes, because the DNA of father and child match more closely than the DNA of unrelated individuals. It is through surviving relatives of Hitler that identification of 'his' skull could be achieved. The remains of another prominent Nazi, Josef Mengele, have already been analysed with the help of DNA fingerprinting. In 1985, the supposed body of this notorious concentration camp doctor was exhumed from a grave outside Sao Paulo in Brazil. DNA samples from the body closely matched samples from Mengele's son and, combined with dental and skeleton analysis, helped to fix the corpse's identity as that of Josef Mengele, Auschwitz's 'Angel of Death'.

GENETIC FINGERPRINTING   Blood is taken from the suspect (1) and from the crime scene (2). DNA is extracted (3) and cut into fragments (4), which are sorted by length (5). The DNA fragments are transferred to a nylon membrane (6). Light-emitting probes locate the fragments of interest (7), and these are photographed (8) for comparison (9). Only 9b matches.

DOUBLES FOR DECEPTION

IN THE INCREASINGLY SOPHISTICATED WORLD OF DELUSION AND DISINFORMATION, LOOKALIKES ARE USED AS DECOYS

Lieutenant M.E. Clifton James was at his desk at the Royal Army Pay Corps in 1944, when he received a telephone call from film star Colonel David Niven, who was serving with the Army Kinematograph section during the Second World War.

The call was the first thread in an elaborate web of deception intended to draw attention away from the imminent Allied invasion of Europe. James, who had fought in the trenches during the First World War, was a peacetime actor who happened to bear an extraordinarily close physical resemblance to General Montgomery, the victor of El Alamein and the commander-in-chief of all ground forces for the Normandy landings of 1944. Security chiefs hatched a plan which involved using James to impersonate Monty. Monty's double was then to be despatched to Gibraltar and North Africa in order to delude the Germans that Monty was going to lead an invasion from southern France, rather than from Normandy.

Under conditions of the utmost secrecy, James was posted as a Sergeant of the Intelligence Corps to Monty's staff so that he could study the general's voice, gestures and mannerisms: the way he saluted, for example, clasped his hands behind his back, or pinched a little roll of his cheek when thinking. As an actor, James had little

I WAS MONTY'S DOUBLE Lookalike Lieutenant Clifton James (left) was asked to impersonate Britain's General Montgomery (right) during the build-up to the D-Day landings in 1944.

HITLER'S DOUBLE The body of the Führer's impersonator, Gustav Weler, was found in the bunker beneath the Reich Chancellery garden with a bullet hole in the forehead.

difficulty in mastering Monty's every movement, but he was more worried about his ability to capture Monty's personality. 'It was so unique and overpowering', he wrote in his classic *I Was Monty's Double*, 'that I despaired of ever *being* him. It was one thing to ape the outside of a man, but quite another to acquire something of his fire and forcefulness.'

James underestimated his abilities. After several rehearsals, he flew as General Montgomery to Gibraltar, where he was greeted by the British Governor and introduced – as if by chance – to several of Hitler's known secret agents. A similar performance was then repeated in Algiers, where he was cheered by British troops. News of 'Monty's' whereabouts travelled fast – transmitted by enemy agents back to the German High Command. James's performance was as fine as any he ever gave and contributed in no small way to the success of what his British Secret Service handler described as 'one of the greatest plans of deception that has ever been attempted'.

The German leader, Adolf Hitler, also employed a double. The man's name was Gustav Weler and he was an employee at the Reich Chancellery in Berlin, occasionally brought out to stand in for the Führer. When Russian troops discovered Weler's corpse in 1945, they believed, at first, that they had found Hitler's body.

In more recent years it has been widely reported that the Iraqi leader, Saddam Hussein, uses a double as a decoy to foil would-be assassins. His 1990 invasion of Kuwait and his savage repression of Shiites and Kurds have made him a prime target; he is known to have survived at least 12 attempts on his life.

THE DEATH OF STALIN

DID THE SOVIET DICTATOR'S POWER-HUNGRY POLITICAL RIVALS ALLOW STALIN TO DIE?

On January 13, 1953, the Russian newspaper *Pravda* announced that security police had arrested nine distinguished doctors and accused them of conspiring to kill Soviet leaders. The prosecution alleged that the conspirators were agents of Zionist and Western intelligence organisations, and among them was V.N. Vinogradov, until recently personal doctor to the Soviet leader, Joseph Stalin.

The trumped-up charges suggested to foreign observers that Stalin was raising the curtain on a new terror, comparable perhaps to that of the 1930s. Particularly disquieting was the fact that six of the nine doctors named were Jewish, provoking concern about a coming pogrom. But all senior party figures must have quivered at the announcement; no one knew who would be accused next.

The dying days of a dictator

Long years of despotic rule had made Stalin suspicious to the point of paranoia, but he had good reason to feel uneasy at this time. He was 73 years old, and ailing in health. Other, ambitious men were waiting in the wings; Stalin had even come to doubt the loyalty of old comrades such as Lavrenti Beria, the Soviet secret police chief, and Nikita Khrushchev, head of the Party secretariat. Early in 1953, Stalin started elevating younger men to positions of authority in order to dilute the power of the old guard.

It was against this backdrop of suspicion and menace that, on March 1, 1953, Stalin suddenly collapsed, apparently from a stroke. At about 10.30 pm an anxious bodyguard broke into his rooms where the Soviet

HARD MAN Notorious for his ruthless repression of dissent, the Soviet leader was born Joseph Djugashvili. Stalin (Russian for 'man of steel') was an adopted name.

leader was found lying on the carpet, partially paralysed and unable to speak. Asked what was wrong, he replied with an incoherent buzzing sound. His pocketwatch and a copy of *Pravda* were lying on the floor beside him. Stalin was moved to a couch and, while Beria and other colleagues were summoned, word was also sent to his family. Stalin's son Vasily had no doubt about what had happened; while the dictator lay dying he raged

around the apartment shouting in a drunken voice: 'They've killed my father!'

Was Stalin murdered – and if so, by whom? If there was foul play, the sinister Beria, who – as well as running the internal security services – administered the Soviet Union's labour camps, or 'gulags', has been singled out as the likeliest candidate for the role of killer. It took Stalin more than three days to die, and throughout the long ordeal

1900 Stalin joins a Georgian revolutionary organisation

1917 The Russian Revolution

1922 Stalin becomes General Secretary of the Communist Party's central committee

1934 Murder of Kirov and the start of the purges

1941 Germany invades Russia, precipitating the Soviet Union's entry into the Second World War

HEIRS APPARENT Marshal Bulganin (above, left) and Nikita Khrushchev (above, right) came to prominence when Stalin died. Beria (right) was tried and executed.

of waiting, while others wept or lay slumped in states of exhaustion around the apartment, the secret police chief was torn by conflicting emotions and interests. As Khrushchev later remembered: 'As soon as Stalin showed signs of consciousness, Beria threw himself on his knees, seized Stalin's hand and started kissing it. When Stalin lost consciousness again and closed his eyes, Beria stood up and spat …spewing hatred.' It was not long, however, before Beria conspicuously took control, behaving as if he were heir apparent to the vast Soviet empire.

Long after Stalin's death, rumours of a

LYING IN STATE Top Soviet statesmen, jockeying for power, conceal their differences at Stalin's death watch.

top-level conspiracy persisted, and indeed the Soviet politician Anastas Mikoyan later confided to the Albanian leader Enver Hoxha that he and others had discussed killing Stalin. However, there is no evidence that he was murdered by anything so compromising as, for example, poisoning or lethal injection.. It is more likely that Stalin suffered a stroke, and that arrangements were subsequently made to deny medical care to the ailing despot. Beria arrived at Stalin's apartment at about 3 o'clock in the morning on March 2, with the Soviet politician Georgi Malenkov. Doctors did not arrive until 8.30 or even 9 am. By then Stalin had been left untreated for at least ten hours. Had Beria been keen for a recovery, medical help would certainly have arrived much sooner.

The struggle for power

The end came for Stalin at 9.50 pm on March 5, 1953. According to his daughter Svetlana, who defected to the West in 1967: 'The death agony was terrible. God grants an easy death only to the just. He literally

---

REIGN OF TERROR

On December 1, 1934, Sergei Kirov, a rising star in the Communist Party and a potential rival, was assassinated – almost certainly at Stalin's instigation. The murder heralded waves of 'show trials' and purges, in which as many as 20 million Russians lost their lives – more than twice the number who died in the Holocaust.

---

choked to death as we watched.'

A savage power struggle ensued immediately. Beria made the early running, ordering

PERSONALITY CULT A propaganda poster of 1939 proclaims: 'Our army and our country are strengthened with the spirit of Stalin!'

tanks and flame-throwers to seal off Moscow and prevent unrest at the dictator's funeral. One of Stalin's top aides later disappeared, and key members of the Politburo were ousted from their posts. But it was Khrushchev who emerged victorious in the end. Beria was accused of conspiracy in July, tried secretly and executed in December. As for the famous doctors' plot, the whole affair was pronounced a 'criminal hoax' and quickly forgotten. Within a month of Stalin's death, the accused physicians were fully rehabilitated and reinstalled in the Kremlin Medical Service.

1953 Stalin dies
Khrushchev consolidates his power and is
appointed First Secretary of the central committee

WAS DAG HAMMARSKJOLD MURDERED?

HOW THE MYSTERIOUS DEATH OF ONE MAN THREATENED THE FUTURE OF THE UNITED NATIONS

No one who becomes Secretary-General of the United Nations can expect an easy life. Sweden's Dag Hammarskjold, who took up the post in 1953, plunged into the anguish of Cold War confrontation, the Suez Crisis of 1956 and the Hungarian rising against Soviet control, also in 1956. In 1960 a new crisis developed in the Congo (now Zaire) where a bloody civil war broke out on the granting of independence to the former Belgian colony in central Africa. While the rebel statesman Moise Tshombe led the secession of the copper-rich Katanga province, Prime Minister Patrice Lumumba was deposed and murdered. Hammarskjold himself faced criticism for the way the United Nations had handled the transition to independence, and condemnation was particularly loud when UN troops from Sweden, Ireland and India were involved in fighting while attempting to end Katanga's secession.

INDEPENDENCE DAY Patrice Lumumba became the first prime minister of an independent Belgian Congo.

This was the turbulent background to Hammarskjold's last flight. In September 1961 the secretary-general received an invitation from the rebel Tshombe to meet for peace talks at Ndola in neutral Northern Rhodesia (now Zambia). The idea was that Hammarskjold should fly from the capital of the Congo, Leopoldville (now Kinshasa), in a DC4 Skymaster plane, but he switched at the last minute to a DC6 airliner in order to evade the crowds of waiting newsmen. The plane took off in the middle of the afternoon, and after about four hours the pilot contacted the control tower at Ndola airport announcing his intention to descend for landing. Oddly, though, the four-engined DC-6B failed to come down at the expected time of arrival. It was not until two and a half hours later that the airliner began to approach the airfield, and when it did so it came in from the south-west, flying from deep inside Rhodesian territory. The assumption was that it had overshot its target by some distance and was now backtracking. There was nothing, however, to suggest any difficulty as the DC6's Swedish pilot radioed that he had the runway lights in sight and was coming down.

Then, as ground staff peered into the darkness, they saw a sudden burst of flame and watched in horror as the burning aircraft crashed, incandescent, into the jungle beyond the runway. When rescue workers reached the wreckage, they found 13 of the 14 passengers dead, including Hammarskjold whose body lay sprawled in the aisle.

Accident or assassination?

It might have been an accident. The DC6 was a UN plane which had been peppered by Congolese anti-aircraft fire on the day before it took off on the fateful flight. It had been only hastily fixed afterwards, and maps detailing the approach to Ndola were missing from the pilot's flight-briefing book. Moreover, the altimeter was faulty, and would have given an incorrect reading of the plane's height above the ground. A Rhodesian enquiry concluded that the

FINAL FAREWELL Dag Hammarskjold (left) confers with an Italian representative at the United Nations, only weeks before his funeral (above).

crash was indeed an accident, and put it down to pilot error. According to the official version, the plane struck a tree with its wingtip as it turned for its final approach.

But such a crash, in the midst of sensitive negotiations, raised inevitable suspicions of foul play. In New Delhi, the Indian Prime Minister Pandit Nehru was among the first to suggest that the plane might have been sabotaged. And it was certainly true that there were people on both sides of the civil war who might have wanted to see the peace talks fail. Dag Hammarskjold was not universally

PRESIDENT ITALY

SMOULDERING RUINS Rescuers work amidst the wreckage of the airliner which crashed in the African bush, 8 miles (13 km) from Ndola, killing 13 passengers including Hammarskjold.

A puzzling detail was supplied by the sole survivor of the disaster, Harold Julian, an American security officer with the United Nations. Terribly burnt, and suffering from broken bones, he was to recover consciousness only for a brief period after the crash.

Unanswered questions

Questioned at his bedside about the missing two hours, when the plane seemed to have overshot Ndola airport, the injured man answered that 'Mr Hammarskjold told us to turn back, he didn't say why', and that, moments later, a series of explosions had preceded the crash. Police at Ndola saw a 'huge flare in the sky, seconds before the crash'.

Harold Julian died without being able to elucidate further. Had the secretary-general

admired. Soviet leader Nikita Khrushchev had dubbed him a 'bloody-handed lackey of the colonial powers', and in the United Nations, the Russian delegate dissociated his government from a communiqué which praised Hammarskjold's leadership. When Khrushchev called for his removal, Hammarskjold responded by claiming that 'by resigning I would ... at the present difficult and dangerous juncture, throw the organisation to the winds'.

In the twisted wreckage of the DC6, scraps of evidence hinted at something more than pilot error. Tucked into the lapel of Dag Hammarskjold's jacket, for example, was a playing card – the Ace of Spades, the mark of death. How did it get there? A revolver was found in the wreckage only a few feet from Hammarskjold's body. There were bullet holes, too, in the fuselage. Were these relics of an earlier attack on the plane, or had there been a gunfight in the cabin? Had someone tampered with the altimeter so that it gave false readings? And how to explain one witness's report of hearing jets whistle above the airport just before the airliner plunged burning into the forest?

REBEL LEADER Moise Tshombe, who headed the breakaway province of Katanga, was imprisoned in Algeria where he died in 1969.

HOMEWARD JOURNEY The coffin holding Dag Hammarskjold's remains is borne by federal policemen towards a plane for its return from Salisbury, Southern Rhodesia, to Sweden.

suddenly doubted the wisdom of the meeting? Had he been warned of something by a fellow passenger? Questions like these torment researchers, and history furnishes no clear answers. Although the Rhodesian enquiry settled for pilot error, the UN's own commission declared the crash 'unexplained'.

1953 Dag Hammarskjold is sworn in as UN Secretary-General

1960 Khrushchev asks for Hammarskjold's resignation
1961 Death of Dag Hammarskjold

WHO KILLED PRESIDENT KENNEDY?

CONSPIRACY THEORIES STILL SURROUND THE MURDER THAT SENT THE WORLD INTO MOURNING

The assassination traumatised the United States, wrenching at the psyche of the world's most powerful nation with such shocking force that the American Dream has never truly recovered.

On Friday, November 22, 1963, cheering crowds lined the streets of Dallas, Texas, as the young President John F. Kennedy moved in a motorcade through the metal-and-glass city sweltering in summer sunshine. The president had been apprehensive about his visit, for Dallas was politically hostile territory, but he needed to reconcile liberal and conservative elements within Texas's Democratic Party, and he hoped to raise funds and political support for his presidential re-election campaign the following year. The crowds were enthusiastic as he waved from his open limousine. 'Mr Kennedy, you can't say Dallas doesn't love you', said Mrs Connally, wife of the Governor of Texas, who was also in the car.

Then, as the motorcade moved slowly through Dealey Plaza just after 12.30 pm, several shots rang out in quick succession. Kennedy lurched; in front of him Governor Connally was hit in the chest and head; there was more gunfire and the president jerked backwards, his head partially exploding in a shower of blood. Jackie Kennedy, in a blood-spattered pink suit, cradled her husband as the driver raced the car to nearby Parkland Hospital. There Connally's life was saved. But there could be no hope for Kennedy. 'The president is gone', Mrs Kennedy was told.

Numb with the shock of the assassination, a worldwide audience was to follow its aftermath with disbelief. Only 45 minutes after the Kennedy shooting, a second murder was reported. A police patrolman had been shot dead a couple of miles from Dealey Plaza, and a young man was arrested in a nearby movie house. The suspect, said to have a pistol in his waistband, was hustled out of the cinema. He was charged in due course not only with the patrolman's murder but also with the assassination of President Kennedy.

The young man's name was Lee Harvey Oswald, and over the next two days he faced

MORNING NEWS A Dallas newspaper announces the shooting. Vice-president Lyndon Baines Johnson swiftly succeeded to the presidency.

IN THE FRAME A cine film taken by Dallas dress manufacturer Abraham Zapruder (right) is the most accurate record of the assassination. Lee Harvey Oswald (below) was presumed to be the assassin.

FATEFUL MOTORCADE A smiling President John F. Kennedy, with Jackie at his side, rides through Dallas only moments before his assassination on November 22, 1963.

1917 Birth of John F. Kennedy

1943 Kennedy heroically rescues a burnt crewman when his torpedo boat is sunk by a Japanese destroyer in the South Pacific

1952 Kennedy is
elected a senator
for Massachusetts

1960 Kennedy is elected president
of the USA, the youngest ever
1963 President Kennedy is assassinated

1979 The House Select
Committee on Assassinations
reports its findings

SUSPECT SLAIN Lee Harvey Oswald, led by detectives, is shot by nightclub owner Jack Ruby bursting forwards in the basement garage of the Dallas police HQ.

intense police questioning. In the police station too, representatives of the world's press managed to put questions to him, so that microphones recorded his emphatic denial of any involvement in the assassination. 'I'm a patsy!' he shouted as he was hustled away, implying that he had been framed.

Lone assassin or conspiracy?

On Sunday, flanked by detectives, Oswald was brought to the basement garage of the police HQ, to be moved to the county jail. As he was being led to a police car, a bystander lunged forwards with a revolver. The assailant was Jack Ruby, a local nightclub owner with underworld connections. Watched by millions of television viewers, Ruby fired one lethal bullet into Oswald's stomach. Within minutes Oswald was dead.

What forces were at work in this nightmare? Had Oswald been silenced to protect others? An official commission was set up to examine the whole affair under the much-respected Chief Justice, Earl Warren. Its conclusions, however, failed to have the calming effect that officialdom may have hoped for. The Warren Commission reported that Lee Harvey Oswald had acted alone in killing President Kennedy. A lonely, left-wing misfit, he was said to have fired three shots from the Texas School Book Depository where he worked. A 'sniper's nest' was found in a sixth-floor corner window, with three empty cartridges and a Mannlicher-Carcano rifle dating from 1940 stashed behind a pile of boxes. The Italian-made rifle, it was alleged, belonged to Oswald. As for Ruby, he testified before the Commission that he killed Oswald on a sudden impulse – to save Jackie Kennedy from the ordeal of a trial – and the Commission accepted his story.

The official verdict provoked a furious

THE SECOND SHOCK The murder of the prime suspect added a new and disquieting dimension to the assassination. Was Lee Harvey Oswald silenced?

controversy that has never died. Critics of the Warren Commission complained that Oswald's guilt was by no means proved, and that whether he was guilty or not, the authorities had wilfully ignored evidence

MURDER WEAPON The gun with which Kennedy was shot was said to be the 6.5mm bolt-action rifle with telescopic sight found in the Book Depository.

1917 Birth of John F. Kennedy

1943 Kennedy heroically rescues a burnt crewman when his torpedo boat is sunk by a Japanese destroyer in the South Pacific

——— Shots fired by Oswald, according to the Warren Commission

——— Six shots fired from possible positions in Dealey Plaza

——— Additional shots fired

Red trajectories
According to the Warren Commission, three shots (in red) were fired from the window of the sixth floor of the Book Depository at 411 Elm Street. One (the so-called 'magic bullet') struck the back of Kennedy's neck and exited to hit Governor Connally in the back, wrist and thigh. Another shot shattered Kennedy's skull. And a third bullet missed the motorcade entirely, landing on the kerb of Main Street.

Black trajectories
According to other versions, six shots (in black) may have been fired. The first (1) from the Dal-Tex building missed completely. The second (2), from the grassy knoll in front, struck Kennedy in the throat. The third (3), from the west end of the Book Depository, hit Connally. The fourth, from either the Book Depository or the Dal-Tex building (4), hit Kennedy in the back and propelled him forwards. The fifth (5), from the grassy knoll, hit Kennedy in the temple, and the sixth (6) from the Book Depository may have struck Connally in the wrist.

Blue trajectories
It seems that several other bullets (in blue) were fired that afternoon in Dallas, in addition to the six already suggested. One of these was probably fired from the Dal-Tex building and landed on the south kerb of Main Street. Another may have come from the western end of the Book Depository and ended up on the north pavement of Elm Street.

that more than one gunman was involved – in other words, there had been a conspiracy. There were several key points of controversy.

The magic bullet

An amateur cameraman in the crowd, Abraham Zapruder, had filmed the motorcade, and his harrowing footage of the entire assassination demonstrated that the shots were all fired within 5.6 seconds. However, the supposed assassination weapon was an old Second World War rifle. Critics complained that it could not have been fired quickly and accurately enough to account for at least two direct hits on Kennedy, plus one miss – and the governor's wounds – in the time available. The Commission, aware of this difficulty, theorised that one bullet, which turned up in pristine state in the hospital, had hit the president and gone on to strike Connally. What stretched credulity was that this so-called 'magic bullet' must

DEALEY PLAZA Oswald allegedly fired from the sixth floor of the Texas School Book Depository, but many witnesses reported shots from the grassy knoll.

have ploughed through two men, smashing bones, veins, arteries and nerves, and fallen out of an exit wound virtually undamaged.

Backthrust

The Zapruder film clearly showed Kennedy being slammed backwards by the second, fatal shot to the head. This was after the car had passed the Texas School Book Depository, strongly suggesting that at least one shot was fired from in front of him. Apologists for the Warren Commission have explained this backwards thrust as a nervous or muscular reaction, but the immediate and obvious impression of the Zapruder film is that Kennedy was hit from the front and propelled backwards. (Only still frames of

WARREN COMMISSION Members of the official investigating team assemble in their Washington meeting-room under the chairmanship of US Supreme Court Chief Justice Earl Warren (fourth from the left).

1952 Kennedy is elected a senator for Massachusetts

1960 Kennedy is elected president of the USA, the youngest ever
1963 President Kennedy is assassinated

1979 The House Select Committee on Assassinations reports its findings the film were made public at the time; moving pictures were first shown on television in March 1975.)

The grassy knoll

Of the many witnesses whose statements were available to the Warren Commission, 49 believed that the shots came from the

Texas School Book Depository and 21 believed that they came from the so-called 'grassy knoll': a tree-topped slope, with a fence and colonnade, facing towards the oncoming motorcade. This would have made an ideal vantage point for a gunman firing from in front, with a car park beyond for a getaway

vehicle. Yet the Warren Commission ignored all testimony relating to it, even though onlookers standing on the knoll itself reported gunfire that came from higher up on the slope behind them. Puffs of smoke were seen there. Patrolman Joe Smith heard a woman cry out 'They're shooting the president from the bushes!' and ran to the grassy knoll where he detected the lingering smell of gunpowder. Others also testified to the acrid scent, and a suspicious figure wearing a sports shirt and sports trousers was seen in the vicinity.

Patrolman Joe Smith and others reported that, when challenged, the mystery man whipped out Secret Service credentials. Only later did the policeman discover that there were no authentic Secret Service agents in the area.

A wealth of further questions have been raised with regard to the Kennedy assassination. Ballistic evidence proved that the 'magic bullet', for example, had definitely been fired by the Mannlicher-Carcano rifle, but it had turned up mysteriously on the hospital floor, having apparently fallen from

a stretcher. No one knew whose stretcher. Had it been planted?

After a bungled autopsy, in which the directions of the bullet wounds were not adequately tracked, the president's damaged brain was removed from the body and preserved 'for future study'. In 1966, however, the brain went missing from the National Archives, along with tissue sections, blood smears and a number of slides. Some claim that the president's brother, Robert Kennedy, disposed of the missing brain to prevent it from being tastelessly displayed; others suspect foul play.

Questions attached themselves also to Oswald and Ruby, two enigmatic characters. Investigation of Oswald's background showed the 24-year-old ex-Marine to be a Marxist, who had lived in Russia for two and a half years and married a Soviet girl. On his return home he had kept up his left-wing activities, carrying 'Viva Castro' banners in the name of the Fair Play for Cuba Committee. The CIA, it is known, had kept a file on Oswald. He

SOVIET SYMPATHIES In 1959 Oswald asked for his US citizenship to be revoked and applied for Soviet citizenship.

FREEDOM FIGHTER? In a controversial photo, Oswald, who distributed pro-Castro propaganda leaflets in New Orleans in 1963, appears to hold the assassination rifle.

1900   1950

1917 Birth of John F. Kennedy

1943 Kennedy heroically rescues a burnt crewman when his torpedo boat is sunk by a Japanese destroyer in the South Pacific

ACCUSED KILLER A nervous Jack Ruby is surrounded by newsmen as he goes for trial in February 1964 for Oswald's murder.

must have been of interest to Soviet intelligence, too. Was he, conceivably, an agent working for one or the other organisation?

Ruby's background was equally dubious. Chicago-born, he had, as a boy, run errands for Al Capone and probably came to Texas as an emissary of the Chicago mob. In Dallas he cultivated members of the local police department, which is one reason why he was able to gain easy access to the police HQ. Ruby also made several trips to Cuba where, the Warren Commission heard, he took part in gun-running for forces hostile to Fidel Castro. Nothing in the Warren version strikes a more unlikely note than that Ruby might have killed Oswald out of sudden chivalrous feelings for Jackie Kennedy. In fact Ruby, who died of cancer in jail in 1967, was to let slip in a TV interview that he did not think the true facts would ever come out, 'because unfortunately these people, who have so much to gain and have such an ulterior motive to put me in the position I'm in, will never let the true facts come above-board to the world'.

Immediately after the assassination, with anti-Soviet feeling strong in the USA, and

FAILED COUP Prisoners – mostly Cuban exiles – are lined up by Castro's soldiers after the ill-fated Bay of Pigs invasion.

Cuba a feature of the histories of both Oswald and Ruby, the popular theory was that Kennedy had been the victim of a communist death plot. But suspicion today focuses much more on the CIA and the Mafia. They had cooperated in coup attempts against Castro, which culminated in the disastrous Bay of Pigs invasion of 1961. About 1200 Cuban exiles tried to invade Castro's island, and their catastrophic failure left a lasting bitterness between Kennedy and the CIA. The exasperated president afterwards told a top official that he wanted to 'splinter the CIA in a thousand pieces and scatter it to the wind'. Agency operatives, meanwhile, felt betrayed by a president who had provided insufficient military back-up. The Mafia also hated Kennedy's administration because it had harassed mob bosses at home. As the investigation proceeded, a belief grew that Kennedy was killed by Mafia marksmen in a plot hatched and covered up by renegade members of the CIA, among whom there must have been someone with special knowledge of Oswald's background.

In 1978, controversial new acoustic evidence was brought before a Congress Assassinations Committee. It was a routine recording of police radio traffic in Dallas on that fateful Friday in 1963. Amid the blur and static, scientists claimed to discern the sound of the rifle shots, recorded on a mov-

ing microphone of a police outrider in the motorcade. There were, it was claimed, four shots, and analysis indicated that gunfire came from in front of the president as well as behind him.

The debate continues

It seemed at the time a complete vindication of all who had campaigned for a review of the case. In the summer of 1979, the Committee reported that President Kennedy probably was assassinated as a result of a conspiracy involving a second gunman. It voiced suspicion that Mafia or anti-Castro elements might have participated, and even named two living mobsters, Carlos Marcello and Santos Trafficante, as men with the requisite motives and means. The Committee believed that Oswald was among the assassins but avoided committing itself on whether he had any links with the CIA.

The Committee's findings have since been criticised, both by those who still believe in the lone gunman theory and by those who claim that Oswald was an innocent fall-guy. On the one hand, the acoustic evidence of the police radio recording has been challenged, while on the other it has been alleged that the original autopsy pictures and X-rays were forged to indicate that the shots came from behind. So far, all the paraphernalia of hi-tech forensic science has failed to solve this deeply troubling mystery.

GEORGE BLAKE'S ESCAPE

IN THE SHADOWY WORLD OF INTERNATIONAL ESPIONAGE, LITTLE IS COMPLETELY CERTAIN

In May 1961 Britons learned with astonishment that a diplomat named George Blake had received a 42 year jail sentence at the Old Bailey. The trial had been held in secret 'for reasons of national security', but it was made known that the exceptionally long sentence was given for espionage. The 38-year-old Blake, it transpired, had worked for many years in Germany, and during this time was alleged to have photographed almost every secret document that came his way and passed on copies to the Soviet Union. His treachery had 'rendered much of this country's efforts completely useless', according to Lord Chief Justice Parker. After the verdict, bowing slightly towards the bench, Blake walked down from the dock to begin one of the most severe sentences imposed by an English court in peacetime.

But Blake never served his full time. In October 1966 his name hit the headlines again when it was reported that the superspy had escaped from Wormwood Scrubs prison in London and that his present whereabouts were unknown. How could so important a prisoner have got free? And where was he now? Reports that he had been spirited away to Moscow were countered by the Soviet authorities, who continued to maintain that he had never been their spy. Blake's escape raised disquieting questions about the efficiency of Britain's security services and awakened renewed interest in the mystery man at the heart of the furore.

In the Resistance

George Blake had a cosmopolitan background. He was born, with the surname of Behar, of a Dutch mother and a father who was an Egyptian Jew with a British passport. As a child he lived for two years with relatives in Egypt, and attended the English School in Cairo. He then returned to the Netherlands and was in Rotterdam when the Nazis invaded in 1940. The young Behar fought bravely in the Dutch Resistance and eventually escaped to England, where he changed his name to Blake. His languages and undercover experience made him a considerable asset to British Intelligence, and when the war ended, employed by MI6, he took up a Foreign Office post.

Blake was a consular official in Seoul in South Korea when the Korean War broke out. He was captured by the communists and held in

MUG SHOT A police portrait of George Blake, taken after his arrest for espionage.

a North Korean interrogation camp for some months. According to the official version, this was the turning point in his life: he was brainwashed and became a communist. Fellow prisoners have, however, cast doubt on this story, claiming that he stood up to his jailers throughout his captivity. And Blake himself has described his conversion to

FREE MAN George Blake arrives in Berlin from Moscow in 1953. He had recently been released from captivity in North Korea.

> ## NOTHING NOW WOULD STOP ME
>
> In his own account of his 1967 escape from Wormwood Scrubs, double agent George Blake described how he kept in contact with Sean Bourke by means of a smuggled walkie-talkie. At the critical moment, Bourke threw the ladder over the wall:
>
> 'In the light of the arc lamps I saw the ladder flash over the wall, writhe for a moment and hang still. It looked incredibly thin and fragile, but the instant I saw it I knew that nothing now would stop me. I pushed the walkie-talkie set into my soaking wet sweater and, bending low, rushed to the wall. I grabbed the ladder and started up. It seemed amazingly easy. In a moment, unseen by the officers in the observation booths at the end of the wall, but watched, I am sure, by several pairs of eyes bursting with excitement from the cell windows, I reached the top of the wall. As I climbed astride it I looked down and saw a car and, beside it, looking up at me with anxious expectation, Sean.
>
> "Let yourself drop", he shouted, his voice high with tension. "Hurry."'

1922 George Blake is born in Rotterdam

1940 Blake fights with the Dutch Resistance

communism as one of intellectual conviction rather than one of compulsion.

After the Korean ceasefire of 1953 Blake was released, and he returned to the Foreign Office, which posted him to Berlin. He received orders from MI6 to infiltrate the Soviet spy networks in the city. This was the period of his greatest reported treachery. Apart from passing over a mass of secret documents, he was said to have betrayed at least 50 British, American and German agents to the KGB. Following the arrest of a Russian agent and the defection of a Pole, however, Blake's cover was blown, and he was arrested in 1961 shortly after being posted to the Middle East.

Break-out

After Blake's secret trial, imprisonment and escape, a few features of the enigmatic man became clearer. For one thing, despite the early Russian denials, he did resurface in Moscow where he was eventually acclaimed as a hero. In February 1970 Soviet officials announced that Blake had been awarded the Order of Lenin with a citation stating that 'Comrade Blake had rendered eminent services over a long period of years and under perilous conditions, and had foiled the operations of the British Secret Service and other hostile organisations'. It became known that Blake had settled down comfortably in Moscow, where he still lives and where he had a job working in the British section of the KGB.

Questions still lingered about his intelligence role, and especially about his prison escape. Blake's own story was that he planned and accomplished his break-out with no help from the KGB, which would have been badly compromised if something went wrong. He knew he would need outside help, however, and in prison made friends with an Irishman, Sean Bourke, who was soon to be released. Bourke managed to smuggle him a walkie-talkie set, with which they communicated regularly after the Irishman left jail. During the break-out, a

THE SECRET TELEPHONE TUNNEL

One of the most notorious acts credited to George Blake was the betrayal of a secret tunnel which the American CIA had dug to tap Soviet telephone lines in East Germany. The tunnel ran for 2000 ft (600 m), from a radar station in the West Berlin suburb of Rudow, under the barbed-wire border, to Alt Glienicke in East Berlin. Its clandestine construction was a remarkable feat: while thousands of tons of earth and rubble were removed on a narrow gauge railway and driven away in covered US Army trucks, steel sections were welded together underground and the walls crammed with recording and amplifying equipment. The switchboard at one end could monitor 432 separate conversations at the same time.

The tunnel functioned for nine months, but on April 2, 1956, the Russians burst in at the eastern end. Alerted by an electric alarm system, the operators left the place deserted – though a coffee percolator was still bubbling in one of the empty chambers. After Soviet and East German Intelligence officers had combed the tunnel for its incriminating evidence, they threw it open for inspection to the people of East Berlin, to display 'the diabolic extent of criminal spying against the socialist countries'.

RUSSIAN PRAISE An article in the Soviet paper *Izvestia* in 1970 reports on Blake's role in thwarting the CIA eavesdropping tunnel.

fellow inmate kicked out a rusty window bar at Wormwood Scrubs. Blake scrambled out on a rainy night, crossed a passageway roof and dropped by way of a gutter down to a rope ladder which Bourke tossed over the wall.

Smuggled out of England

The pair of them lay low for some time, knowing that ports and airfields were being watched. In hiding in London, they were aided by two sympathetic peace campaigners, Patrick Pottle and Michael Randle, whom they had met in prison. During this period, the getaway car was traced back to Bourke, which meant that he had to flee the country too. Blake was smuggled across the Channel in a secret compartment built into the Randle family's Dormobile van. Bourke followed by a different means soon after. Both reached the Soviet Union via East Berlin, but while Blake stayed on behind the Iron Curtain, Bourke appears to have become homesick and returned to Ireland where he wrote his own account of

OVER THE WALL Michael Randle (left) and Patrick Pottle (right) point in 1989 to the spot where Blake escaped from Wormwood Scrubs in 1966.

the break-out. He died in his early forties, living destitute in a caravan in a seaside resort.

It is unlikely that Blake's account contains the whole truth. In his version, Sean Bourke almost single-handedly engineered the escape, while Pottle and Randle found the money to finance the operation and smuggled him out of England. Was the KGB more deeply involved? Did Blake have help from traitors in the British security services? Or was it conceivable that Blake was really a triple agent, allowed to escape in order to work for Britain inside the Moscow KGB?

IRISH AID An Irishman called Sean Bourke smuggled a walkie-talkie into prison to assist Blake's escape.

LIN BIAO'S MYSTERY CRASH

WAS CHINA'S VICE-CHAIRMAN THE VICTIM OF A VIOLENT POLITICAL STRUGGLE?

The news did not come out of Beijing (Peking) until November 1971, and when it came the details were sparse. In the early hours of September 13, the reports announced, Chairman Mao's appointed heir, Marshal Lin Biao, had died when his military aircraft crashed in the desert in Outer Mongolia. Later came announcements that Lin had died fleeing to the Soviet Union in the wake of an abortive coup.

To China-watchers everywhere, these statements were electrifying. Lin was a hard-line leftwinger who had seemed destined to inherit the supreme leadership of 800 million people and thereby stamp his personality on the whole history of the world. Yet it was known that, in recent months, he and Chairman Mao had fallen out over certain key aspects of policy. Mao, for example, favoured the opening of doors to the United States. Lin Biao's sympathies, in contrast, leaned more towards the Soviet Union. Mao feared the growing influence of the army in politics; Lin, on the other hand, had strong support among the generals. Above all, Mao mistrusted the personal ambition which Lin was beginning to exhibit, which could only threaten Mao's own authority.

Party politics

Tension between the two statesmen had started to come into the open in the autumn of 1970, when Mao began to purge Lin's allies and to clip the wings of the military. As the moves intensified, the marshal's supporters

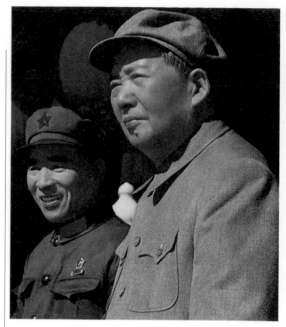

COMRADES IN ARMS Lin Biao (left) poses with Mao Ze-dong at a conference.

grew desperate and Lin's impetuous son, Lin Liguo, a deputy commander in the air force, began to plan a coup d'état against the revered chairman.

Most information about the plot comes from official Chinese sources which are impossible to verify. They describe how the coup was code-named '571' which, when pronounced in Chinese, can also mean 'armed uprising'. According to official reports, the conspirators made various attempts on Mao's life: through poison in his food; explosives planted in his train, and even by the strafing of his mansion by air force fighters. Some commentators have doubted whether Lin would have involved himself in assassination attempts, but it is not unlikely that his hot-headed son Liguo might have done so. Certainly, the autumn of 1971 seems to have been a nerve-racking time for Mao, for he made no publicised appearances at this time and moved out of his main residence at South and Central lakes, reportedly fearing its infiltration by his enemies.

The attempts on Mao's life failed, however, and according to the official story, their collapse caused Lin and his wife to plan to flee to Moscow. However, Lin's

CHEER LEADER Vice-Chairman Lin Biao (left) and Chairman Mao celebrate the 20th anniversary of the founding of the People's Republic of China in 1969. This was the year in which Lin was proclaimed as Mao's successor.

29-year-old daughter, Lin Liheng, baulked at this proposal and tipped off the authorities. The family was staying at the seaside resort of Beidaihe at the time, and now raced to the local airport in a convoy of cars. A hostile guard, shot by Liguo, was pushed from a speeding vehicle; suspicious ground crew at the airport tried to block the aircraft's take-off by parking two trucks across the runway.

BOOK MEN Party workers and Lin Biao (centre right) brandish copies of *Quotations from Chairman Mao Ze-dong,* the little red book that became the bible of the Cultural Revolution; it was first published in 1964.

1900
1907 Lin Biao born
1921 Founding of Communist Party of China
1927 Lin Biao joins Mao's Red Army
1950

PARTY PEOPLE Chairman and Vice-chairman commemorate the 50th anniversary of the Communist Party of China in 1971. 'The thoughts of Chairman Mao are always correct', claimed the sycophantic Lin Biao.

Lin's Trident managed to take off amid gunfire, and with damage to a fuel tank which began leaking. Some 155 miles (250 km) beyond the Chinese border, the plane ran out of fuel and crashed in flames just short of the Mongolian capital, Ulan Bator. Lin, his wife Ye Qun, his son and six other people on board all perished.

A thrilling tale – but it was greeted with scepticism in many quarters. For one thing, it is known that Mao had convened a top-level meeting at the Great Hall of the People in Beijing before the dramatic flight from Beidaihe, and there stripped Lin and his supporters of office. This suggests a more active role than merely following a tip-off from Lin's daughter. Mao was out to get Lin, and the aircraft crash was a suspiciously convenient accident. 'It was probably murder', wrote the author Ross Terrill, in his biography of the chairman. Terrill points out that Lin had not in fact been seen in public since June 3. He may have been arrested – perhaps executed – at the time of the meeting in the Great Hall, or even long before.

The case has many curiosities.

HISTORIC HANDSHAKE Chairman Mao welcomes US President Nixon to Beijing in February 1972.

According to Moscow, some of the nine charred bodies found at the Mongolian crash site were riddled with bullet holes. Beijing confirmed this – but only after the Russians had reported the fact. Were the gunshot wounds relics of the airport shootout? Or of a confrontation inside the airborne Trident?

Accidental death?

More controversially, Moscow at first declared that none of the nine bodies was of a person over 50 years of age – implying that 63-year-old Lin was not aboard, or that he had survived the crash. This may, however, have been a mischievous assertion, designed to worry Mao with the possibility that his rival was alive and talking to the Russians; in reality, the bodies seem to have been too charred for their age or identities to be determined, and in due course the Soviet authorities quietly dropped their 'under 50' assertion.

It is simply not known whether Lin died in the Mongolian wreckage or in Chinese detention beforehand; even if he was on the fateful flight, the crash may not have been an accident. What is certain is that the crisis involved a great shake-up in China. In that second week of September, not just Lin but five other members of the Politburo died violent deaths. While the huge blow-up photographs of Lin disappeared from Chinese street parades, Mao steered his vast nation, as he had planned, in the direction of a rapprochement with the USA.

In February 1972, in one of the most astonishing twists of 20th-century diplomacy, the ageing chairman welcomed President Nixon into China and entertained him at his house in the Forbidden City in Beijing.

1966 Cultural Revolution begins
1969 Lin Biao designated Mao's successor
1971 Death of Lin Biao

THE KOREAN JET CRASH

WHY DID THE SOVIET UNION DESTROY A BOEING 747, KILLING 269 INNOCENT CIVILIANS ON BOARD?

Waves of horror and alarm rippled all around the world on September 1, 1983, when the Russian government admitted shooting down a civilian airliner that had strayed into Soviet airspace. A total of 269 lives – including 61 Americans – were lost in the missile attack on Korean Airlines' Boeing 747 flight KAL 007 from Anchorage, in Alaska, to Seoul. And although it was night-time and visibility was poor, there was no question of an accident on the Soviet side. In the diplomatic furore which followed the tragedy, US officials played a tape at the United Nations of what the fighter pilot had said on the fateful night: 'I am closing in on the target . . . I am in lock-in. I have executed the launch. The target is destroyed.'

Red alert

But the Soviet Union's version of events was very different from the American. According to Moscow, the South Korean airliner did not stray accidentally but was on a spying flight over sensitive military installations off Siberia. 'The

DAILY NEWS

SOVIETS SHOOT DOWN JETLINER

30 Yanks among 269 victims; U.S. demands 'full accounting;' Congress angry; Ron returning

Eight pages of stories and pictures start on page 2

FIRST REACTIONS The American press registered outrage at the shooting and the loss of American lives (61, in fact, rather than 30). Later came questions about the plane's flight path.

What was the truth? The plane had certainly swung wildly off course; it was 365 miles (587 km) to the north of its intended flight path. And in straying from its planned route, it passed over a Soviet area of high security which greatly interested US aerial intelligence. As KAL 007 crossed the tip of the Kamchatka Peninsula, it passed over the Soviet town of Petropavlosk, a base for

Soviet nuclear submarines with an arsenal of ballistic missiles. The Red Army was due to test a new item of weaponry at the base at dawn that very day. As the foreign airliner approached, the weapon test was cancelled and a flight of fighters was scrambled to try to compel the intruder to land. The Russian pilots went through the usual drill of waggling their wings, switching their lights on and off, and as a last resort calling up the captain on the mayday frequency. But, according to the Soviets, the Korean pilot appeared not to see the warplanes, nor to hear the emergency signals instructing him to land.

As it happened, the airliner survived this first interception. The Soviet warplanes turned back as KAL 007 stubbornly stuck to its course, clearing the tip of the peninsula and flying on over the Sea of Okhotsk. But the captain's luck ran out when he reached the far side of the Sea and approached the strategic air bases on Sakhalin Island. This time the Russian interceptors closed in – and when a burst of cannon shells failed to win the pilot's attention, the fatal Anab heat-seeking missiles were fired.

Amid the bitter recriminations which followed the Soviet action, a puzzle remained.

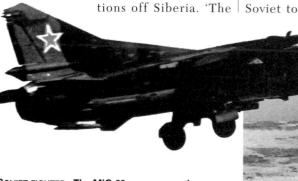

SOVIET FIGHTER The MiG-23 was among the fighter planes scrambled by the Soviets to intercept the Boeing 747.

Soviet government expresses regret over the death of innocent people and shares the sorrow of bereaved relatives and friends.' However, 'the entire responsibility for this tragedy rests wholly and fully' with the American leadership.

THE SEARCHERS Three Japanese villagers scour a beach at Hamatonbetsu, looking for fragments of the Korean jet wreckage 11 days after the plane was shot down.

USSR NAVAL BASE
USSR AIR BASE
USSR SUBMARINE BASE
USSR MISSILE BASE
ACTUAL ROUTE OF KAL 007
INTENDED ROUTE OF KAL 007

Seoul

Sakhalin Island
Sea of Okhotsk

Kamchatka
Peninsular

Anchorage

18.26 GMT
Hit by a missile fired from a
Soviet Sukhoi fighter, KAL 007
crashes into the sea, 365 miles
off course

18.00 GMT
KAL 007 crosses the Sea of
Okhotsk, still tracked by Soviet
radar. Soviet fighter planes are
scrambled

17.00 GMT
KAL 007 overflies the Soviet port of
Petropavlosk, where the Soviets
claim they first warned the pilot

15.51 GMT
The Soviets use radar to track the
plane as it deviates from its
correct route, maintaining a
constant magnetic heading 246°

COUNTDOWN TO CATASTROPHE
KAL 007 took off from
Anchorage at 13.00 GMT,
deviating farther and farther
from its intended route, on its
journey to oblivion.

BOEING JET This 747 jumbo jet from the
Korean Airlines fleet is similar to the one
shot down by the Soviets.

that, from the outset, the plane was following a wrong course: an unswerving 246°
magnetic heading. KAL 007 was 6 miles
(10 km) north of its intended path as it left
the limits of Anchorage radar, and the dis-
crepancy grew steadily. Perhaps the darkness
and bad weather made the pilot unaware of
the Soviet warnings as the plane followed its
computer-controlled track to oblivion.

Why did the airliner follow such a wrong
course? The captain, Chun Byung-in, was a
veteran fighter pilot who had been in civil
aviation for 11 years, and whose flawless
record of service had placed him among the
elite eligible to fly the South Korean
President. Had he, perhaps, been briefed to
fly over the Russian bases so that US intelligence could monitor the Soviet response?

Or was there a mechanical or pilot error?
The Korean airliner was equipped with a
computer-controlled Inertial Navigation
System (INS). This determines the aircraft's
position, calculates altitude and guides the
automatic pilot, all with a high degree of
accuracy. However, if even slightly wrong data
is fed into it in the first place, the error may
be magnified on a long flight. It is evident

ANGRY DEMONSTRATORS Protesters filled
the streets of South Korea's capital, Seoul,
in the days after the shooting.

1983 The Soviet
Union brings down a
Korean Airlines jet

1991 President
Yeltsin apologises for
the shooting

MYSTERY AIR CRASHES

FROM METAL FATIGUE TO MECHANICAL FAULTS, PILOT ERROR TO POLITICAL TERRORISM, THE CAUSES OF AEROPLANE DISASTERS ARE THE SUBJECT OF INTENSE INVESTIGATION

In May 1952, with much celebration in the press, a BOAC Comet aircraft launched the world's first scheduled jet service, from England to South Africa. Less than a year later the Comet had brought Tokyo within 36 hours of London. Before long, orders for this, the triumph of British aero-engineering, were pouring in from all over the world. And then disaster struck. At 10.15 one Sunday morning in January 1954, a Comet flying from Rome to London crashed into the sea off the island of Elba. Early thoughts of sabotage were followed by the realisation that a Comet had recently gone down in stormy weather on a flight from Calcutta. Had the bad weather been at fault? Or was there a fault in the aircraft? Three months after the Elba crash, despite modifications to all Comet jets, another came to grief en route for Johannesburg. The British Government immediately ordered the grounding of all Comet jet airliners, and production was stopped at the Hatfield works where they were manufactured.

What had caused the mystery crashes? After painstaking research and testing, the experts diagnosed a new ailment for the revolutionary jet age. All the Comet disasters, it was discovered, had occurred when the planes reached or approached maximum altitude at full power. Scientists at the Royal Aircraft Establishment in Farnborough were able to identify the problem as 'metal fatigue' – a deterioration which occurred through vibration when stresses went above a critical limit. This was to become a consideration of key importance in the future design of high-speed aircraft.

SALVAGE OPERATION   British sailors recover fragments of the Comet airliner which crashed into the Mediterranean off Elba.

Black box

Aircraft are lost every year around the world, and if they are prestige products, or carry important political figures on board, suspicions of sabotage are often voiced. Amid the twisted wreckage of a disaster, it is not always easy to discover the cause of the calamity. For the investigators, the main puzzle-solvers are the flight data recorder and cockpit voice recorder. Known as 'black boxes', they are really bright red so that they can be spotted immediately amid the debris. The flight data recorder tracks the operation of key instruments such as airspeed and altitude indicators, and the cockpit voice recorder picks up the conversation of the crew. Both boxes are walled in steel and capable of withstanding the temperatures of a crash inferno. Black boxes are generally more useful in discovering the cause of an accident than in identifying the symptoms of foul play, for evidence of sabotage is not always easy to detect.

Concordski explodes

One of the more suspicious air crashes of recent decades occurred at the Paris International Air Show in June 1973, when the star attraction, a Russian Tupolev-144 supersonic airliner, exploded in mid-air in front of 200 000 spectators. Known to the world's press as 'Concordski', the plane had been built following a brilliant espionage coup mounted by Soviet Intelligence to probe the industrial secrets of the UK, France and West Germany. This enabled the Russians to build their own version of the Anglo-French Concorde.

When the Russian 'Concordski' exploded in 1973, its crew of six

THE RUSSIAN CONCORDE   The debris of the Tupolev-144, which exploded in 1973, damaged a French town near the airfield at Le Bourget.

was killed instantly. Nine more people died, and 28 were injured, as the wreckage landed on the town of Goussainville, north of Paris. Experts put the disaster down to pilot error, but widespread whispers of sabotage have never been entirely silenced. Recent reports indicate that a French spy plane, taking photographs of the Soviet machine, inadvertently crossed the path of Concordski and forced the pilot to take the evasive action which caused the crash.

The Lockerbie disaster

Foul play was certainly involved on December 21, 1988, when a jumbo jet on Pan Am flight 103 crashed onto the town of Lockerbie in Scotland, killing all 259 passengers as well as 11 people on the ground. The plane broke up in mid-air, causing bodies and debris to rain from the sky in Britain's worst-ever air disaster. American embassies had received a warning that the plane would be a terrorist target; the mystery in this case was: who had planted the bomb?

Two days after their arrival in Scotland, investigators found a piece of twisted metal pitted with the tell-tale evidence of high-intensity explosives. The bomb, it was determined, had gone off in a brown Samsonite suitcase in the baggage area. A fragment of the timing device bore the name of a Zürich firm, which declared it to be one of a consignment delivered to a Libyan official. Also in the suitcase had been a shirt which came from a boutique in Malta called Mary's Shop. When investigators questioned the boutique owner, he recalled that in December 1988 a man with a Libyan accent had surprised staff by buying a whole batch of clothing

CRASH SITE In a hangar (above) investigators piece together the jumbo jet's remains, which landed in and around Lockerbie (below).

regardless of size or shape. FBI laboratory artists drew up an Identikit picture of the man in the boutique, and matched it against photographs of known Libyan intelligence officers.

He was identified as Abdel Basset Ali al-Megrahii, who had arrived in Malta with a former Libyan Arab Airlines official named Lamen Khalifa Fhimah; they had been carrying a dark Samsonite suitcase. Fhimah placed the lethal luggage on an Air Malta flight which connected at Frankfurt with Pan Am 103. In November 1991, Basset and Fhimah were charged with the outrage, but Libya refused to hand them over. It was hardly a satisfactory outcome for human justice – but it bore witness to a remarkable feat of international detection. In July 1996, piecing together the evidence from the TWA crash off Long Island proved to be just as challenging.

THE RWANDA TRAGEDY

HOW A MYSTERY PLANE CRASH SPARKED A VICIOUS ORGY OF TRIBAL BLOOD-LETTING

A horrific eruption of tribal genocide in Africa's most densely populated country, the central state of Rwanda, resulted in an estimated one million people being

EXECUTIVE WRECKAGE   A tangle of twisted metal is all that remains of the jet aircraft whose crash killed two African presidents.

killed in a single three-month frenzy. More than a million more fled as refugees from the country. Yet what triggered the calamity was a plane crash that remains a mystery to this day.

On April 6, 1994, the leaders of Rwanda and Burundi were both killed when their executive jet crashed as it came in to land at the airport at Kigali, Rwanda's capital. President Juvenal Habyarimana of Rwanda and President Cyprien Ntaryamira of Burundi had been returning from a meeting in Dar es Salaam, Tanzania, aimed at ending ethnic hostilities between members of the Hutu and Tutsi tribes. At the meeting, Habyarimana had finally given way to international pressure for democratic reform.

RWANDAN REFUGEES   Hundreds of thousands of civilians took to the roads, to flee the violence that shook Rwanda in 1994.

Early reports suggested that the aeroplane, a French Mystère-Falcon jet, had been shot down: a Rwandan official said that the aircraft was hit by two rockets, and Kigali residents said that they heard explosions followed by sporadic shooting, and glimpsed a small plane circling the airport in distress. But others declared the crash an accident, and United Nations officials were unable to mount a proper investigation.

SLAIN PREMIER   The Rwandan prime minister, Agathe Uwilingiyimana, was killed in the Kigali crash's bloody aftermath.

Mobs on the rampage

The violence in Rwanda was rooted in long-standing rivalries. The country had already endured a four-year civil war between its Hutu majority and Tutsi minority. But peace agreements had been signed, and there were serious hopes for a healing of the wounds at the time when the crash occurred. Though both of the dead statesmen were members of the Hutu tribe, President Ntaryamira of Burundi was a noted campaigner against tribal hatred, who had promoted Tutsis to positions of authority in his government. If the plane was shot down, the culprits may just as well have been hard-line Hutu opponents of compromise as Tutsi rebels.

Although much remains to be learned about the plane crash itself, there can be no doubt of its consequences. Suspecting a Tutsi assassination plot, mobs of youths, egged on by Hutu extremists and armed with clubs and machetes, rampaged through the streets of Kigali seeking vengeance. While parts of the armed forces tried to restore order, special units of the Rwandan army and the presidential guard, which were fiercely loyal to the late President Habyarimana, ran amok. Within days, a full-scale civil war had broken out. Rwanda's acting prime minister, the Hutu moderate Agathe Uwilingiyimana, was murdered by a mob after fleeing from the presidential palace to a UN compound; the Belgian UN peacekeepers guarding her were surrounded, disarmed and then killed. Other moderate government ministers, nuns, priests and aid workers also fell victim to the rampaging death squads. Anarchy reigned, and while the world's media began to focus its attention on terrible tales of atrocity and the plight of the refugees, both in Rwanda and in neighbouring Burundi, the puzzling spark that had detonated the catastrophe – the plane crash at Kigali – was almost forgotten.

1900   2000

1959 Rwanda gains
independence from
Belgium

1972 Ethnic violence
between Hutus and Tutsis
leaves 300 000 dead

1994 Plane crash
is followed by
massacres

STRANGE DISAPPEARANCES

THOUSANDS OF PEOPLE GO MISSING EVERY YEAR, FOR PERFECTLY MUNDANE REASONS. PLAGUED BY FINANCIAL WORRIES OR BY UNHAPPY RELATIONSHIPS, THEY WALK OUT OF THEIR HOMES NEVER TO RETURN. OTHER VANISHING ACTS ARE FAR MORE BAFFLING, HOWEVER, AND SINISTER FORCES WERE MOST CERTAINLY AT WORK IN THE DISAPPEARANCES OF THE AMERICAN UNION BOSS JIMMY HOFFA, FOR EXAMPLE, AND THE SWEDISH BUSINESSMAN AND DIPLOMAT RAOUL WALLENBERG.

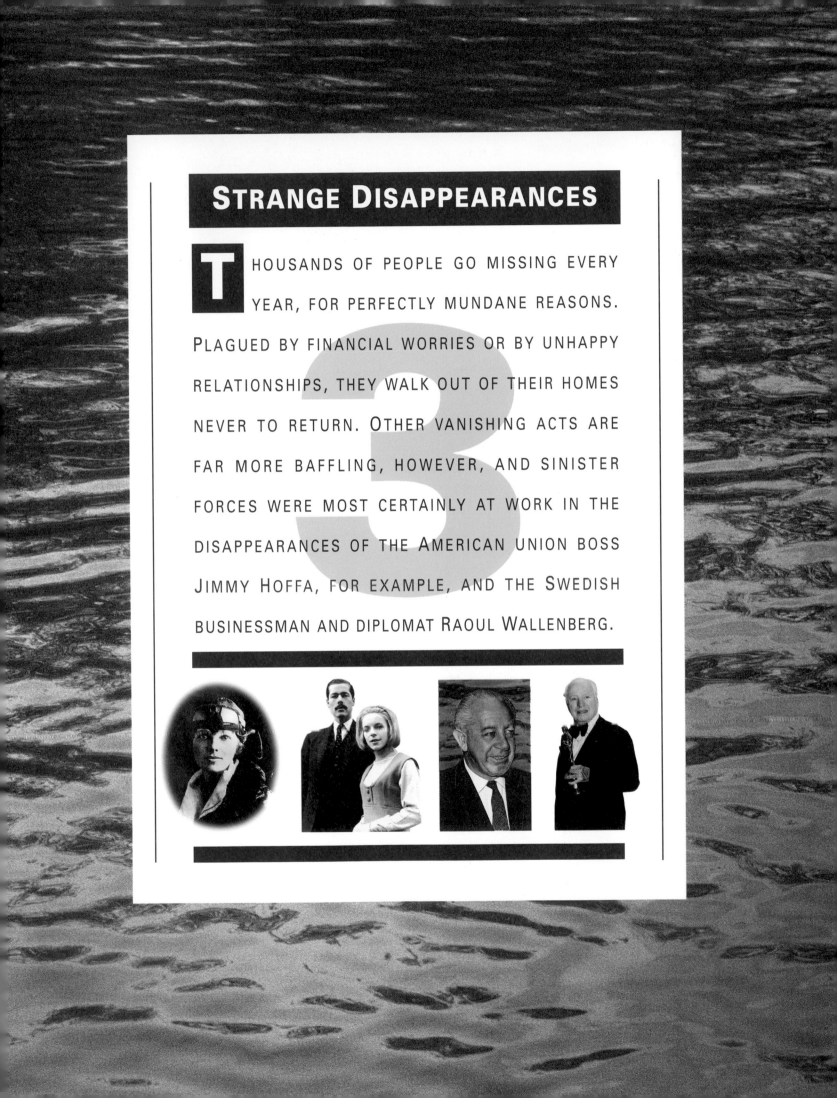

THE GREATEST AGATHA CHRISTIE MYSTERY OF ALL

MORE WHYDUNNIT THAN WHODUNNIT: A CASE THAT WOULD HAVE BAFFLED HERCULE POIROT

The story was as intriguing as the plots she so cleverly crafted for her detective novels. In 1926 the crime writer Agatha Christie disappeared from her Berkshire home for 11 days. On Friday, December 3, dressed in a velour hat, grey cardigan and green knitted skirt, the 36-year-old novelist walked out into the wintry night. The following morning her two-seater Morris was found about half a mile (0.8 km) away with its front wheels over the edge of a deep chalk pit. The brakes were off and the ignition switched on; the car was empty.

Agatha Christie had vanished. And while the press speculated wildly about suicide, kidnapping and murder, the police mounted a nationwide hunt for the missing novelist (who was moderately famous at that time).

Then, on December 14, newspapers announced that the search had ended – hundreds of miles from her home. Staff at the Hydro Hotel in the spa town of Harrogate, Yorkshire, had noticed a marked similarity between a newspaper photograph of the missing Mrs Christie and a guest named 'Theresa Neele' claiming to come from South Africa. Colonel Archibald Christie, the writer's husband, was brought north to the scene and there, outside the dining room – reading a newspaper report of her own disappearance – he identified the hotel guest as his wife. However, when he approached Agatha, according to the hotel manager, she seemed rather dazed and confused. Colonel Christie stated at the time that she did not know where she was or who she was. She was taken home by her husband, and there doctors diagnosed that she was suffering from some form of amnesia.

'When one thing goes wrong'

Agatha always maintained that she had no recollection of how she came to be in Yorkshire. Even her autobiography makes no direct reference to it, although the book does acknowledge that 1926 was a traumatic year for her. She wrote: 'As so often in life, when one thing goes wrong, everything goes wrong.' First, her mother died and the writer – already feeling run down – was

QUEEN OF CRIME Agatha Christie is still one of the most widely read authors in the world, with translations into 103 languages.

MURDER HUNT Agatha's abandoned car prompted a massive police investigation.

December 3, 1926 Agatha Christie vanishes
1928 Agatha Christie divorces her husband
1930 Agatha Christie remarries

reduced to a state of exhaustion clearing out her crowded house. Then Archie, her husband, confessed that he had fallen for another woman and asked Agatha for a divorce. This shattering news seems to have been what triggered the novelist's flight. And some deep psychological need was obviously answered by her escapade, for the surname she chose to live under in Harrogate – Neele

NEW LOVE In 1930 Agatha Christie married the eminent archaeologist Professor Max Mallowan. His work abroad allowed her to indulge her passion for foreign travel.

– was the same as that of Archie's new love. There was talk that the whole affair might have been a publicity stunt. But questions remained to be answered. Just how considered were Agatha Christie's plans? Did she drive to the chalk pit in a suicide bid, and leave the scene dazedly when the attempt failed? Or did she orchestrate a sensational disappearance to humiliate her errant husband – or perhaps even to implicate him in a murder investigation?

One aspect of the mystery that has never been revealed is the question of the three letters Agatha wrote at the time of her disappearance. Two she left behind for her husband and her secretary. The third was received in the post by her brother-in-law a couple of days later. Both her husband and her brother-in-law destroyed their letters. Her secretary handed over her letter to the police, sealed in an envelope to be opened only in the event of an inquest. The contents of all three letters remain a secret.

History records only that the Christie divorce went ahead, and that Agatha herself remarried in 1930. She shunned publicity until her death in 1976 and always refused to discuss her disappearance – the curious enigma of 1926 went with her to the grave.

MISSING PERSONS

Every year in Britain there are an estimated 250 000 reports of missing persons, according to the Missing Persons Helpline – a national charity set up in 1992 by friends of the Suzy Lamplugh Trust. Of these, about 65 per cent of cases are resolved – in other words, these people are found, they stay missing because they want to (but have made contact to express their wishes), or are dead as a result of foul play. However, only a small minority – about 5 per cent – come into the last category. Far more consist of teenagers on the run from unhappy homes, or fugitive wives or husbands plagued by debts who – in classic cases – go out to the shops and do not come back. Many people under stress have breakdowns when, for days or months on end, they forget who they are and where they live – as, perhaps, in the case of Agatha Christie.

Worldwide, no one knows just how great the problem is. Missing persons, where no crime is involved, challenge already overstretched police manpower and there are limits to the public resources that can be expended on an individual's disappearance. Few countries, other than France and Britain, have independent bureaux set up to deal with missing persons of any age, so there are few statistics available. In the United States, however, the self-explanatory National Center for Missing & Exploited Children (NCMEC) estimates that more than 750 000 children under the age of 18 disappear there every year.

Police in Britain and the USA now possess national computerised databases of missing persons, and have devised a new technological aid to assist in the task of identification. This is the Photosketch, a computerised machine that can 'age' old photographs of people who have gone missing years before, to produce an image of how they might look now. A photograph of the individual is fed into the machine with photographs of parents, brothers and sisters. Because many facial features are hereditary, it has proved possible to predict how people will change as they age: with, for example, the coming of wrinkles. First employed by the FBI in 1991, it can also alter the photograph of a toddler into a teenager and then adulthood. In one early case it helped to trace a 14-year-old girl who had disappeared when she was four.

STEP ONE Last known photograph of child before her abduction at three-years old

STEP TWO The child's photograph is scanned into the computer and stretched.

STEP THREE The stretched photo is merged with a photo of the nine-year-old brother.

STEP FOUR Hairstyle and dress of a nine-year-old girl is taken from a reference file of images.

STEP FIVE This is merged with the missing child's aged image to produce a final result.

STEP SIX What she really looked like. A photo of the girl after she had been found.

GOODTIME JOE GOES MISSING

DID NEW YORK JUDGE JOSEPH CRATER DISAPPEAR OF HIS OWN FREE WILL OR WAS HE DISPOSED OF?

In the United States to this day, the expression to 'pull a Crater' means to disappear suddenly from a tricky situation. The phrase dates back to a summer's day in 1930 when Judge Joseph F. Crater hailed a taxi in New York, stepped inside and vanished.

Known in high society as Goodtime Joe, Crater had started his career as a respected law professor at New York University. But his love of money – and associating with showgirls – led him into bad company. In particular he became associated with the Tammany Hall crowd, the Democratic Party organisation in New York City, which was notorious for political corruption. There was some evidence that he had bought his appointment as a judge – a position of influence that soon paid off. One of Crater's coups was to act as receiver for the bankrupt Libby Hotel which he sold to a finance company for $75 000. Two months later, the city agreed to buy it back for demolition in a street widening plan. The price was nearly $3 million. Did Crater receive a cut?

A new life

By the time of his disappearance Crater was a justice of New York's Supreme Court and a very wealthy man. While holidaying with his wife at their summer cottage in Maine, he received a phone message that called him back to New York. 'I've got to straighten some fellows out,' he told his wife before leaving the house.

Back in the city, on August 6, he cashed cheques for over $5000 and spent the afternoon sorting out office papers, and stuffing documents into briefcases. He told an assistant he was going 'up Westchester way for a few days', but did not leave immediately, for that evening he dined at a West 45th Street restaurant with glamorous showgirl, Sally Lou Ritz. He was planning to go on to a Broadway show when, after saying goodbye, he hailed the taxi and disappeared.

Was he murdered by crooked associates who feared that he might reveal their crimes? Sally Lou Ritz herself disappeared a

MISSING PERSON   A photograph of Joseph Force Crater appears against the Manhattan skyline. This picture was one of the last ever taken of the vanishing judge.

few weeks after Crater, prompting whispers that she knew more than was good for her. Others believed that Crater had fled to start a new life elsewhere; sightings in Canada, Europe and the Caribbean were reported.

As late as the 1950s, Dutch clairvoyant Gerard Croiset was brought in by writer Murray Bloom to examine the mystery. When a photograph of Crater was turned face down in front of Croiset, he went into a trance and drew a map of New York City and its suburbs. Croiset believed that Crater had

been murdered and buried at a house in Yonkers, just over the city line. When, in 1959, investigators dug a hole in the backyard of the house, no body was found.

Still unsolved, the mystery which fascinated the American public in the 1930s remains one of the most baffling on file.

1900 ▬▬▬▬▬▬▬▬▬▬▬▬▬▬▬▬▬▬▬▬▬ 2000

1930 Judge Crater
disappears

1959 Excavations at a
house in Yonkers reveal
nothing

CORPSES THAT WERE SPIRITED AWAY

**NOT FOR THE FAINT-HEARTED, THE MACABRE AND GHOULISH PRACTICE OF
BODYSNATCHING HAS HAD SOME UNLIKELY EXPONENTS**

T he embalmed body of Eva Perón, the glamorous wife of Argentina's dictator, Juan Perón, went missing for 16 years – an event that assumed enormous significance in the recent political history of South America. Evita ('little Eva') was worshipped by the poor, and when she died of cancer on July 26, 1952, an incredible two million people filed past her coffin.

Three years later, when roaring inflation led to her husband's overthrow, Eva's embalmed corpse vanished from its temporary resting place in the Confederacion General de Trabajadores (CGT) building in the capital, Buenos Aires. Rioting crowds demanded its return; but it was not until 1971 that it reappeared. It turned out to have been shipped abroad in a packing case and shuttled via Brussels, Bonn and Rome to a Milan cemetery where it was buried in lot 86 of the Musocco Cemetry in Milan.

The plot had been the work of the military-led coup that had deposed Juan Perón in 1955. Headed by General Aramburu, the military had felt that there was

SCENE OF PLUNDER Shock and speculation greeted the news that Charlie Chaplin's body had been stolen from this tiny cemetery at Corsier-sur-Vevey, Switzerland.

DIVINE WORSHIP In life and in death, the cult of Eva Perón was so powerful that even her corpse became an important political weapon.

much to fear in the cult of Evita. Ironically enough, a right-wing Peronist guerrilla group, the Montoneros, went on to kill Aramburu in 1970 and use his corpse as a means of trying to get Eva back. Her body was actually returned to her husband in Madrid in 1971 as part of a political deal by another military regime, and has been back in Buenos Aires since 1974 buried in a tomb 15 ft (5 m) under the ground.

When the corpse of Charlie Chaplin was snatched from its grave in a cemetery in Switzerland on March 1, 1978, the motives were much less clear. For two months, speculation about the mysterious body-snatch was rife – it was even rumoured that the corpse had been seized by Chaplin cult worshippers for reburial in England. It transpired that the culprits were two East European motor mechanics trying to extract a £330 000 ransom from the Chaplin family – relatives had kept silent to protect the police investigation. So inept were the kidnappers that when they were caught they couldn't pinpoint exactly where they had hidden the corpse. The police had to use mine detectors so that the body could be found and restored to its original resting place.

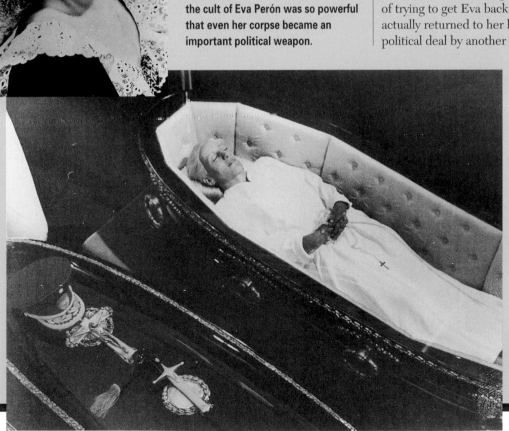

WHAT HAPPENED TO AMELIA EARHART?

LAST SEEN OVER NEW GUINEA: THE FLIGHT INTO OBLIVION OF AMERICA'S DARLING

A particular mystique has always attached itself to women flyers, and none is more fondly remembered than Amelia Earhart. A fresh-faced, Kansas-born

RECORD BREAKER Following her historic transatlantic flight of 1932, Amelia Earhart became the first woman to fly solo across the Pacific Ocean, in 1935.

tomboy, she was the toast of America in 1932 when she became the first woman to fly solo across the Atlantic. This adventure, soon to be followed by many others, seemed to naturally culminate in plans for a round-the-world flight.

On June 1, 1937, Amelia set off from Oakland, California, in a twin-engined Lockheed Electra with an experienced flyer named Fred Noonan as navigator. One by one, their targets were met: Florida, Brazil, West Africa, East Africa, Pakistan, India, Burma, Singapore and New Guinea. At 10am on July 2 the pair set off from Lae in New Guinea to begin the last lap – the long haul across the Pacific Ocean.

'No landfall ... position doubtful'

Their aim was to land next on tiny Howland Island, a mere pin-prick on the vast map of the Pacific, and they took off into a headwind, with storm clouds looming, over a stretch of ocean never before flown. The crew of an American coastguard cutter, *Itasca*, waited anxiously off Howland Island, transmitting homing signals that would help the couple to locate the speck of land which was their destination.

As the scheduled time of arrival came and went, the *Itasca* and other ships picked up broken messages from Amelia: '30 minutes' gas remaining, no landfall ... Circling, trying to pick up island landfall, position doubtful ...' And then there was silence.

Despite a massive two-week search by ships and aircraft of the US Pacific fleet, the pair were never found. According to the official story, Amelia and her navigator must

HELPING HAND All flight publicity was handled by husband George Putnam: above, with Amelia in New Jersey, 1931.

have run out of fuel and drowned at sea. But this was not the only version of events. It was said that, after the aircraft had vanished, ham radio operators had picked up messages indicating that the Lockheed had landed on a coral atoll. Jacqueline Cochran, a close friend of Amelia's and an alleged psychic,

WINGS OF DESIRE Amelia's Lockheed took off from Oakland Airport in California on the ill-fated round-the-world attempt.

1932 Earhart is the first woman to cross the Atlantic solo

1937 Earhart sets off on her round-the-world flight

THE PACIFIC ROUTE Flying eastward, the Lockheed met all its targets as far as New Guinea – then just disappeared off the map.

added fuel to the controversy by insisting she could sense that the pair had ditched in the sea and were still afloat.

Later, following the outbreak of the Second World War, a startling new theory emerged. 'Amelia Earhart – college head thinks flyer is Jap captive', announced the *San Francisco Chronicle* in April 1943. Dr Brittain, president of Georgia Tech University, suggested that Amelia had been on a surveillance mission for the US Government, with orders to fly over the Marshall Islands – about 650 miles (1040 km) northwest of Howland. She was said to have been taken prisoner while trying to discover whether the Japanese were illegally fortifying the islands.

Long after the end of the war this theory continued to fascinate. From various scattered sightings of a white female pilot or 'American spy lady', author Fred Goerner claimed to have evidence that the pair had ditched at Mili atoll in the southeastern Marshalls and been taken for questioning to Saipan, Japan's military headquarters in the Pacific. There, he suggested, they had been interrogated and, presumably, executed.

More theories proliferated. One outlandish hypothesis suggested that Amelia was still alive and well and living in New Jersey under the name of Irene Craig Bolam. This myth was exploded when the real Irene Bolam sued. In 1992 an expedition to the South Pacific unearthed what were taken for historic remains: a size 9 shoe and a fragment of aircraft that was supposedly part of

TRIUMPH AND TRAGEDY Cheers greet Amelia after her 1932 transatlantic flight; inset, with round-the-world navigator Fred Noonan.

Amelia's Lockheed Electra. However, the shoe size was not a match for Earheart or her navigator – and another theory crashed.

A government agent?

The most enduring notion has been that Amelia Earhart was a spy for the US government, and that officials covered up information about her secret role when she disappeared. In 1994 a book claiming to substantiate the theory was published by

aviation historian Randall Brink. He believes that Amelia switched aircraft for the last fatal lap of her round-the-world journey, flying instead a specially fitted-out Lockheed with holes cut out of the interior to accommodate spy cameras.

Sceptics remain dubious. It is more than likely that the US military supplied Amelia with substantial financial and technical assistance, probably because the US President, Franklin D. Roosevelt, appreciated the flight's value in boosting national morale. If there was any element of official cover-up, though, it was perhaps to protect the public from the knowledge of Amelia's failings as a pilot. She should have delayed take-off from Lae until the weather improved; she should have kept in regular radio contact with those monitoring her progress; and she should also have carried flares.

Among all the exotic theories that surround her disappearance, the likeliest is the most dull and humdrum; for all her charisma and bravery, Amelia Earhart was a normal, mortal woman – who paid the ultimate price for human failings.

1992 South Pacific expedition falsely builds up hope that Earhart's plane has been found

THE LAST SERENADE OF GLENN MILLER

MISSING, PRESUMED DEAD: THE LOSS OF THE SWING LEGEND WAS MOURNED BY THOUSANDS

Smooth, muted brass was the instantly recognisable trademark of American bandleader Glenn Miller, whose swing tunes survive among the most evocative hits of the Second World War. In 1941 he volunteered for active service but was persuaded that he could do more for the war effort through his music. So, joining the air force, he put together a United States Army Air Force Band to entertain troops abroad.

When Paris fell to the Allies late in 1944, Major Glenn Miller and his 60-piece orchestra were scheduled to perform in the French capital. His intention was to travel ahead of the band, and on December 14 he and another officer assembled with a pilot at an airfield a few miles from Bedford in England. Fog had been rolling in all day but, despite bad weather warnings, they took off for France. Their plane, a single-engined Norseman D-64, then vanished with its occupants into the fog.

No one realised that the aircraft had gone missing until two days later, when the rest of the band arrived in Paris. The show took place without him, but with hope that he was still alive. After three days, when searches revealed neither plane nor wreckage, Glenn Miller was reported missing, and people began to accept that he might be dead.

A fatal crash in the sea was the problable explanation, although there were no records of a plane being shot over the Channel on that day. According to one widespread theory the aircraft had iced up, stalled and fallen from the sky. Alternatively there may have been a mechanical failure, or the pilot may have lost his way and run out of fuel.

Did Miller reach Paris?

The shock of the tragedy, combined with the delay in official announcements, allowed alternative stories to circulate. Miller's wife Helen refused to believe the worst and hoped throughout the war that her husband might have survived as a German POW. A later theory proposed that Miller was shot down in error by an RAF fighter, a tragic

KING OF SWING   Some rumours had Glenn Miller being shot down by an RAF fighter; others said that he had a fractured skull from a brothel brawl in a seedy area of Paris.

mistake which was covered up by the authorities. An even more extraordinary cover-up was proposed by an ex-RAF officer called John Edwards. He was to suggest in 1976 that Miller was not aboard the crashed Norseman at all, but reached Paris in a Dakota and died there of a fractured skull

following a brothel brawl in the seedy Pigalle district. In a variation of this story, Miller was flown from Paris, badly injured, to the USA – where he died in a military hospital.

The wreckage of Second World War aircraft has occasionally been discovered in the Channel, but the Norseman has never been located. Unless it turns up, the enigma of Glenn Miller's death is likely to remain shrouded in suppositions as misty as the fog that engulfed southern England on that fateful night in wartime.

1939 Miller achieves world fame as big-band leader
1941 Miller joins US Air Force
1944 Miller disappears between England and France

LOST FLIERS OF THE SECOND WORLD WAR

THERE WERE OTHER VICTIMS – APART FROM AMERICAN BANDLEADER GLENN MILLER – OF PUZZLING AIRCRAFT CRASHES DURING THE SECOND WORLD WAR

Britain's best-loved female aviation pioneer and a successful movie star, a famous French novelist and the exiled Polish leader all vanished during the 1939-45 conflict.

Amy Johnson, 1941

Britain's pioneer of aviation worked for the Air Transport Auxiliary when the Second World War broke out. On January 5, 1941, while ferrying a plane, she baled out over the Thames Estuary and vanished into the waters. The puzzle was that she was 100 miles (161 km) from her destination and two hours late. Moreover, witnesses thought they saw two figures drop into the waves.

Conspiracy theorists have pictured the aviator returning from a mission in France, perhaps with a secret agent. However, Johnson was flying without a radio in bad conditions. Probably, she went off course, running out of fuel in the process. As for her companion, this was probably the rear exit door – which she had to jettison to make the jump.

PEOPLE'S DARLING   The British couldn't accept Amy Johnson's disappearance.

General Sikorski, 1943

Foul play was suspected from the moment news came through that General Wladyslaw Sikorski, the prime minister of the Polish government in exile, had died in an aircrash over Gibraltar on July 24, 1943. With Poland partitioned between Germany and the Soviet Union, the outspoken leader had made many political enemies – and was seen by many as a liability to the

FLIGHT OF FANCY   Saint-Exupéry (right) with an air mechanic before the Paris to Saigon Race, 1936.

Allies. There was an official investigation of the crash, but nothing concrete was revealed that could prove an assassination.

Antoine de Saint-Exupéry, 1944

The great French novelist was also a pioneer aviator who had flown mail in North Africa and South America. Although he was 43 when Paris fell to the Germans, Saint-Exupéry joined the Free French Air Force.

On July 31, 1944, he took off from base at Bastia in Corsica, on a mapping mission east of Lyons, and was never seen again. Mischievous rumours at the time hinted that he had been assassinated by the Gaullists – but his disappearance was probably no more sinister than that of many others lost on wartime flights. People close to Saint-Exupéry believed that he had long been courting death. 'If I disappear,' he told one friend, 'you can be sure it will be without regrets.' He had bequeathed his chess set to another, saying: 'Keep it. We'll play again on another planet.'

Leslie Howard, 1943

Leslie Howard, one of Britain's best-known movie stars of the 1930s, returned from Hollywood at the outbreak of war in order to make patriotic films such as *Pimpernel Smith*. In April 1943 he flew to Lisbon to lecture on cinema and drama in neutral Spain and Portugal. Though his talks had no propaganda value, his business partner took the opportunity to arrange film distribution; as a result, 900 Spanish cinemas were to show British war films. Returning on June 1, Howard took off from Lisbon on a DC3 civil airliner. As the aircraft passed over the Bay of Biscay, it was shot down by German Junkers fighters. No traces of Howard, the 12 other passengers or the aircraft were ever found. The Nazis' excuse for shooting down the plane was that the DC3 had been mistaken for an enemy bomber. But it was whispered that Howard – a potent ambassador for Britain – might have been a deliberate target.

HOLLYWOOD HEARTTHROB Leslie Howard's glittering career and life were cut short.

LAST PARADE   General Wladyslaw Sikorski reviews British soldiers in Gibraltar, July 1943. This was the last photograph ever taken of him.

ON THE TRAIL OF MARTIN BORMANN

THE NAZI WAR CRIMINAL WHO WAS OFTEN 'SIGHTED' BUT NEVER BROUGHT TO JUSTICE

When Hitler's top henchmen were sentenced to death for war crimes at the Nuremberg Trials of 1945-46, judgment was passed on one high-ranking SS man in his absence. This was Martin Bormann, the Führer's personal secretary since 1942, whose ultimate fate has never been completely ascertained to this day.

He is known to have served as witness when Hitler married Eva Braun in the Berlin bunker under the Reich Chancellery on April 29. The next day, when Hitler and Braun committed suicide in the bunker, Bormann was seen trying to commandeer a tank to escape the devastated capital. As he approached the vehicle, a shell burst close by. According to one witness (Hitler's

WANTED FOR WAR CRIMES Hitler's personal secretary, Martin Bormann was sentenced to death in his absence at the Nuremberg Trials.

chauffeur, Erich Kempka) there was a blinding flash, and when he looked again Bormann had vanished. It was assumed that he had died in the explosion, but there were other versions of events. It was rumoured that he had been spirited away and was later helped by the ODESSA organisation, which was run by Nazi sympathisers to assist former members of the SS escape retribution by the Allies.

He was 'sighted' time and again in South America: in Brazil, Argentina and Chile. In 1959, a grave thought to be Bormann's was opened up near Asuncion in Paraguay – to reveal only the bones of a Paraguayan named Hormoncilla. In 1967, police in Guatemala arrested a man answering the missing Nazi's description – he turned out to be an elderly carpenter named Martinez.

The bodies in the park

In 1971 new and sensational claims were made by Reinhard Gehlen, Hitler's chief of intelligence against the Soviet Union, who worked for the CIA after the war. Gehlen claimed that Bormann had been a Soviet agent and that he had escaped in 1945, and lived for many years behind the Iron Curtain, acting as an adviser on German affairs for the Russians. Few today believe this amazing claim, which was probably designed to sell Gehlen's memoirs.

Equally extraordinary is a theory put forward in 1995 by the author Christopher Creighton. He proposed that Bormann was smuggled out of the Berlin bunker on the orders of British Prime Minister Winston Churchill, taken to England and given plastic surgery. In an attempt to prise from him the secret of hidden Nazi gold deposits, the British authorities installed him in a village on the Berkshire-Hampshire border, where he died in 1989. According to the theory, he was then buried in an unmarked grave in a local churchyard.

The simplest and most likely story of Bormann's fate is that he died on May 1, 1945, in the neighbourhood of the Lehrt Station, during the bombardment of Berlin. After the unconditional surrender by Germany on May 7, 1945, the Russians found this whole area strewn with the bodies of German men, women and children, and ordered them to be buried in three mass

SINISTER SECRETS Bormann was known to be a great admirer of his Führer. A witness at Hitler's marriage to Eva Braun, he disappeared on the day of their suicide pact.

graves in a neighbouring park. Bormann's body was recognised among the corpses by one of those ordered to dig the graves. The park was dug up in 1965, when a large number of bones were found. In 1972 another search near the Lehrt Station yielded a skull

MISTAKEN IDENTITY An Italian monk named Martini (left) and the Guatemalan Martinez (right) were both thought to be Bormann.

thought by forensic experts 'with near certainty' to be Bormann's. This evidence, at least, was sufficient for the authorities in Bonn. In April 1973 the West German government confirmed Bormann's death, and closed the file on the Nazi war criminal.

1900   2000

April 30, 1945 Bormann vanishes, presumed dead   1959 Grave is opened up in Paraguay   1967 Man thought to be Bormann is arrested in Guatemala

THE HUNT FOR VANISHED NAZIS

**WANTED FOR CRIMES AGAINST HUMANITY: MANY SS MEN SPENT YEARS EVADING
CAPTURE – BUT THEY RECKONED WITHOUT THE DEATH CAMP SURVIVORS**

Frederick Forsyth's bestselling novel *The Odessa File* took its name from a real-life organisation operated by SS loyalists to help former members evade arrest by Allied authorities and so escape prosecution as war criminals. The acronym ODESSA stood for Organisation der ehemaliger SS Angehorigen (Organisation of former SS members). Founded in 1947 and posing as a charitable body, the organisation secretly assisted Nazi fugitives with contacts, money and forged papers. Thousands of Nazis are thought to have vanished in this way. Many passed through Italy, finding aid among circles close to the Vatican, before reaching countries in South America.

Among the escapees was Adolf Eichmann, a monstrous mass murderer who never actually felt the blood of his victims on his hands. Responsible for 'cleansing' Europe of Jews and any other groups deemed not to fit in with the Aryan masterplan, Eichmann was the technician who orchestrated the so-called 'final solution' on behalf of the Third Reich. It was thanks to him that the entire horrendous scheme was made possible – from rounding-up victims to organising the trains that took them to the Holocaust death camps.

At the end of the Second World War Eichmann was captured twice by American

THE INVESTIGATOR Simon Wiesenthal, a survivor of the death camps, has made it his mission in life to hunt down the perpetrators of war crimes.

THE EXTERMINATOR Adolf Eichmann in his Gestapo uniform in the 1940s, right, and how he looked when he was captured by Israelis in 1960, above.

troops – but both times managed to escape without being identified, despite the enormous price on his head. Subsequently he lived for four years as a lumberjack in Germany under an alias before he was able to flee via Austria to an Italian monastery, where he was issued with false papers in the name of 'Ricardo Klement'. Under that identity he obtained an Argentine visa and went to live in Buenos Aires, where in 1952 his wife, Vera, and two children joined him. As far as the world was concerned, Eichmann had vanished – whereas he was actually enjoying a comfortable post under his false identity with the firm of Mercedes-Benz.

The enigma of his fate was solved in 1960 when he was tracked down and kidnapped by a team of Israeli agents. They brought him back from South America to face trial in Jerusalem, where he was convicted and hanged for his war crimes in 1962.

Eichmann had been located with the aid of Simon Wiesenthal, a prominent Austrian investigator of Nazi crimes who had himself spent three years in concentration camps. Head of the Jewish Documentation Centre in Vienna since 1961, Wiesenthal has helped to track down more than 1000 missing war criminals. However, the fate and whereabouts of others remain a mystery, including Heinrich Mueller, chief of the Gestapo; Richard Gluecks, inspector-general of the concentration camps; and Walter Rauff, who supervised the provision of gas trucks for the 'final solution'.

THE WALLENBERG IRONY

THE HERO WHO RESCUED THOUSANDS BUT WAS POWERLESS TO SAVE HIMSELF

It has been said that Swedish diplomat and businessman Raoul Wallenberg saved more lives during the Second World War than any single government. As part of an American plan to rescue the last remaining large Jewish population in Europe, he spent the latter half of 1944 in Hungary. There he and his helpers provided shelter in protected 'safe' houses, supplied passports and even followed the trains to the concentration camps, distributing food, clothing and money. Yet the man who is credited with saving perhaps as many as 20 000 lives was powerless to save himself from a tragic fate, which remains unsolved.

Towards the end of the war, when fleeing German troops were being replaced by victorious Soviet forces in Budapest, Wallenberg decided to try to ensure the safety of his rescued Jews. He left under Russian escort en route

COLD WAR VICTIM Decades have been spent trying to track down the missing Raoul Wallenberg.

to Debrecen (150 miles/ 241 km away) to negotiate with Russian military leaders in January 1945. He was never seen again.

At first, it is thought, the Russians arrested Wallenberg on suspicion of Nazi connections – because of his dealings with Eichmann in saving Jews from the camps. Later, it seems, the Russians suspected that he might have been an American spy. Whatever the initial reason for his arrest, the Russian version reports Wallenberg's death from a heart attack in Lubianka Prison, Moscow, in 1947. But no body was produced, and, over the decades, many reports from freed Soviet prisoners suggested he was still alive in a Siberian camp or elsewhere – caught in a no-man's land of denied existence because of the Cold War.

The international enquiry

In 1981 the US President and the Swedish Prime Minister jointly pledged to continue the search for Wallenberg. The new period of *glasnost*, or openness, in Russia strengthened hopes, and in 1989 the KGB handed over some of Wallenberg's effects. The Russians still insisted that he was dead, but this did not prevent an international

AFTER OCCUPATION Wallenberg disappeared amidst the chaotic legacy of booby-trap bombs and devastation left by the Germans.

commission from asserting the opposite in 1990. Their report included eyewitness sightings of the diplomat within the Soviet Union, as well as the views of the late Andrei Sakharov, the Nobel prize-winning human rights activist. 'The evidence is incontrovertible that he did not die in 1947 as the Soviets claim,' said the report.

Sadly, as investigation continued, it began to seem likelier that the missing diplomat did perish soon after the war's end. In 1992 a former KGB man declared on Swedish television that Wallenberg died in 1947 during interrogation, and the following year a Danish newspaper claimed that he had been executed. There are still some who believe that Wallenberg survived – but with every year that passes, the chances of finding him alive are slimmer. Wallenberg was born in 1912; he would be in his eighties by now.

ENTER THE VICTORIOUS The arrival of Soviet troops spelt saviour in Budapest, but not, ironically, for Raoul Wallenberg.

July 1944 Wallenberg arrives in Budapest
January 1945 Wallenberg leaves Budapest with Soviet escort, bound for Debrecen
1947 Official date of death, in Lubianka Prison, according to the Soviets

1990 International enquiry reports that Wallenberg is probably still alive

GLASNOST RATTLES THE SKELETONS

BURIED TREASURES AND MACABRE LONG-LOST SECRETS WERE JUST SOME OF THE REVELATIONS OF MIKHAIL GORBACHEV'S NEW POLICIES IN THE SOVIET UNION

CRACKS IN THE ICE Talks between Gorbachev and Reagan at the Geneva Summit in 1985 heralded a new era in East-West relations.

I n 1986 Mikhail Gorbachev, the new leader of the Soviet Union, sparked a massive upheaval in his country with a speech to the 27th Communist Party congress. Mincing no words, he strongly criticised the corrupt Soviet bureaucracy, its centralised economy and the record of former President Leonid Brezhnev. Prominent Soviet dissidents were released that year, and in January 1987 Gorbachev ushered in a new democratic age with a call for electoral reform and a policy of *glasnost* – or openness – in social and cultural life.

Gorbachev's democratic reforms had ramifications on politics worldwide. And as glasnost fostered a free investigative spirit within the Soviet Union, long-sealed doors were opened and secret files came to light. Many a historic puzzle was solved as a result. Through glasnost, researchers were able to locate and unearth the long-hidden skeletons of the Russian royal family and send them for DNA testing. For the first time, journalists were allowed to enter and film

LOST LOOT Last seen in Berlin, the Gold of Troy was among the art treasures from Germany that turned up in Moscow.

in the notorious *Gulag*. This Russian archipelago of labour camps and prisons is where thousands of political prisoners and exiles disappeared under Stalin and his successors.

No certain conclusions have been reached about the fate of the missing Swedish diplomat Raoul Wallenberg, but many other wartime mysteries have been cleared up. At last, officials have admitted Soviet responsibility for the Katyn Massacre, when 4500 Polish officers were shot and buried in mass graves in a forest near Smolensk. Many paintings, sculptures and other art treasures taken from Germany by the Red Army at the end of the Second World War have been located. They include the celebrated Gold of Troy discovered by German archaeologist Heinrich Schliemann, which had vanished from Berlin and recently turned up in the basement of the Pushkin Museum in Moscow.

Perhaps the most remarkable finds, though, have been the items relating to Hitler's death, long kept secret from the public by the KGB.

File I-G-23, which was discovered in the State Special Trophy Archive in Moscow, turned out to comprise six buff-coloured files of documents, plus charts and photographs,

REVOLUTIONARY ART New attitudes in the Soviet Union paved the way for open expression, as in this anti-Stalin poster.

reporting what went on in Berlin at the time of the Führer's death. At the same time, in the State Archive of the Russian Federation (also in Moscow), another astonishing find was made: Hitler's charred and tattered uniforms, watercolours and personal photographs, and even what appeared to be fragments of his skull. The skull had been kept in a crumbling cardboard box originally used for biro refills.

THE FROGMAN WHO NEVER SURFACED

WAS LIONEL 'BUSTER' CRABB SOLD DOWN THE RIVER BY THE BRITISH GOVERNMENT?

Much publicity surrounded the eight-day visit to Britain in 1956 of the new Soviet leaders, Nikita Khrushchev and Nikolai Bulganin. The heirs to Stalin came for talks with the British Government, and

THE MISSING MAN **Buster Crabb in 1950 during work in Tobermory Bay, where he was employed to locate a sunken galleon.**

arrived on the *Ordzhonikidze*, an impressive new cruiser which had been admired for its speed and manoeuvrability. Accompanied by two destroyers, the warship anchored outside Portsmouth Harbour.

On the day before the Russians arrived, April 17, 1956, a dapper little man named Lionel 'Buster' Crabb checked into the Sallyport Hotel in Portsmouth. He had served as a frogman in the Royal Navy, and his expertise in dangerous underwater work had earned him a George Medal in the Second World War. Officially at least, Commander Crabb was now a civilian employee of a company in the espresso coffee business. But speculation would soon be rife that Crabb still did underwater work – albeit of a somewhat hush-hush nature.

The day after the Russians' arrival in Portsmouth, Buster Crabb went missing from his hotel. A companion of his, who had given his name as 'Mr Smith', cleared out all his luggage, and some time later a CID man turned up and tore out all of the April pages from the hotel register. He gave no explanation, merely cautioning the staff under the Official Secrets Act to say nothing about the visit of Crabb. When a friend later telephoned the Admiralty in an attempt to contact the missing diver, he was told that the frogman was dead.

The headless corpse

Soon it was being whispered among journalists that Crabb had come to grief while taking part in an underwater spying mission to investigate the unusual hull and rudder of the *Ordzhonikidze*. But while the sensitive Anglo-Soviet talks were going on, all enquiries about the missing frogman met official silence.

It was only after the Russian delegation left that the government admitted that Crabb had gone missing – presumed dead – while carrying out 'trials with certain underwater apparatus' near the Soviet cruiser. In the House of Commons, the Prime Minister, Sir Anthony Eden, declared that it would not be in the public interest to disclose more about these particular circumstances.

The Foreign Office did acknowledge, however, that a frogman who had been sighted by a Russian look-out swimming between the two Soviet destroyers 'was to all appearances Commander Crabb'. They were keen to point out, though, that his presence near the destroyers had occurred 'without any permission whatever and Her Majesty's Government express their regret for the incident'. Inevitably, Soviet newspapers railed against this 'shameful underwater espionage', but did the Russian authorities know more than they let on? Indeed, in Britain, the absence of a body prompted speculation that Buster Crabb had perhaps been captured alive and taken back to the Soviet Union for interrogation.

In June the following year there came a sensational development: Crabb's body had reportedly been found in the sea near Chichester Harbour. The corpse lacked its head and hands, but the lower part of the body was reasonably well protected by a diver's suit, and the left leg bore what looked like a distinctive scar the missing frogman had acquired in wartime.

The coroner declared himself satisfied that the remains were those of Commander Crabb, and the body was buried at Portsmouth. But not everyone accepted this

MACABRE FIND **Two fishermen, Ted Gilby (left) and D.L. Randall (right), found Crabb's supposed – and headless – corpse.**

verdict. Was it not strange that the head and the hands, which would have provided a truly positive identification, were missing? Was it not all too convenient?

Was the body planted?

Suspicions inevitably deepened when it became known that three Soviet submarines had passed through the English Channel just a few days before the corpse had made its appearance near Chichester Harbour. It was rumoured that one of them could have slipped the headless body into the sea near to where it came ashore.

This hypothesis was taken up by the journalist J. Bernard Hutton, who published two sensational books about the case. He claimed to have evidence that the body washed ashore was a plant, and that the real Buster Crabb lived on as 'L.L. Korablov,' a frogman instructor in the Soviet Union.

Hutton's story alleged that the Russians had taken Commander Crabb back to the Soviet Union and, after interrogation,

offered him the alternative of death or a career passing on his submariner's skills to recruits in the Russian Navy.

Sceptics regard Hutton's version as far-fetched, but it is not inconceivable that Crabb was recovered from the water, alive or dead, and removed from the scene on that particular night in April 1956. A disastrous diplomatic incident would have put the crucial Anglo-Soviet talks – billed at the time as being conducted 'in a spirit of candour and realism' – in serious jeopardy. Whether the headless corpse returned to the Channel was that of Crabb or a substitute must remain open to some doubt. What is certain is that if someone sent it floating towards Chichester Harbour – almost a year later – that person wanted the case closed once and for all.

DO SVIDANYA, BRITAIN Bidding farewell, from left to right, Nikita Khrushchev, Dr Ivan Kurchatov (Atom Chief), Nikolai Bulganin and A.N. Tupolev (Soviet aircraft designer).

STILL WATERS The Russian cruiser *Ordzhonikidze* (foreground), alleged to be Crabb's intelligence target, berthed outside Portsmouth Harbour with two destroyers.

April 17, 1956 Buster Crabb checks into Portsmouth Hotel
April 18, 1956 Khrushchev and Bulganin arrive in England for talks
April 19, 1956 Buster Crabb goes missing

THE MISSING PRIME MINISTER

AUSTRALIA'S HAROLD HOLT PLUNGES INTO THE SURF – NEVER TO BE SEEN AGAIN

Crowds of Australian holidaymakers watched and waited near a beach on the Victoria coast, while soldiers checked the sands over a 30-mile (48 km) front and helicopters flew low over the waves. Hundreds of divers, including navy frogmen, searched underwater for signs of the missing statesman. The date was Sunday, December 17, 1967, and Australia's Prime Minister, Harold Holt, had vanished into the sea.

As leader of Australia's Liberal Party, Harold Holt headed a coalition government which he had been struggling for some time to hold together. Two days before he disappeared the usually ebullient politician had seemed to journalists to be tired and withdrawn. But that had not stopped him from entertaining weekend guests and playing vigorous tennis at his house in Portsea some 60 miles (96 km) from Melbourne. On that Sunday morning, he and a group of friends had driven to Cheviot Beach for a swim. The waters here were well known for their treacherous currents, and most of the prime minister's friends were reluctant to go in. But Holt took the plunge and swam powerfully out to sea, followed by a young businessman named Alan Stewart.

Some distance from the shore, Stewart felt an alarming undertow and decided to turn back. Holt however, forged on ahead, swimming strongly. Back on the beach, a witness called Marjorie Gillespie became worried for the prime minister and ran down to the surf's edge. 'The water became turbulent around him very suddenly. It seemed to boil and these conditions seemed to swamp him.'

After that, Holt was gone. And despite a full-scale six-day search, his body was never found washed ashore.

An astonishing allegation

While US President Lyndon Johnson and other world statesmen gathered in Australia for Holt's memorial service, some inevitable questions were raised. Why had the 59-year-

FAMILY MAN Keen fisherman Harold Holt and his wife, Zara, play in a speedboat with their grandson during a weekend of relaxation on the Victoria coast.

against his support for the Vietnam War; it was rumoured that his own party wanted to ditch him. While friends and family repudiated the idea of suicide as wholly against Holt's character, there were some in the parliamentary opposition who felt that he had showed signs of an impending breakdown.

In 1983, however, a much more controversial claim was made. In a book called *The Prime Minister was a Spy*, the British journalist and author Anthony Grey argued that Holt had not drowned off the Victoria coast at all. He swam out to a waiting submarine, was pulled down by frogmen who provided breathing apparatus, and was whisked away to the People's Republic of China. This astonishing allegation was based on unverifiable information from Chinese sources that Holt was a spy for Chairman Mao Ze-dong. He had (it was claimed) been a socialist sympathiser since the 1930s, passed information to Red China, and made his escape when he thought exposure was imminent.

Critics laughed at the theory, though this would not have been the only escape through a fake drowning. Britain's John Stonehouse, a Labour MP and former minister, had apparently drowned when his clothes were found on a Miami beach. In December 1974 he turned up living in Australia on a false passport, and he was subsequently brought back to England to face charges of fraud and theft. In the case of Harold Holt, such a secret getaway seems implausible, though the lack of a body has left room for the imagination to wander.

THE SEARCH CONTINUES A newspaper (above) of Monday, December 18, 1967, describes continuing attempts to find Australia's missing Prime Minister, Harold Holt, photographed in 1966 (left).

old prime minister swum with such determination so far out into the notoriously dangerous waters? Some theorised that he had committed suicide as a way out of his increasingly fraught political position. Holt's coalition was shaky; he had been under pressure from protesters demonstrating

1900 ── 2000

1908 Harold Holt
born in Sydney

1966 Harold Holt succeeds
Sir Robert Menzies as
prime minister

1983 Anthony Grey's *The
Prime Minister was a Spy*

THE VANISHED SKYJACKER

HOW A MYSTERY MAN KNOWN ONLY AS D.B. COOPER ENDED HIS DARING COUP WITH A PARACHUTE LEAP

The quiet, clean-shaven man in dark glasses boarded a Northwest Airlines Boeing 727 at Portland, Oregon, giving his name as D.B. Cooper (which was all that was ever known about him). About half an hour after takeoff, he pushed a button overhead to call the stewardess who came with a tray to take his order for a drink. But Cooper asked for no liquid refreshment. Instead, he passed her a note warning that he had a bomb with him, and that unless he was given $200 000 in cash he would blow the plane to bits. Then he opened the canvas carrier bag on his lap to reveal the sticks of dynamite and the detonator.

It was Thanksgiving Day – November 24, 1971 – a date that would long be remembered among students of 20th-century crime. For that night, D.B. Cooper pulled off a coup that led him to be dubbed the world's only successful skyjacker.

Notified of the danger, the pilot, Captain Bill Scott, managed to radio a coded alert about the hijack, so that when the plane landed some 400 miles (640 km) away at Seattle, Washington State, squads of police, airline officials and FBI men were already assembled on the ground. But they could see that the risk was real enough and acceded to Cooper's requests. A sack containing the

$200 000 was brought to the aircraft, along with a selection of four parachutes that he had requested in return for the safe release of the hostages. Oblivious of the dramatic events unfolding around them, the passengers on board were then allowed to leave before the plane took off once again with Cooper and the three-man flight crew.

At 8.13 pm, 32 minutes after leaving Seattle, with the jetliner flying at 200 mph (320 km/h) over the Lewis river, Cooper opened the rear exit door and leapt out.

His fate is unknown to this day. Cooper jumped into high altitude winds and freezing rain wearing only his lightweight lounge suit and a raincoat. Some believe that he would have perished in the air, or on hitting the thickly wooded mountains, but neither aerial searches by spotter planes nor satellite surveillance photographs revealed any trace of his parachute canopy. And the authorities were further confounded when, three weeks after the hijack, a typed letter purportedly written by D.B. Cooper arrived at the offices of a Los Angeles newspaper. 'I am no modern-day Robin Hood,' the writer declared, 'unfortunately I have only 14 months to live. The hijacking was the fastest and most profitable way to gain a few last grains of peace of mind. I didn't rob Northwest because I thought it would be romantic, or heroic, or any of the other euphemisms that seem to attach themselves to situations of high risk.'

The money in the mud

Was the letter genuine? Or a fake? It was hard to tell since the vanishing skyjacker had started to acquire a cult following in the United States, prompting everything from scrawled graffiti to newspaper cartoons, proposals of marriage from impressionable women, and record dedications by disc jockeys. But as time passed,

MONEY IN THE BANK Investigators dig a trench at the spot in the river bank where thousands of dollars of the skyjack loot were found by picnickers in 1980.

the forests of Washington State began to yield some real and tantalising clues. In 1979, a deer hunter in the woods above Kelso village came upon a plastic warning sign from the rear door hatch of a Boeing 727. Then, in 1980, a full nine years after his disappearing act, about $3000 of the marked bills from Cooper's haul were recovered from the shore of the Columbia river.

For some, the implication of the muddied cash was that D.B. Cooper must have perished after all, and that his bones lay somewhere in the forest, or in the riverbed, upstream. Further searches, though, revealed nothing, and others have pictured him injured but still alive making a cunning escape from the forest with the bulk of his ransom money. No one can say for certain unless Cooper really did survive and secretly lives on, enjoying the proceeds of his audacious coup.

MYSTERY PASSENGER As part of the police investigation into the identity and fate of D.B. Cooper, artists attempted to capture his likeness from eyewitness accounts.

1971 D.B. Cooper disappears
1976 FBI officially close the file on D.B. Cooper
1980 Dollar bills found on bank of river

VIETNAM'S MISSING GIS

WERE AMERICAN SERVICEMEN LEFT BEHIND IN SOUTH-EAST ASIA AFTER THE END OF THE WAR?

On March 29, 1973 – two months after peace talks had brought the Vietnam War to an end – the last prisoners officially held by the North Vietnamese in Hoa Lo Prison (known as the Hanoi Hilton) boarded an Air Force plane at Gia Kam airfield near Hanoi. Their release prompted an immense outpouring of joy and relief from the crowds who gathered in the United States to greet them. But the trauma of this bitter and divisive war was not over yet. Still unaccounted for at the war's end were more than 2400

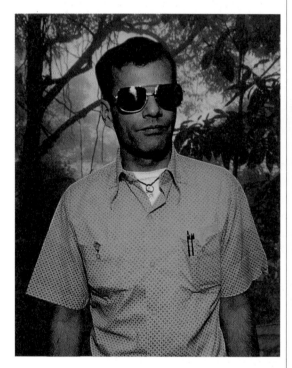

MARINE'S RETURN Private Robert Garwood, captured in 1965, escaped from Vietnam in 1979 and brought back reports of other American POWs still alive there.

servicemen and civilians who had disappeared during the struggle in South-east Asia, some 1800 in Vietnam itself. These were the MIAs – the Missing in Action – who had been involved in combat with the enemy but had been listed neither as killed in action nor as prisoners of war.

Obviously, in the chaos of a long jungle war, many lives might be lost unaccountably. But the number of the missing was exceptionally high in relation to the handful of released prisoners of war. Only 591 Americans regained their freedom following the signing of the Paris peace accords in January 1973. Had others been left behind?

The official silence

Suspicions were aroused in June 1973 when a North Vietnamese defector called Nguyen Thanh Son told newsmen that he had recently seen six prisoners who he believed were Americans who had not yet been released. As other Vietnamese refugees turned up telling similar stories, families of the MIAs became alarmed by Washington's seeming inactivity. Accusations of a cover-up were to be levelled against the US government.

What possible motive could there be for

MAN WITH A MISSION 'Bo' Gritz, a former Special Forces officer, led a rescue team to recover American GIs who were believed to have been left behind in South-east Asia.

government secrecy? Part of the problem was reputedly that the missing personnel included troops lost during the secret wars in Laos and Cambodia – conflicts long denied by officialdom. To acknowledge the prisoners would be to admit an involvement in covert operations. It has also been alleged that President Nixon had secretly agreed to provide more than $3 billion to help pay for postwar reconstruction in Vietnam in

exchange for prisoners of war. But Congress had refused the aid money – so the POWs' liberty became forfeit.

One missing serviceman who did turn up was a Marine, Private Robert Garwood, who had been captured near Da Nang in 1965, when barely 19 years old. After the war he had worked as a mechanic in the motor pool of a prison camp, repairing American vehicles left behind in Vietnam. In 1979, he managed to smuggle a message out of Vietnam to the BBC via a neutral diplomat, telling the world that he wanted to go back to the United States. On his return, however, he was accused of being a turncoat who had collaborated with the enemy, been given preferential treatment in the camps, and had on one occasion struck a fellow American prisoner. At his court martial, Garwood insisted that he had been isolated from other POWs and forced to live with his Vietnamese guards because of his gift for languages. Either way, he disproved Hanoi's claim that there were no Americans left in Vietnam.

And Garwood insisted that other GIs were still alive in South-east Asia. He claimed to have been in a camp with other American prisoners when he heard former Secretary of State Henry Kissinger assert over the camp radio: 'There are no more live POWs in Vietnam.' This was a devastating blow to all of them, and their guards had taunted them with their government's desertion. Garwood claimed that he could name other American prisoners still alive in Vietnam, but was reluctant to do so because if he identified them by name they were liable to be killed.

A secret expedition

Another extraordinary story came to light when it was reported that a retired Special Forces soldier named Lt Colonel James 'Bo' Gritz had led a mission in 1981 to recover American servicemen left behind in South-east Asia. The rescue team had investigated a suspected prison site, said to have been located on several satellite photographs, but had found no Americans. After a two-year silence, the Department of Defense acknowledged that Gritz had headed just such an expedition.

PUZZLE PICTURE This grainy black-and-white photograph, dated 1990, was alleged to depict three captive pilots shot down during the Vietnam War: (from left to right) Col John Robertson, Major Albro Lundy and Lt Larry Stevens. Relatives were convinced that the photograph of the middle-aged men, last seen 25 years before, was genuine.

The whole issue was now becoming a national scandal, and a vigorous campaign was conducted by the National League of Families of American Prisoners and Missing in South-east Asia. Many individual cases became known to the increasingly concerned public. A Colonel David Hrdlicka, shot down

TRAGIC TOLL During a ceremony at Hanoi airport in 1985, American service personnel salute the remains of 26 MIAs handed over by the Vietnamese and returned to the USA.

in 1965, had been photographed and was thought to have made a radio broadcast as a prisoner, but was not among the returnees of 1973. The wife of a serviceman named Captain James Grace, shot down in 1968, identified her husband as the bearded man shown on a Soviet propaganda film on prisoners made during the war. What had happened to these men, and others like them?

President Ronald Reagan himself asserted that the missing servicemen's fate was a matter of top priority for his administration. In 1986 a high-powered US delegation visited Vietnam for talks to resolve the problem. Hanoi officials acknowledged that there might be some Americans still held captive in remote areas of Vietnam not fully under government control, and later that year the US government agreed to help Hanoi in tracing and accounting for the MIAs.

But the mystery of the missing GIs was still not resolved to everyone's satisfaction. In January 1993, a US Senate report declared that in its eagerness to see an end to the war the Nixon administration had 'shunted aside' the possibility that the POWs were left behind. The same year, a report made by a North Vietnamese general, Tran Van Qang,

in 1972 was discovered in the archives of the Soviet Communist Party in Moscow. The document said that North Vietnam was

MY GOD! LOOK!

Scott Barnes, a freelance specialist in covert operations, has claimed that in the course of a CIA mission into Laos in 1981, in company with an American named Jerrold 'Hog' Daniels, he saw US prisoners being kept in a jungle compound:

'He assembled the cameras – one had the longest lens I'd ever seen; then radio equipment with what looked like a satellite dish . . . In a valley below, I saw what seemed like a triangular camp, surrounded by a fence, with a watchtower at three points. One building was larger than the others and was surrounded by large drums. Outside the walled compound were fields, one to the left and the other facing us, where men worked under armed guard. At the furthest point there was a kind of tunnel into the thick jungle.

'Suddenly Daniels shouted, "My God! Look!" I took the binoculars and saw two Caucasians under armed escort, walking to the compound. He shouted, "We really did leave them behind!"'

holding 1205 Americans in 11 camps; at that time Hanoi publicly acknowledged only 368. A White House envoy who verified the authenticity of the document claimed that it was an exaggeration.

Its discovery did nothing to allay the worries of concerned relatives. In July 1993, President Clinton said that he would not lift a crippling US trade embargo on Vietnam unless the country did more to resolve the fate of the American servicemen still listed as missing in action. And, at the request of relatives, the former world boxing champion Muhammad Ali even visited Vietnam to try to persuade top officials to continue their investigations. The trade embargo was lifted the following year, but when, in 1995, the United States formally renewed diplomatic ties with Vietnam there was a public outcry. The uncertainties lingered on, long after the conclusion of the harrowing war in South-east Asia.

1950   2000

1965 US government commits the first fighting American soldiers to the Vietnam War   1973 US government withdraws troops; POWs returned   1979 Robert Garwood returns home   1981 'Bo' Gritz's secret mission   1994 Trade embargo lifted

LORD LUCAN FLEES THE SCENE

THE SENSATIONAL CASE OF THE MISSING EARL AND THE MURDERED NANNY

It was a cold November night in 1974 in London and Veronica, Countess of Lucan, sat watching television in the bedroom of her home at 46 Lower Belgrave Street. Her daughter Frances was with her; the other two children were in bed. Just before 9 pm the 29-year-old nanny, Sandra Rivett, put her head round the door, offering to make a pot of tea, and Lady Lucan gratefully accepted. But the nanny never returned, and after about 20 minutes the puzzled Lady Lucan went down to the kitchen three floors below. There the horror began.

In the dark basement kitchen she glimpsed the tall, shadowy form of a man who was bundling the nanny's corpse into a canvas mailsack. Lady Lucan screamed in terror and the figure came after her, battering her about the head. In the account she gave to the police and then to the Coroner's Court, Lady Lucan could not identify her assailant at first. But when he told her to 'shut up', she recognised his voice as that of her estranged husband, Richard John Bingham – the 7th Earl of Lucan.

After a brief struggle, Lady Lucan was

MAN ABOUT TOWN The police always believed that the 7th Earl of Lucan, a professional gambler, was the murderer.

able to calm her husband down and persuade him to help her back upstairs to her bedroom. But, while he was fetching a cloth to clean up her face, she dashed from the house and ran, barefoot and bloodstained, into the saloon bar of the nearby Plumbers Arms pub calling out 'Help me! Help me! I've just escaped from a murderer. He's still in the house. My children! My children!' The police, inevitably, wanted to question Lord Lucan as a matter of urgency, but by the time they arrived in Lower Belgrave Street the Earl had long since fled the scene.

Why kill the nanny?

Lucan's flight that night in 1974 was for many a compelling argument that he was, in fact, the basement murderer. And it was not hard to find motives for the attack: Lord and Lady Lucan had separated acrimoniously and fought a £40 000 High Court case for custody of their

children. Despite attempts by Lord Lucan to prove that his wife was too mentally unstable to look after their children, Lady Lucan had won. 'Lucky' (as friends called him, despite his losing streak) was known to be bitter and distraught about the case. Although a gambler and man-about-town, he was deeply attached to his children and felt their loss intensely. Police believed that he went to the house with the intention of killing his wife and disposing of her body so that he could get custody of the children. But why kill the nanny? Perhaps it was a simple case of mistaken identity. Sandra Rivett normally had Thursday evenings off, but as chance would have it she had decided to stay in that night. The theory was that Lord Lucan murdered her in the dark basement kitchen, mistaking her for his estranged wife.

A CASE OF MISTAKEN IDENTITY? Did Lord Lucan kill the nanny, Sandra Rivett (left), mistaking her in the dark for his estranged wife Veronica (right)?

The police view was also the verdict at the coroner's inquest, held in June 1975. The jury named Lord Lucan as the killer; if the missing earl reappeared, he would face a murder trial at the Old Bailey.

There was an alternative version of events, however, supplied by the fugitive earl. After the horror in Lower Belgrave Street, Lucan sped in a borrowed Ford

HAPPY COUPLE Lord Bingham (as Lucan was called before his father's death in 1964) poses with his fiancée, Miss Veronica Duncan, for an engagement photograph in 1963.

1934 Richard John Bingham is born in London, into an aristocratic family with the motto 'In Christ lies my hope'

1947 Lord Bingham is sent to Eton College

CRIME RECONSTRUCTION At 8.30 pm Lord Lucan arrives at the Clermont Club (1) and chats to the doorman to establish an alibi, before letting himself into the family home in Lower Belgrave Street (2) and waiting in the darkened basement. Here, at around 9.00 pm, he attacks nanny Sandra Rivett by mistake (3) but is disturbed by his wife (4). Lucan attacks her on the stairs; she calms him down before escaping at 9.50 pm to the nearby Plumbers Arms (5). Lucan leaves the house (6) and drives to Uckfield in Sussex (7). From the home of the Maxwell-Scotts he telephones his mother, the Dowager Countess of Lucan (8). He later abandons his car near the ferry terminal at Newhaven (9), where it is discovered the next morning.

1950   2000

1953 Lord Bingham serves
with the Coldstream
Guards in Germany

1963 Bingham
marries Veronica
Duncan

1974 Lord and Lady Lucan separate
1975 At the Coroner's Court, a jury finds Lord Lucan
guilty of murder, in his absence

Corsair to the home of close friends in Uckfield, Sussex, and gave Susan Maxwell-Scott his own story. The earl claimed that he had been walking past his wife's home and, through the venetian blinds of the basement, had seen a man attacking her. He quickly let himself in and drove the intruder off, but when he ran upstairs to comfort Lady Lucan she became hysterical and accused him of having hired the killer himself.

Lord Lucan did not, however, stay around to offer his story to the police. 'The circumstantial evidence against me is strong,' he argued in one of two letters written from the Maxwell-Scott home. 'Veronica will say it was all my doing.' Around 1.15 am, he said goodbye to Mrs Maxwell-Scott and drove off. It was the last time that he was sighted for certain. The following day the Ford Corsair was found abandoned at the ferry port of Newhaven in Sussex. Bloodstains matching the types of Lady Lucan and the nanny were found in the abandoned car, with a piece of the same lead pipe which had been used to bludgeon Sandra Rivett. Though it was conceivable that Lucan had snatched the weapon from the 'intruder', this was a particularly incriminating piece of evidence. And the location of the car at a ferry port which runs regular cross-Channel services to Dieppe in France carried the clear implication that Lucan had fled the country.

A polite silence

Where did he go? In the months and years which followed, the missing earl was reported in South Africa and the Seychelles, in

AROUND THE WORLD Every year there are still around 50 'sightings' of the missing earl (some of the more plausible of which are shown on the map above); but, to the police's frustration, no positive trace of Lucan has yet been found.

Cherbourg, Las Vegas, Rio de Janeiro, Dublin, Bogotá ... yet despite an international police effort the leads were never proved to be correct. Some investigators came to doubt that he had left the country at all, for immigration checks in both England and France produced no evidence that he had been aboard the only ferry to leave Newhaven that day. Did he commit suicide at the Channel port? Divers searched the harbour, and helicopters equipped with infra-red cameras scanned large areas of the surrounding countryside. But no body was ever found.

If Lucan fled abroad or lay low in England, someone must have helped him. Police questioned many members of his circle, but their efforts were not aided by the polite silence of the many wealthy socialites who were the earl's friends. All their instincts, it appeared, were to club together to protect one of their own. According to Detective Chief Superintendent Roy Ranson, they were 'living in their own world, quite apart from the rest of us'.

The earl's fate remains a mystery to this day. More than 20 years after the murder, with no confirmed sighting, many have come to believe that Lord Lucan must be dead: that he committed suicide out of guilt. Perhaps he had left the car at Newhaven to allow doubt to remain about his innocence

FRIENDS IN NEED After the murder, Lord Lucan drove to Grants Hill House, the home of Susan and Ian Maxwell-Scott in Uckfield, Sussex. Mrs Maxwell-Scott gave him a drink and listened to Lucan's account of his 'nightmarish experience'.

and freedom, and then had a friend dispose of his body to spare his children the misery of learning the truth. Yet his name still appears in *Who's Who*, the directory of living persons of influence and interest, and it is not beyond credence that Lord Lucan really is still alive and in hiding, shielded from the law – but ruined by the nightmarish events which unfolded that November night.

THE TEAMSTERS' LEADER

WHATEVER HAPPENED TO THE NOTORIOUS AMERICAN UNION BOSS, JIMMY HOFFA?

At 12.30 pm on July 30, 1975, Jimmy Hoffa kissed his wife Josephine goodbye and climbed into the bullet-proof limousine waiting outside his luxury home in Orion, Michigan. The former president of America's giant International Brotherhood of Teamsters, a truck drivers' union, was on his way to a luncheon appointment with 'a couple of guys' at the Machus Red Fox Restaurant in a Detroit suburb. But the men he was to dine with seem not to have turned up, for some hours later Hoffa phoned an aide to find out if they had tried to contact him. An eyewitness that afternoon glimpsed Hoffa in the back seat of a car with a number of other men. And then he vanished.

Hoffa was one of the most notorious figures in American public life. Appointed president of the Teamsters' union in 1957, he was to be accused of milking the organisation of almost $2 million and of using vicious gangster tactics to maintain power. Hoffa

UNION MAN Jimmy Hoffa, the Teamsters' leader, appears at a press conference after the Union's quarterly meeting, at Miami Beach in 1960.

became the prime target of Robert Kennedy, attorney-general between 1961 and 1964, who called his union leadership a 'conspiracy of evil' and initiated enquiries that absorbed the energies of 13 grand juries, 16 lawyers and 30 FBI agents.

The efforts of the 'Get Hoffa Squad', as it was soon dubbed, finally came to fruition. On March 7, 1967, the Teamsters' boss was sent to Lewisburg Penitentiary in Pennsylvania for a total of 13 years on two separate convictions (with sentences to run consecutively) for jury fixing and defrauding the union's pension fund.

The abandoned car

Richard Nixon, whose presidential election campaigns in 1960 and 1968 had been generously funded by the union, commuted Hoffa's prison sentence to four years – on the condition that he should hold no union office until 1980. When Hoffa emerged from jail in 1971, however, he immediately embarked on a campaign to get President Nixon's ban lifted. And he also began manoeuvring against a one-time colleague, Frank Fitzsimmons, who had replaced him as Teamster president in 1967.

This was the setting for Hoffa's disappearance – and there has been no shortage of theories about his fate. In one version, he was killed by a rival faction within the Teamsters' union. In another, he was murdered by the Mafia in order to prevent him from exposing details of the corrupt relationship between the union and organised crime – or even from revealing details of plots, involving the CIA, to assassinate

ARCH ENEMIES Jimmy Hoffa jabs his finger at Robert Kennedy, chief counsel for the Senate Rackets Committee, in an angry clash in 1959 (above). Below: At the age of 67, Frank Fitzsimmons succeeded Hoffa as leader of the Teamsters – with 2.2 million members, America's biggest transport union.

Fidel Castro of Cuba. And still there remains a third possibility that, knowing that his life was in danger from a broad selection of different enemies, Hoffa stage-managed his own disappearance.

Hoffa's car, located after an anonymous phone call to the police, offered no clues. Inside was a pair of white gloves, neatly folded on the back seat. But there was no sign of a struggle. In the months that followed, police and private citizens – encouraged by the hope of a $300 000 reward offered by Hoffa's family and friends – searched through landfills, woods and rubbish dumps in the hope of discovering the corpse.

But of Jimmy Hoffa – alive or dead (and his family believe that he must have been murdered) – nothing has been seen again.

WHAT HAPPENED TO SHERGAR?

THE KIDNAP RIDDLE OF THE WORLD'S MOST FAMOUS RACEHORSE REMAINS UNSOLVED

On the evening of Tuesday, February 8, 1983, armed men burst into the home of James Fitzgerald, head groom at Ballymany stud, the Aga Khan's stable in County Kildare in the Irish Republic. The intruders locked the groom's family in a downstairs room and then, at gunpoint, forced Jim Fitzgerald to identify the security stable housing Shergar, a handsome bay stallion with a distinctive white blaze, who was one of the world's most valuable horses.

Another member of the gang (police estimated that more than six were involved) required a ransom of £2 million, and then driven in a van to the outskirts of a village 20 miles (32 km) away. From here he had to make his own way home – some four hours after the break-in. Shergar, meanwhile, vanished with his kidnappers into the night.

Hoax calls

Shergar's kidnapping prompted a massive farm-by-farm search. While police issued Identikit pictures of three men they wanted to question in connection with the theft, more than 100 000 farmers throughout the country combed their land, sheds and barns for traces of the missing steed. Nicknamed the 'wonder horse' after winning the Derby in 1981 by a record margin

up to be covered by the Derby-winner in 1983 alone.

Reports circulated that huge ransoms had been asked for Shergar, but throughout the period of the search the police were bedevilled by hoax calls; the syndicate of 34 shareholders which owned Shergar countered such rumours by claiming that no ransom had been demanded. According to some reports, Shergar had been smuggled to Libya or the Middle East. But early in April an anonymous caller to RTE, the Irish radio and television station, indicated that the stallion was still in the country, and said that unless £1.5 million ransom was paid, the head of Shergar would be cut off and deposited at a location in Dublin.

The IRA connection

In May the horse's insurers decided to pay theft claims on Shergar – a fact indicating that they expected no swift return of the horse from the kidnappers. With the passing months, and then years, fears for Shergar's safety deepened into a widespread conviction that the horse must be dead. In 1986 a book claimed that Shergar had been killed by the IRA, and a TV drama was broadcast based on this version of events. In 1991, however, hopes for the horse were revived when the deputy chairman of Lloyd's bloodstock committee revealed that he had been contacted by a bounty hunter claiming that Shergar was still alive.

In December 1992 a former IRA police informer imprisoned in Northern Ireland claimed to reveal the definitive version of events. Sean O'Callaghan, serving a life sentence for two murders, told *Sunday Times* journalists that Shergar was killed within hours of being kidnapped. In this account, the Derby-winner was shot because he had panicked in captivity and could not be controlled by his kidnappers. The five-year-old stallion was then buried in thick woodland 100 miles (160 km) from the Aga Khan's stud farm. Although this version of events has been widely accepted, Shergar's remains have yet to be located and identified.

WONDER HORSE Shergar (inset) wins the Epsom Derby in 1981 (above), ridden by jockey Walter Swinburn.

reversed a scruffy light-blue or green horse-trailer to the stall, and Shergar was pushed inside, with the reluctant help of the head groom. Mr Fitzgerald was taken back to his house, told by the kidnappers that they of 10 lengths, Shergar was syndicated at £10 million – although with a value of perhaps three times that amount on the open market – and had been seized only a week before the breeding season started. The Aga Khan, one of the richest men in the world, and other members of the syndicate who owned the champion stood to lose £70 000 for each of the 50 or so mares which had been lined

1981 Shergar wins Epsom Derby
1983 Shergar kidnapped

PARANORMAL PHENOMENA

THE 19TH-CENTURY POET PERCY BYSSHE SHELLEY RECALLED HOW 'WHILE YET A BOY I SOUGHT FOR GHOSTS'. IN THE 20TH CENTURY, TOO, ENQUIRING INDIVIDUALS HAVE CONTINUED TO HUNT FOR SPECTRES. SPACE-AGE MAN, IT SEEMS, SHARES HUMANKIND'S AGE-OLD FASCINATION WITH REPORTS OF UNIDENTIFIED FLYING OBJECTS, MONSTERS, MIRACLES, UNCANNY PHENOMENA AND HAUNTINGS. IN OUR TECHNOLOGICAL AGE, THE DREAM OF AN OTHERWORLD STILL PERSISTS.

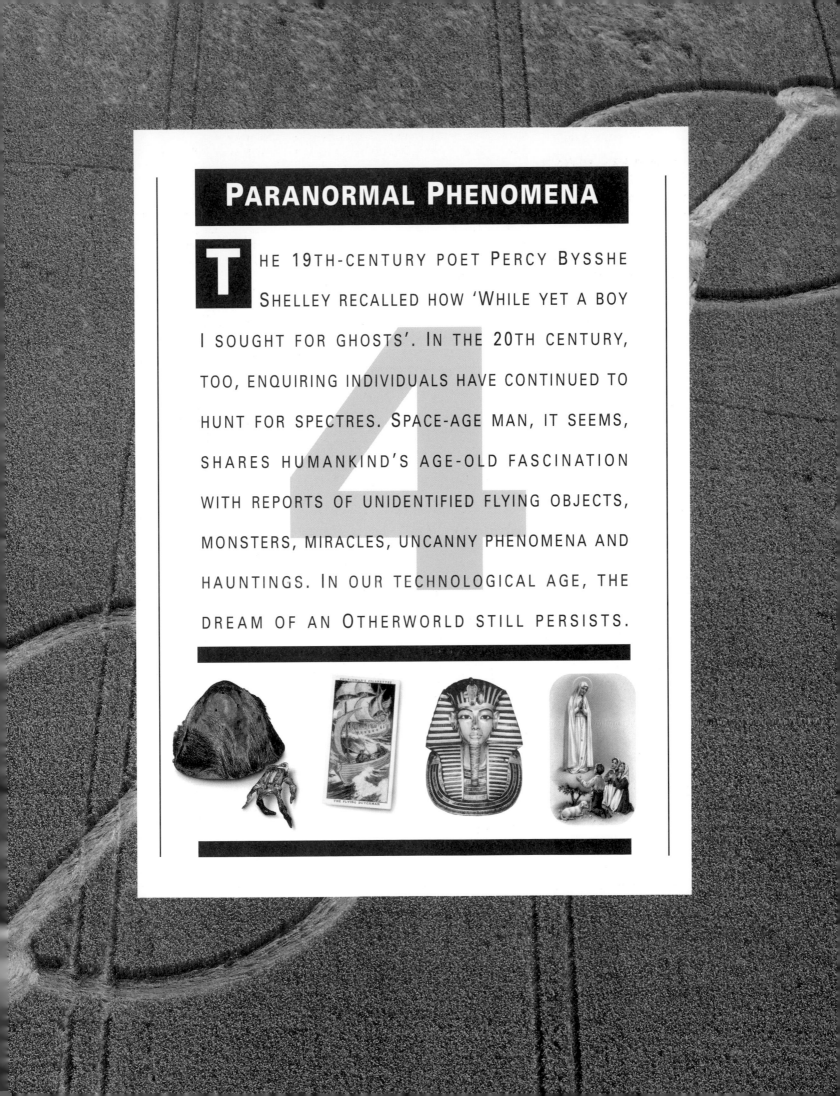

THE ANGELS OF MONS

HOW A PIECE OF POPULAR FICTION BEGAN A FIRST WORLD WAR MYTH THAT WOULD NOT BE EXPLODED

On August 23, 1914, during the early engagements of the First World War, British and French troops fighting near the village of Mons were overwhelmed by a larger German force and began to retreat.

In September of the same year, the writer Arthur Machen published a story called 'The Bowmen' in the *London Evening News*. In it, he told how struggling soldiers were saved from the advancing Germans by a vision of St George and the bowmen of Agincourt (not far from Mons). Although Machen's story was a piece of fiction it was taken for fact by a number of readers, and found its way as a true story into a number of magazines. Reports were published of winged and robed 'angels' who suddenly appeared at Mons between the Allied troops and the Germans, causing the enemy to fall back in disarray. When Machen told the press that he had made the original story up, many people refused to believe him.

Enemy propaganda?

The case might be taken as a classic example of how easily people are deceived, especially at times of stress when the need to believe outweighs common sense.
And many

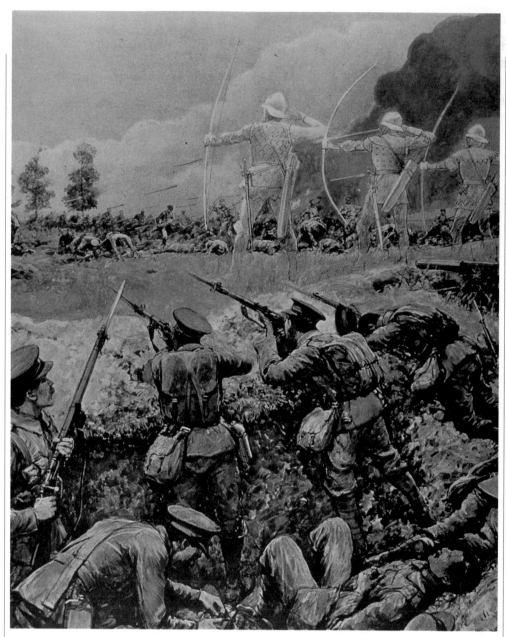

APPARITIONS 'The Bowmen of Mons' as they appeared in a Christmas issue of the *Illustrated London News*, 1915.

troops who served at Mons continued to insist that they did see angels. An affidavit was sworn in August 1915 by Private Robert Cleaver of the 1st Cheshire regiment that 'I personally was at Mons and saw the vision of Angels with my own eyes'.

It has also been reported that weeks before Machen published his story, Brigadier General John Charteris wrote to his family that 'the Angel of the Lord on the traditional white horse, clad all in white with

LEGEND COMES ALIVE Arthur Machen's fictional tale began a long-lasting controversy. Some who fought at Mons said that it was true.

flaming sword, faced the Germans and forbade their further progress'.

The debate was revived in 1930 when Friedrich Herzenwirth, a man claiming to have been a member of German Military Intelligence, told a New York newspaper that German aviators at Mons had projected movie images onto the white cloudbanks over Flanders to prove that God was on their side. 'What we had not figured on,' he said, 'was that the English should turn the vision to their own benefit.' Controversy deepened when a member of the German War Office declared the story a hoax and asserted that there was no such person as Herzenwirth.

Products of propaganda? Hallucinations? False memories? Or bona fide apparitions? The Angels of Mons have not yet been explained to everyone's satisfaction.

1900

1914 Battle of Mons
Arthur Machen writes
'The Bowmen'

1930 Claims that
Germans projected
'angels' at Mons

2000

MIRACLES AT FATIMA

HOW THE HOLY VIRGIN TOLD HER SECRETS TO THREE CHILDREN IN A PORTUGUESE VILLAGE

Three shepherd children at the grazing ground of Cova da Iria outside the Portuguese village of Fatima reported being visited by a 'Lady from Heaven'. Lucia (aged ten) and her two cousins, Jacinta (aged seven) and Francisco Marto (aged nine), saw a white-clad image of a beautiful, shimmering

THE VISION The shining lady who appeared before shepherd children at Fatima told them that she was the Lady of the Rosary, who wanted to save souls and bring peace.

woman on a cloud above a small oak. The date was May 13, 1917, and the children reported that the vision asked them to come back at the same hour on the thirteenth of each month for the next six months. Ever larger crowds gathered with the children each month, but the Lady was visible only

TERRIBLE SECRET Pope John XXIII is said to have almost fainted when he learnt the third secret of Fatima.

THE WITNESSES The children who saw the vision, photographed in 1917. From the left: Jacinta, Francisco and Lucia.

to their eyes. Their claims were doubted so strongly that they were arrested and interrogated, but they stuck to their story.

The final visitation

At the final sighting on October 13, a crowd of about 70 000 people assembled in pouring rain. Once again the shining lady showed herself only to the children, who reported that she called herself Our Lady of the Rosary, and told them three secrets about the future.

After this visitation, the rain suddenly stopped. Then, through a gap in the clouds, the sun appeared and seemed to spin and plunge earthwards, giving off heat as it approached. There was considerable panic in the terrified crowd, some of whom feared that the end of the world was nigh. Then the sun returned to its normal position, but onlookers found that their clothes, which had been soaked by the rain, were dry.

The so-called 'miracle of the sun', which lasted ten minutes, was observed many miles away, and documentation of the episode was so persuasive that, in 1927, the Catholic

Church authorised pilgrimages to the village of Fatima, which today is the site of a shrine for Our Lady of the Rosary of Fatima.

The two youngest children, Francisco and Jacinta, both died during the great influenza epidemic which swept war-weakened Europe in 1918-19. But Lucia, the oldest child, lived on to become a Carmelite nun called Lucia dos Santos, and to record in

---

VISIONS OF THE PAST

Only a handful of 20th-century apparitions have been authenticated by the Catholic Church: Fatima, Portugal (1917); Beauraing, Belgium (1932-3); and Banneaux, Belgium (1933). Historically, the best-known visions of the Virgin Mary were seen at Lourdes in France in 1050 by the 14-year-old peasant girl Bernadette Soubirous, who was canonised in 1933. The most famous modern Visions of the Blessed Virgin Mary were reported in 1981 by children at Medjogorje in former Yugoslavia.

---

writing the three secrets that the Lady of the Rosary had told to her and her two cousins. The first 'secret' was a vision of hell, and the second has been taken as a warning of the outbreak of the Second World War.

The third secret has never been disclosed to the world and was known to no one but Lucia dos Santos until 1960, when it was allegedly read by Pope John XXIII. It has been reported that what the Pope read so horrified him that he almost fainted.

1900   2000

1917 The vision appears at Fatima   **1927** Pilgrimages to Fatima are authorised   **1948** Lucia becomes a Carmelite nun   **1967** Lucia and Pope Paul VI visit the shrine   **1981** Sightings of the Virgin at Medjogorje begin

A DISSOLUTE DEMON AT THE TSAR'S COURT

WAS THE 'MAD MONK' RASPUTIN A WOMANISING CHARLATAN OR A TRUE HOLY MAN?

Psychic energy does not submit easily to scientific analysis, yet certain historical figures have undoubtedly possessed an ability to direct others' actions – for good or evil – through a kind of personal magnetism. And few had more influence on 20th-century history than Grigori Yefimovich, who became known as Rasputin, the 'mad monk' or 'holy devil' of Tsarist Russia. 'Rasputin' is a term meaning dissolute which Grigori, the son of Yefim Novykh, welcomed as his nickname from the local villagers in his home province of Tobolsk. Rasputin was born around 1872 into a peasant family and received no education. To the end of his life he was unable to write properly. Nonetheless, he experienced some kind of spiritual awakening, and left his native village to devote himself to religion. His adopted views were those of a sect called the Khlysty who believed that salvation could only be won through sinning followed by repentance. 'Sin in order that you may obtain forgiveness' was their doctrine – and one well suited to a man of Rasputin's lusty temperament.

An uncouth, hard-drinking womaniser, he was an unlikely candidate for a divine calling. Still, he cannot have been a complete charlatan, for he made pilgrimages to Mount Athos and Jerusalem and spent some time in monasteries before returning to his village as

MAGNETIC PERSONALITY Above: Rasputin among his many lady admirers. Right: the monk with the vivid blue eyes captured the tsar's family in his spell.

a mysterious itinerant holy man. In 1903 he appeared in St Petersburg and presented himself to the city's most revered holy man, Father John of Kronstadt. Rasputin was a compelling personality and a spellbinding preacher and rapidly made a name for himself. In 1905, certain admiring Russian churchmen allowed him to be presented at the royal court.

Trying to kill a holy man

When Alexis, the son of Tsar Nicholas II and Tsarina Alexandra, began bleeding uncontrollably, they were persuaded to call for Rasputin, who was rumoured to have mysterious healing powers. Rasputin's apparent cure of her haemophiliac son made a deep impression on Alexandra, who became Rasputin's main champion.

The charismatic but illiterate holy man with the 'exceptionally brilliant' pale blue eyes won immense sway over the royal family, and it was not long before he was advising the tsar and tsarina on affairs of state. In consequence he developed immense power over the Russian Government, and high offices were granted to his corrupt and incompetent hangers-on. By 1915 he and the tsarina virtually controlled domestic affairs while the tsar occupied himself with Russia's entry into the First World War.

Tales of the slovenly monk's behaviour both within and outside the royal court in St Petersburg, and of his debaucheries and liaisons with numerous mistresses, including court ladies, were rife. Rumours even circulated of an illicit affair with Tsarina Alexandra herself. But when some officials complained to the tsar, they found themselves 'transferred' to remote regions of the empire. The scandalous tales about Rasputin, and his growing power, aggravated his increasing unpopularity. Finally, with the prospect of revolution

NOBLE CONSPIRATOR Prince Yusupov was an aristocratic murderer. Rasputin was poisoned, shot and beaten at Yusupov's palace.

in the air, a group of ultra-conservative noblemen decided to murder the monk in order to save the monarchy's reputation.

On December 29, 1916, Prince Yusupov, a former admirer of Rasputin, invited him to supper at his palace. Poisoned wine and cake were laid out for the unsuspecting guest and just as the conspirators planned, he helped himself – in copious quantities – to the lethal refreshments. Amazingly though, Rasputin seemed unaffected by the poison. Prince Yusupov resorted to a gun and shot Rasputin in the back. The monk then fell to the floor where he was pronounced dead.

The noblemen's plan was to dump the murdered monk in the river Neva, but when they came to pick up the body Rasputin sprang to life again. Dragging himself along on his hands and knees, he chased the terrified Yusupov up a flight of stairs. Only when he was shot twice more did Rasputin finally crumple. The conspirators then kicked and bludgeoned his apparently lifeless form, took the corpse to the river, broke a hole in the ice and lowered him in.

An unshakeable belief

The tsarina never doubted Rasputin's holiness. She had his corpse recovered from the river three days later. Incredibly, he was discovered to have lungs full of the freezing water and was reportedly making a sign of benediction, with three fingers laid across his breast. Rasputin must still have been alive when he was finally dumped – poisoned, shot and beaten – into the river.

Alexandra had a special chapel built to hold Rasputin's body and she went every night to pray at his grave.

How, other than occult powers, to account for the incredible resistance

of the 'mad monk' to poison and bullets? There are rational explanations. Rasputin was a powerfully built man whose sheer physical strength may have enabled him to survive, at least temporarily, gunshot wounds and battering. Alcohol, which he drank in

TWO CHARISMATICS The Russian mystic and bon viveur George Gurdjieff (left) and the English magician Aleister Crowley (right) attracted cult followings.

prodigious quantities, can nullify the toxic effects of cyanide, and its presence in the lining of his stomach may account for Rasputin's miraculous survival of the poisoning attempt.

And what of his cure for haemophilia? Alexis's health did improve around the time that Rasputin came to court, but this could have been coincidence. There is no scientific evidence that the monk 'cured haemophilia'.

The deeper mystery lies in Rasputin's personal magnetism. Even his opponents paid tribute to his mesmerising presence. 'Rasputin's eyes,' wrote Yusupov, 'shone with a kind of phosphorescent light. From them came two rays that flowed into each other and merged into a glowing circle.' When Rasputin stared at him intently, said Yusupov, he became paralysed. The same spiritual force has been attributed to other 20th-century occultists, such as the Russian George Gurdjieff and the British magician Aleister Crowley. The great evangelists, faith healers, cult leaders and demagogues all seem to tap the same inexplicable psychic energy which remains one of the greatest of all human mysteries.

THE WOLF CHILDREN OF MIDNAPORE

HOW A STARTLING DISCOVERY IN INDIA GAVE NEW CREDENCE TO OLD FABLES

From the Roman legend of Romulus and Remus – the twins cared for by wolves – to the more recent story of Tarzan – a child reared by apes – the idea of children adopted by wild animals has gripped the human imagination. From the jungles of Bengal in the 19th century came several reports of children reared by wolves, a concept which was immortalised by Rudyard Kipling in 1895 in *The Jungle Book*, a tale of a lost boy, Mowgli, who is cared for by the jungle ani-

AMAZING FIND Two children were found curled up with the wolf cubs in the den (above). They ran on all fours (right).

mals. The most celebrated real-life case was reported by a 20th-century missionary, the Reverend J.A.L. Singh, during an evangelistic tour of the district of Midnapore (Bengal), India, in 1920. The missionary heard curious reports of two *manush-baghas* ('man-ghosts') – small, phantasmal creatures with blazing eyes who were neither human nor animal. The ghostly beings were said to frequent the forests near Denganalia and to run with the wolves, terrifying the local people.

Reverend Singh decided to get to the bottom of the curious tale, and by hiding in a tree one night he managed to glimpse the creatures at their lair, an abandoned ant-heap. From what he saw he came to the conclusion that the *manush-baghas* were in fact human children – albeit hideous in appearance – who were living with a pack of wolves and ran on all fours.

On October 17, he returned to the mound with a party of local beaters in order to dig out the wolf den. As soon as excavation began, two wolves bolted from the lair and fled. Then a mother wolf appeared and attacked the diggers in a fury; before Mr Singh could prevent it, the beaters had killed the animal with arrows.

An amazing discovery

When the ant-heap was opened, two small children were found huddled in a ball alongside two wolf cubs. Both children were female; the elder girl was about eight years old and the younger about one and a half.

The four creatures proved difficult to separate, clinging together furiously, but eventually the human and wolf children were prised apart. The tribesmen sold the wolf cubs off, and Mr Singh took the little girls to Midnapore Orphanage, to be looked after by his wife.

Mrs Singh named the younger child Amala and the elder one Kamala. But their newly acquired names were their only human characteristic. They astonished everyone by running on all fours, howling like wolves, and shunning daylight. They were said to be confirmed carnivores too, exhibiting a marked preference for raw meat – even carrion – over vegetable and cereal foods. The girls avoided human company and made friends with the dogs at the orphanage.

Amala died of dysentery within a year of being taken captive, but her sister, Kamala, lived for nine years and in time learned to walk upright, to eat more like a human than a wolf, and to speak 30 words of English.

Despite the copious documentation of the Midnapore case, some people doubt whether it is possible that the children were nurtured by wild animals. It has been disputed, in particular, whether Mr Singh

CAPTIVE CARE Mrs Singh feeds biscuits to Kamala soon after her capture (above left). By 1926 Kamala could stand upright and would tolerate clothes (above right).

really was present at the time when the children were discovered. However, the writer Charles Maclean concluded in his 1977 study *The Wolf Children*, based on diaries and eyewitness reports, that Singh's account was broadly true.

The child psychologist Bruno Bettelheim argued in 1959 that the Midnapore girls were abandoned autistic children. He suggested a number of characteristics that they shared with autistic children, such as speech difficulties and howling noises, the urges to run about naked and to bite humans, and uncontrolled urination and defecation. Bettelheim suggested that to observers who believe children to have been reared by wild beasts, any animal-like behaviour is seen as evidence of an animal upbringing.

Reports of wild children have continued since the Midnapore discovery. Can children really be raised by animals or do the stories reflect a deep-rooted longing in humans for some lost harmony with nature?

REPORTS OF WILD CHILDREN

Long before the present century, children have been found whom observers assumed to be youngsters reared by animals. As far back as 1344, documents record the capture of a 'wolf-boy' in the German principality of Hesse. He was allegedly seized from the wolves by hunters, ran on all fours and could jump prodigiously. Other historic characters include the 17th-century Bear-Boy of Lithuania and a Swine-Girl of Salzburg who had lived during the 1820s in a hog-sty, sitting cross-legged; according to one account: 'She grunted like a hog, and her gestures were brutishly unseemly.'

Were they really raised by beasts? Typical characteristics of wild children include the habits of walking on all fours, making animal-like sounds, and eating and drinking like animals. All could be the traits of retarded children abandoned by their parents. Another often-reported characteristic is an insensitivity to heat and cold. In a famous 18th-century case, Victor, the wild boy of Aveyron, would squat naked in the chill, driving rain without apparent discomfort, and could pluck hot potatoes out of boiling water. Such a remarkable resistance to extremes of heat and cold is often found among autistic children.

Where the youngsters have been reported running with packs of wild animals, the case is rather different. The wolf children of Midnapore have provided the 20th century with its most thoroughly documented case, but there have been others. In 1971 the distinguished anthropologist Jean-Claude Armen wrote of a gazelle-boy moving in leaps and bounds among herds in the Spanish Sahara; he participated in their games and knew their sign language. 'I have watched him approach gazelles and lick their foreheads as a sign of recognition,' claimed Armen. The anthropologist further described the wild boy as roughly ten years old, with a pleasant, open expression. His disproportionately thick ankles presumably derived from his practice of leaping with the herd, and he left footprints that hardly made any impression in the sand, 'revealing a rare suppleness, the human prints blending with the rhythm of the bounding prints of the gazelles'.

1950   2000

1959 Psychologist suggests the girls were autistic   1971 Armen reports a gazelle-boy in the Spanish Sahara   1977 *The Wolf Children* published

ABOMINABLE SNOWMEN

LOCAL LEGENDS OF HUGE APE-LIKE CREATURES HAVE PROVOKED WORLDWIDE CURIOSITY

Reports of a bizarre man-like creature in the Himalayas had circulated in the early years of the 20th century, but it was only as the 'Abominable Snowman' that the creature made headlines worldwide.

In 1921 a British expedition, led by Colonel C.K. Howard-Bury, made an attempt on the northern face of Mount Everest. At about 17 000 ft (5200 m) they saw through their binoculars a number of dark figures moving about in a snowfield far above them. On reaching the place where the creatures had been, they discovered huge footprints, 'three times the size of those of normal humans'. The colonel thought the footprints were probably those of 'a very large stray, grey wolf'. But excited Sherpas in the group identified them as the tracks of semi-human creatures, which they called by a variety of names, including *yeti* and *mehtohkangmi* (snow or wild creature). When a journalist freely translated this local name as 'Abominable Snowman', a legend was born.

Creatures of the snows

The Sherpas – mountain people of Tibet and Nepal – believe yeti to be hairy, human-like creatures that live in the mountains and forage in the valleys. Some even believe that the yeti will carry off humans. In 1913, for example, a Sherpa girl was allegedly abducted from her village by a yeti. Also, several sensational reports of attacks by the Abominable Snowman have appeared in the press in the decades following Howard-Bury's expedition.

Sceptics have explained away the numerous reported sightings as sightings of bears, large langur monkeys which live in the Himalayas, or even the hardy Hindu hermits known as sadhu.

Material evidence for the yeti's existence has been presented too. In 1951 the respected mountaineer Eric Shipton published photographs of what he believed was a trail of yeti footprints, found in the Menlung Basin in Nepal. One close-up revealed a foot some 13 in (33 cm) long that did not belong to any recognisable creature. It has been suggested that snow melting around normal-sized tracks may enlarge and distort their shape and produce these mysterious tracks.

Rather less impressive was a so-called 'yeti scalp' prized by certain Sherpa villagers, which turned out to be made of goatskin. Nonetheless, the idea of some unknown creature existing in the mountains has been sufficiently credible to interest serious scientists and explorers. In 1958, the Soviet Academy of Sciences sent teams to various parts of Asia where semi-human creatures had been reported. The team eventually concluded that some kind of primitive hominid lives in the mountains of Asia.

The American Indians of British Columbia and northern California, meanwhile, have their own legends of a ferocious

YETI OR YAK? Many villagers living in the mountains have seen 'Yeti' relics. One 'Yeti scalp' turned out to be goatskin.

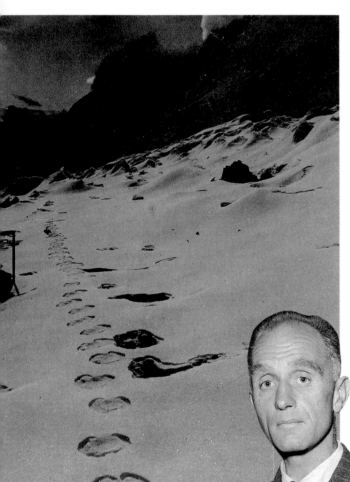

STRANGE FOOTPRINTS The mountaineer Eric Shipton with the alleged 'Yeti tracks' that he found in Nepal.

ITS HEAD WAS HIGH AND POINTED

In March 1949 a herdsman named Mingma at Pangboche in the Himalayas heard a strange, half-human cry and saw something coming towards him through the rocks. Taking refuge in a hut, Mingma observed a creature which he assumed was a yeti. He later described it to Charles Stonor, former Assistant Curator at the London Zoo:

'It was a squat, thickset creature, of the size and proportions of a small man, covered with reddish and black hair. The hair was not very long, and looked to be slanting upwards above the waist, and downwards below it, and was rather longer about the feet.

'The head was high and pointed, with a crest of hair on the top; the face was bare, except for some hair on the sides of the cheeks, brown in colour, not so flat as a monkey but flatter than a man, and with a squashed-in nose. It had no tail. As I watched it, the yeti stood slightly stooping, its arms hanging down by its sides; I noticed particularly that the hands looked to be larger and stronger than a man's. It moved about in front of the hut with long strides . . .'

'Sasquatch' or 'Bigfoot', which appears on carved totem poles and masks. In his book *The Wilderness Hunter*, published in 1893, American President Theodore Roosevelt reported a sighting by two trappers of a 'great body' with a 'strong wild beast odour'. In October 1967, at Bluff Creek in northern

1913 Yeti allegedly carries off a child

1921 Everest expedition sees footprints

ODD SOUVENIRS A former rodeo rider called Roger Patterson caught a large, ape-like figure on film as it loped away from a campsite (below). He also managed to take plaster casts of its tracks (right).

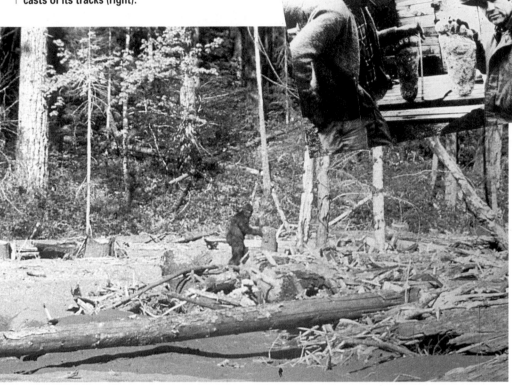

different from that of humans and general primates.

The Chinese take reports of their Wildman seriously. Much of the evidence supporting its existence comes from a year-long expedition in 1977 by the Chinese Academy of Science. Perhaps the creature is a descendant of *Gigantopithecus*, a great ape known to have roamed central south China 500 000 years ago. Alternatively, some unknown species of ape, even

FABULOUS FINDS

Sceptics may doubt whether a large humanoid such as the Yeti could evade discovery for long, but astonishing zoological finds have been made even in the 20th century. These include the mule-sized Okapi (1901), the 12 ft (3.6 m) Komodo Dragon (1912), the supposedly extinct Coelecanth fish (1938) and the long-nosed or Chacoan Peccary, a 100 lb (45 kg) pig-like creature thought to have died out 2 million years ago, which was found in 1975, roaming the wilds of Paraguay.

a group of surviving Orang-Utang, which were believed to have become extinct in China many years ago, could explain the consistent Wildman sightings.

Sasquatch, Bigfoot, Wildman or Yeti – the legends persist because we can never really know what is hiding in the mountains.

California, an alleged Bigfoot was caught on cinefilm by a camper called Roger Patterson. The film seems to show a giant female ambling across a forest clearing.

The Wildman of China

The small town of Wan Xian, half-way down the Chang Jiang (Yangtze River) in southern China, is the home of the Wildman Institute, where information on thousands of reported sightings of China's own version of 'bigfoot' and 'yeti' are collected, as well as material evidence.

The Wildman is said to be a red-haired creature, 6 ft (2 m) tall. The collection at Wan Xian includes pickled hands and feet said to have been from a Wildman, but which have turned out to belong to a previously unknown species of monkey. Other relics include the skeletal remains of a small child with a skull that appears to be half human, half ape. Huge clumps of bright red 'Wildman

BUILDING STORIES FROM BONES These remains found in the Chinese highlands are supposedly the skeletons of some of the Wildmen said to inhabit remotest China.

hairs' have also been collected. Analysis by electron microscope has yielded disputed results. According to one report in 1990, six out of twelve samples of the hair were found to have an iron-to-zinc ratio which was

1950

1951 Eric Shipton
photographs
strange footprints

1967 Bluff
Creek film of
'Big Foot'

1977 China's
year-long search
for the Wildman

1995 Second major
Chinese expedition
in search of Wildman

2000

THE CURSE OF TUTANKHAMUN

ARE WARNINGS TO THIEVES CARVED ON EGYPT'S ROYAL TOMBS IDLE THREATS OR EVIL PROMISES?

When archaeologist Howard Carter finally broke into the tomb of ancient Egypt's boy king Tutankhamun on November 26, 1922, he was struck dumb by the shimmering splendours inside. There were effigies of strange animals, statues and gold everywhere. Behind him his sponsor, Lord Carnarvon, could barely stand the suspense.

MAKING THE FIRST CUT The moment of the first incision in Tutankhamun's wrappings is captured on film. Inset: Carter at the tomb.

'Can you see anything?'

'Yes,' Carter breathed, 'wonderful things!' They had unearthed one of the most magnificent treasures ever found. But did they also unleash an ancient curse?

Some months later Lord Carnarvon was bitten by a mosquito. The bite became infected and he died on April 5, 1923, in a Cairo hotel. At a news conference in Paris, a French Egyptologist and occultist, J.S. Mardus, declared that the Englishman had paid the penalty for profaning the pharaoh's resting place.

Mardus said that the tomb had been protected by the ancient priests against such a violation. Thus the legend of the pharaoh's

ETERNAL GAZE The death mask of Tutankhamun, who became pharaoh at the age of 11 and ruled from 1361 to 1352 BC.

curse was born, and it grew, nourished by a widespread fascination with Egyptian mummification and by reports of strange events at Tutankhamun's tomb. It was said, for example, that on the day that the burial place was first opened, a sandstorm had sprung up and a hawk, sacred emblem of the pharaohs, had soared over the tomb and flown off to the west – the Egyptian Land of the Dead.

It was also said that, on entering the pharaoh's tomb, the archaeologists had come upon an inscription which read: 'Death will come to those who disturb the sleep of the Pharaohs.' No such text was ever really found, but there did seem to be a large number of deaths involving people connected with the tomb.

However, on closer examination the toll was not especially high. Herbert E. Winlock, director of the Metropolitan Museum of Art in New York, calculated that of the 22 people present at the tomb opening in 1922, only six had died by 1934, some of whom were ill before visiting Egypt. Their deaths were all of natural causes, and if some victims succumbed to disease in Egypt that was hardly surprising for foreigners unaccustomed to local conditions.

Howard Carter himself always scoffed at the idea of a curse and lived to the age of 66, dying peacefully in 1939. Still, the unremarkable statistics have not prevented the public imagination from being captured by Tutankhamun's curse, and the papers regularly report eerie mishaps connected with the treasures. Most famously, in 1966, while the Egyptian authorities were considering sending the treasures to Paris for an exhibition, the Director of Antiquities, Mohammed Ibrahim, was run over by a car. Was the accident a common coincidence or an ancient Pharaoh's curse?

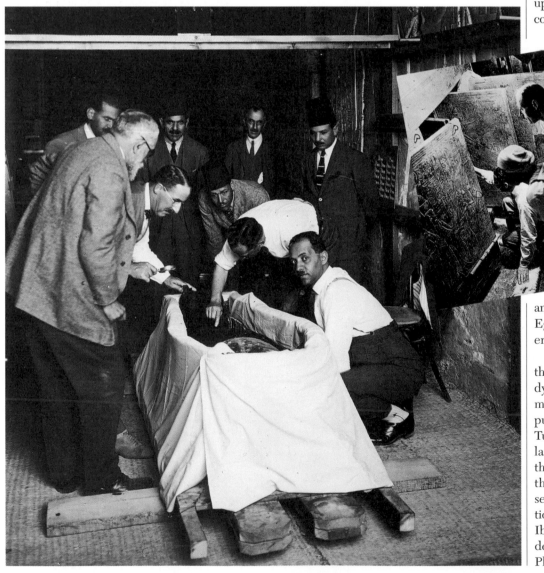

1900 ▮▮▮▮▮▮▮▮▮▮▮▮▮▮▮▮▮▮▮▮▮▮ 2000

1922 Tutankhamun's tomb opened   1939 Howard   1966 Egyptian
1923 Lord Carnarvon dies   Carter dies   curator killed
                                 peacefully   by a car

CURSE OR COINCIDENCE?

WHEN LIFE THROWS UP STRANGER-THAN-FICTION COINCIDENCES, SHOULD THEY BE BLAMED ON CHANCE OR ON THE SHADOWY WORKING OF SOME UNKNOWN POWER?

O n the seventh day of the seventh month (July) of 1977, a woman named Mrs Severn became 77. As human beings we relish such curiosities, perhaps because they hint at the presence of inexplicable forces working behind the scenes of everyday life.

More compelling still are those coincidences with a moral dimension. When Lord Carnarvon and others died after helping to open Tutankhamun's tomb, it seemed a retribution for breaking into an ancient place of burial. The idea of a curse is darkly attractive to the superstitious mind. Perhaps we consider Fate, however stern, to be more alluring than a cold, material universe, wholly indifferent to how we behave.

Hard-headed statisticians have no difficulty in explaining coincidences in terms of the law of averages. In the case of Mrs Severn, the odds are that once in a while someone of her unusual surname will celebrate a birthday on a date with many sevens in it. The event is less striking if set against the innumerable days on which people of the surname 'Seven' or 'Severn' celebrate birthdays without sets of seven in the date.

Statisticians have also denied that there is anything exceptional about the number of deaths associated with the opening of Tutankhamun's tomb. In any group of adults assembled for whatever reason, a certain number are likely to die within a few succeeding years. Deaths will follow the opening of a garden fete as surely as they will follow the opening of a pharaoh's tomb.

Stranger in its way is the famous coincidence of the *Titanic* prophecy. In 1898 author Morgan Robertson penned a novel called *Futility* which bore striking similarities to the loss of the real-life liner 14 years later. Robertson's ship was the largest vessel afloat with the most modern equipment, but it lacked sufficient lifeboats to accommodate everyone on board. The ship went down in April (like her real-life counterpart) after an encounter with an iceberg – and her name was the *Titan*.

Was this prophetic fiction? Not according to the sceptics who have put many

MORBID REMINDERS Lord Carnarvon's death certificate. Four months after opening Tutankhamun's tomb he was dead, having fatally infected a mosquito bite while shaving.

details down to good research. The threat to shipping from icebergs, for example, was a known hazard of Atlantic travel, and Robertson was perspicacious (but not psychic) in observing how regulations about lifeboat numbers did not change to match the modern liners' increase in size. In one view, the only outstanding coincidence was the choice of *Titan* as a name – and even there, Roberston did not have that many options in naming his giant liner. *Emperor, Colossus, Giant ...* the odds on settling on *Titan* were not very long.

The law of averages operates in ways that may be surprising to the layman. For example, how many people are needed in a group before there is a 50-50 probability of two of them sharing the same day and month of birth? Commonsense may suggest 365 people; yet statistically this coincidence is likely to occur when only 22 people are gathered together.

Many people believe, however, that there is more to the mechanism of coincidence than blind chance. According to the pioneering psychologist, and believer in the paranormal, Carl Jung, events may be meaningfully connected, although there is no discernible cause. He called this principle 'synchronicity'.

Jung quoted an incident from his own life as an example of synchronicity: one day a young female patient was describing a dream to him. She had dreamt of being given a golden scarab beetle, an ancient symbol of rebirth. As the patient told the psychologist about her dream, a scarabaeid beetle (*Cetonia aurata*), the nearest thing to a golden scarab beetle that can be found in the northerly latitudes, flew into the room.

This apparently significant coincidence began the patient's healing process. It seemed to Jung that the presence of a real-life scarabaeid beetle had indeed produced a real, psychological rebirth – yet more synchronicity.

SYMBOLIC BEETLE The scarab beetle – a symbol of rebirth – played a part in developing Jung's theory of synchronicity.

THE FLYING DUTCHMAN

HOW A PHANTOM SHIP TERRIFIED SUN-SEEKERS ON A BEACH IN SOUTH AFRICA

On a blazing hot day in March 1939, about 60 people were relaxing on the sands of Glencairn beach, South Africa. Suddenly an apparition of a high-pooped 17th-century merchantman (sailing ship) emerged from the sea haze. A newspaper later reported that all her sails were billowing, although there was not a breath of wind at the time. According to the *British South*

with talk of a mirage or a mass hallucination. But the witnesses on the beach were sure that what they had seen that day was the fabled *Flying Dutchman*.

According to sea lore, the *Flying Dutchman* is the ghost of a 17th-century ship whose Dutch captain refused to find safe port during a wild gale on the Cape of Good Hope, despite the pleas of his passengers and crew.

Punishment from God

The maniacal captain lashed himself to the wheel of his ship and sang blasphemous songs, leaving the terrified passengers to throw themselves on the mercy of God. As

MY GOD, IT'S A GHOST SHIP

A ship thought to be the *Flying Dutchman* was sighted on January 26, 1923, by seamen rounding the Cape of Good Hope on a voyage from Australia to England. At about 00.15 am a strange light was noticed on the port bow. Fourth Officer N.K. Stone described what happened:

'It was a very dark night, overcast, with no moon. We looked through binoculars and the ship's telescope, and made out what appeared to be the hull of a sailing ship, luminous, with two distinct masts carrying bare yards, also luminous; no sails were visible, but there was a luminous haze between the masts. There were no navigation lights, and she appeared to be coming close to us and at the same speed as ourselves. When first sighted she was about two-three miles away, and when she was within about a half-mile of us she suddenly disappeared.

There were four witnesses of this spectacle, the 2nd Officer, a cadet, the helmsman and myself. I shall never forget the 2nd Officer's startled expression - "My God, Stone, it's a ghost ship." '

WAGNERIAN SCENE A German print illustrates the legend of the *Flying Dutchman*, which was the inspiration for one of Wagner's best-known operas.

Africa Annual of 1939, 'The ship sailed steadily on as the beach-folk, shaken from their lethargy, stood about keenly discussing the whys and wherefores of the vessel, which seemed to be bent on self-destruction on the sands of Strandfontein. Just as the excitement reached its climax, however, the ship vanished as strangely as it had come.'

Sceptics have explained the phenomenon

punishment, the captain was condemned to sail round the Cape for ever, bringing bad luck to all those who saw him.

Perhaps one of the most famous sightings of the *Flying Dutchman* was that by George, Prince of Wales, later King George V, in 1881. At the time the prince was a young naval officer aboard HMS *Bacchante*. In his private journal, he recorded the appearance of a strange red light, 'in the midst of which

POPULAR IMAGE The legend of the *Flying Dutchman* has inspired novels, poems, films, plays and even cigarette cards (right).

the masts, spars and sails of a brig stood out in strong relief as she came across our port bow. The lookout man reported her as close on the port bow, but there was no vestige or sign of a material ship.' The phantom ship, true to legend, brought bad luck. The seaman who had first reported the *Flying Dutchman* fell from the mast later that day and was killed.

CHURCHMAN'S CIGARETTES

THE FLYING DUTCHMAN

VISIONS, ILLUSIONS AND HALLUCINATIONS

CAN YOU REALLY TRUST WHAT YOU SEE WITH YOUR OWN EYES – WHEN IT COULD BE AN OPTICAL ILLUSION, A MAGICIAN'S SLEIGHT OF HAND OR A TIRED BRAIN PLAYING TRICKS?

Sceptics often explain phenomena, from shared visions of the Virgin Mary to group sightings of the *Flying Dutchman*, as 'mass hallucinations'. But in doing so, they employ an explanation that in itself requires some explaining. What is a hallucination? And how can a whole crowd of people participate in it? In medical terminology, a hallucination is something very different from an illusion.

Illusions result from misinterpreting real, physical events. For example, through sleight of hand a professional magician may be able to trick members of an audience into believing that they have seen him cause a playing card to disappear, when it has in fact been deftly slipped up his sleeve. Also using trickery, Hindu fakirs (miracle-workers) have famously created great illusions of levitation.

Illusions may occur naturally, too. For example, on summer days, when the air near the ground is much hotter than the air above, light rays are often refracted, or bent, creating the illusion, or mirage, of a shimmering lake.

The effect of light being refracted by the sea can also create the illusion of a 'ghost ship' by distorting the image of a real vessel which is sailing below the horizon, and therefore not visible, and making it seem nearby. Perhaps this is the physical explanation for the persistent reports of the legendary phantom ship *Flying Dutchman*.

Hallucinations differ from illusions, arising as they do out of the private imagination. A hallucination occurs when the person mistakenly believes that he or she can see or hear something that is happening only in his or her fantasy realm. Schizophrenic patients, for example, may 'hear' voices, and 'see' threatening visions.

But healthy people experience hallucinations too. In a sense, everybody hallucinates when they dream, and people are also prone to hallucinate in states of deep concentration, emotional arousal, excitement, fear, ecstasy, or tense anticipation. Some religious and magical ceremonies are designed to encourage just such states, so that participants see visions and hear spirit voices.

Sceptics believe that disorientation encourages participants to hallucinate, and to mistake private fantasies for external reality. In the doubters' view, a mass hallucination could be triggered by one member of a crowd declaring that he can see a vision, prompting others who are already in a state of anticipation and arousal to fantasise along the same lines.

In a devout Catholic community, for example, the image of the Virgin Mary is so embedded in everyone's psyche that it may take surprisingly little stimulus to trigger a shared holy vision.

ST ELMO'S FIRE Atmospheric electricity during stormy weather can cause a ship's mast to glow.

DECEPTION OR HALLUCINATION? Saint Giuseppe di Copertino is said to have levitated before Pope Urban VIII. Was it a hallucination or a clever variant on the famous Indian rope trick?

WELCOME TO 'ENGLAND'S MOST HAUNTED HOUSE'

EERIE NOISES, GHOSTLY WRITING AND A PHANTOM NUN EARNED BORLEY RECTORY ITS REPUTATION

The damp and draughty Victorian rectory at Borley in Essex was built by the Reverend Henry Bull in 1863, supposedly on the site of a medieval monastery where some gruesome tragedy had previously unfolded. This gloomy edifice became the subject of intense psychical investigation during the 1930s, when it won a reputation as 'the most haunted house in England'.

When the Reverend G.E. Smith and his wife arrived to take up residence in 1929, they were warned against it by the previous occupants. Rumours soon started to fly. National newspapers described how the Smith family had been startled by strange noises, a phantom nun, headless coachmen and a spectral coach and horses.

One night Mr Smith, armed with a hockey stick, lay in wait for one of the ghosts. When the sound of footsteps began in the room, he lashed out at the place from which the noise seemed to be coming. But the stick whistled through the air and the steps continued across the room.

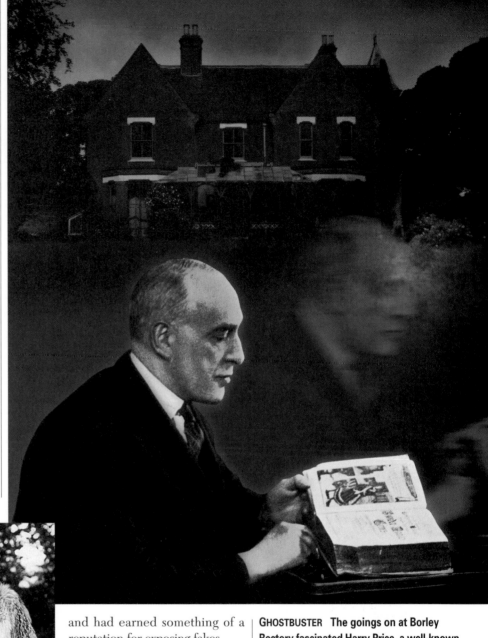

GHOSTBUSTER The goings on at Borley Rectory fascinated Harry Price, a well-known investigator of paranormal phenomena.

PLAGUED BY SPIRITS The Reverend G.E. Smith (left) and his wife (right) suffered the haunting for nine months before they fled.

The Borley haunting attracted the attention of the renowned ghost hunter Harry Price. Price was the founder of the National Laboratory of Psychical Research in London and had earned something of a reputation for exposing fakes.

Price compiled a file of bizarre happenings: strange whispers, a woman's voice that moaned 'Don't, Carlos, don't', banging doors and ringing bells, objects apparently moving of their own accord, inexplicably smashed pottery, and mysterious writing on the walls. Price himself heard bells and saw objects crashing down the stairs.

All change at the rectory

The Smith family left after only nine months at the rectory. Price, however, maintained a keen interest in the place for many years.

When the new occupants, the Reverend L.A. Foyster and his family, moved in, the ghostly activity continued. Foyster's wife Marianne was especially troubled by violent poltergeist activity. Weird notes addressed to her appeared scribbled on the rectory walls.

Price suspected that Marianne – who admitted hating the rectory – might have been responsible for some of these events. Much younger than her husband, Marianne had, by all accounts, a succession of lovers, and at the time of their residence at Borley was having an affair with a man named Frank

1900   1950

1929 Smith family take up residence
1930 Foyster family move in
1939 Borley Rectory burns down

Pearless who lived in an adjoining cottage. Foyster knew about Marianne's affair, and perhaps in this tense emotional situation the vicar, his wife and her lover played poltergeist pranks on each other.

After the Foysters left, Price rented the rectory himself for a year in order to conduct

ANOTHER TROUBLED STAY The Foyster family pose outside the rectory with Harry Price. They too suffered ghostly activity.

experiments. With a showman's instincts he advertised in *The Times* for assistants. The advertisement read: 'HAUNTED HOUSE – Responsible persons of leisure and intelligence, intrepid, critical, and unbiased, are invited to join rota of observers in a year's night and day investigation of alleged haunted house'. From some 200 replies, he recruited 40 volunteers.

A year-long study

Some volunteers left disappointed at an early stage, but others were less dubious. Bricks and candlesticks were said to have hurled themselves about. One researcher, Dr C.E.M. Joad of the BBC's Brains Trust panel, registered an inexplicable 10° drop in temperature in one room. Another volunteer, a Cambridge undergraduate called Charles Wintour, said: 'I went to Borley with an entirely open mind. As far as I could make out there were manifestations occurring. It wasn't at all frightening. We took precautions to make sure no one could enter rooms or passages by placing cotton strands across the entrances. But pencil marks started appearing on the walls. We would circle each mark and time and date them, but new ones kept appearing. Once I saw a pencil mark moving along a wall.'

Price held seances at Borley Rectory. At one of these, the spirit of a French nun named 'Marie Lairre' communicated with mediums, claiming to have been murdered by a member of the local Waldegrave family in 1667. At another seance, held on March 27, 1938, a message claimed that 'Sunex Amures and one of his men' would burn the house down that night.

Ghosts dance in the flames

The fire did not happen as predicted, but the rectory was detroyed by a fire, started by an accidentally overturned paraffin lamp, on February 27, 1939. While the house was burning, witnesses, including a policeman, claimed to have seen mysterious figures flitting among the flames.

After Borley Rectory was burned down, strange phenomena were reported at nearby Borley Church. Researchers recorded strange knockings and rappings, and reported the cowled figure of a

LENDING A HAND Price advertised for help to investigate Borley Rectory. Professor Joad (left) was among the volunteers.

nun. During one session in the 1960s researchers found their tape recorder smashed. In 1974, film director Denny Densham recorded several inexplicable noises, including the opening and closing of a heavy door, with the drawing of a rusty bolt. Did Borley Rectory's unquiet spirits survive the fire and migrate from the lost rectory to the nearby church?

After Harry Price's death in 1948, critics challenged both his ability and his integrity. One even claimed to have caught Price faking paranormal effects by hiding pebbles in his pockets, which he would toss to create noisy 'phenomena'. But paranormal events were reported at Borley long before Harry Price became connected with the place and they have persisted long since.

TROUBLE AT BORLEY CHURCH

Long after the haunted rectory at Borley burned down in 1939, people reported strange phenomena at Borley Church. In the 1980s Pamela Bullock visited the church with her husband Frederick and daughter Lucille:

'Before we went into the church we heard what sounded like an organ playing – it was rather beautiful. As we entered the music stopped. There was not a soul in the church and the organ console was padlocked. I stood in the central aisle facing the altar, to the right of the Waldegrave tomb. Suddenly we were aware of the sound of pebbles falling, or being thrown, on to the floor of the altar. It was very distinctive, but we couldn't find any evidence of pebbles.'

ENIGMA OF LOCH NESS

HI-TECH EQUIPMENT IS USED TO SEARCH FOR AN ANCIENT MONSTER IN THE PEAT-BLACK WATERS

Tales of a huge 'beastie' in Loch Ness go back at least as far as AD 700, when St Columba reportedly encountered Scotland's most famous monster. The legend – of a secretive throwback to a dinosaur age living in the loch – has survived, and it continues to fascinate, even as the 20th century draws to its close.

Loch Ness is the largest freshwater body of water in the British Isles. It is 24 miles (38 km) long and almost severs northern Scotland from the rest of the nation. The loch was once thought to be bottomless, and

its immense waters are so dark and peaty that underwater photography will not reveal with any clarity anything that is more than a few feet from the lens. Here is the ideal environment for a secretive monster, or colony of monsters – for if Nessie has any zoological reality, the creature must be capable of breeding.

Nessie's modern history

Modern press coverage of the monster in the loch began in May 1933 when the *Inverness Courier* reported how Mr and Mrs John Mackay had seen an enormous animal that rolled and plunged in the water. Publication of the story prompted many other witnesses to come forward with sightings of their own, and by the end of the year 20 or 30 reports had appeared in the press. The monster had become a focus of worldwide media interest.

From the sightings, a profile of Nessie began to take the shape of a huge, hump-backed creature with a long, flexible neck that would occasionally break the surface of

the loch. The image was fixed in April 1934 when a photograph was published.

The picture, which was reportedly taken from a promontory north of Invermoriston by a London gynaecologist, Robert Kenneth

Wilson, showed the dark silhouette of a head and neck moving through the loch. The so-called 'Surgeon's Photograph' remained one of the most persuasive pieces of evidence for Nessie's existence until March 1994, when the world learned that it had been a hoax. Just before he died, Christian Spurling, the

SURGEON'S PHOTO This shot was finally exposed as a fraud after fooling the public for 60 years. But an earlier glimpse of Nessie (inset) taken in 1933 by Hugh Gray, which has been dismissed by some as 'a dog with a stick', remains controversial.

last surviving member of the group of tricksters, confessed to Loch Ness researchers how a group of conspirators had created the picture by propelling the foot-high head of a fake serpent through the water, attached to a clockwork submarine.

Telling testimonies

Nessie might be taken for a national joke were it not for the sheer number of sightings reported by people from every walk of life. Alex Campbell, the water bailiff of Loch Ness, reported 18 encounters with the monster, which he once saw fleeing trawlers. He said: 'Suddenly there was this upsurge of water...I was stunned. I shut my eyes three times to make sure I was not imagining things. The head and the huge, humped body were perfectly clear.'

Another convincing tale was that of Father Gregory Brusey who in October 1971, watching with a visitor in the grounds of a Benedictine Abbey at Fort Augustus, saw the creature rear its head 7 ft (2 m) above the water before swimming off. 'We felt a sort of awe and amazement,' he said.

Some believe that what these witnesses saw was a Loch Ness monster. Many people have long favoured the notion that a small breeding population of relic dinosaurs – perhaps a left-over group of long-necked plesiosaurus, which supposedly died out 65 million years ago – inhabit a network of caves and tunnels deep beneath the surface of the loch.

Doubters prefer to explain sightings in terms of giant eels, or outsize otters. Motor boats could account for reports of a monster travelling at great speed. And occasionally, logs and debris floating up from the loch bed may burst to the surface in a gaseous mass that might be misinterpreted as the upsurge of a huge marine creature.

Project Urquhart seeks the truth

In recent decades all the paraphernalia of hi-tech underwater search equipment has been brought to bear on the loch. In the 1970s expeditions by the Academy of Applied Science, led by Dr Robert H. Rines, investigated its murky waters with sonar equipment triggering a camera and strobe light. The apparatus yielded much-publicised underwater pictures that were said to show the torso, neck and head of the monster. But the latest scientific findings tend to reinforce the doubts of the sceptics.

In 1992, under *Project Urquhart*, Loch Ness was surveyed by sonar to chart its underwater topography. Vessels cruised the whole lake and, in a fan-shaped sweep of its bed, produced 7 million depth readings. The loch's lowest point was found to be a forbidding 787 ft (240 m) down, northeast of Invermoriston. Computer-interpretation of the data allowed scientists to produce virtual reality images of the submarine terrain. Loch Ness proved to possess steep sides plunging to a fairly level lake bed. Labyrinthine caves and tunnels simply do not exist. Where in this stern, rock-walled habitat could Nessie make a den?

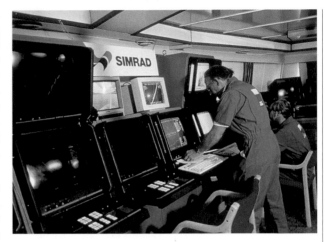

SOUNDING OUT THE LOCH The sonar room aboard MV *Simrad*, Project Urquhart's research vessel, which performed a sonic survey of the bed of Loch Ness in 1992.

SCIENTIFIC SEEKER In 1975 Dr Rines' team from the Academy of Applied Science used underwater cameras (right) to produce the grainy image above.

> ### TREMENDOUS UPHEAVAL ANNOUNCED ON THE LOCH
>
> The first substantial news story about the Loch Ness Monster appeared in the *Inverness Courier* of May 2, 1933, under the headline 'STRANGE SPECTACLE ON LOCH NESS - What was it?'
>
> 'Loch Ness has for generations been credited with being the home of a fearsome-looking monster, but, somehow or other, the "water kelpie", as this legendary creature is called, has always been regarded as a myth, if not a joke. Now, however, comes the news that the beast has been seen once more, for, on Friday of last week, a well-known business man who lives near Inverness, and his wife (a University graduate), when motoring along the north shore of the loch, not far from Abriachan Pier, were startled to see a tremendous upheaval on the loch, which, previously, had been as calm as the proverbial mill-pond. The lady was the first to notice the disturbance, which occurred fully three-quarters of a mile from the shore, and it was her sudden cries to stop that drew her husband's attention to the water.
>
> 'There, the creature disported itself, rolling and plunging for fully a minute, and the water cascading and churning like a simmering cauldron. Soon, however, it disappeared in a boiling mass of foam. Both onlookers confessed that there was something uncanny about the whole thing, for they realised that here was no ordinary denizen of the depths, because, apart from its enormous size, the beast, in taking the final plunge, sent out waves that were big enough to have been caused by a passing steamer. The watchers waited for almost half-an-hour in the hope that the monster (if such it was) would come to the surface again: but they had seen the last of it.'

THE BERMUDA TRIANGLE

IS THE WORK OF PARANORMAL FORCES BEHIND THE REPUTATION OF THIS NOTORIOUS SEAWAY?

In June 1991 the *Deep See* underwater research vessel was using hi-tech equipment to search for sunken Spanish galleons off the coast of Miami. Instead the instruments revealed five Second World War bombers stacked neatly together on the sea floor. One of the aircraft bore the same number and call-sign as the leader of Flight 19, an ill-fated bomber squadron which had set out from its base at 3.15 on the afternoon of December 5, 1945 – never to return. The excited crew of the *Deep See* had expected to find treasure, not to solve one of the mysteries of the Bermuda Triangle.

Flight 19, made up of five TBM (Torpedo Bomber Medium) Avenger aircraft, successfully completed a US Navy training exercise around the Bimini islands on December 5, and was due to fly back to base at Fort Lauderdale, Florida. It never arrived and a five-day search of the ocean found nothing.

Many believe that the aircraft and their occupants fell victim to the strange forces of

the Bermuda Triangle, an expanse of sea between Bermuda, Puerto Rico and Miami. Here, it is alleged, ships and aircraft are prone to vanish eerily, instruments to fail and compasses to swing wildly. Some have blamed 'interference from other worlds', while others have speculated that an irregularity in the Earth's magnetic field may account for the disappearances.

The truth behind the hype

Sceptics, however, cite the Flight 19 case as the classic example of a so-called mystery cranked up by slipshod research, misrepresentation and sensationalism.

Disquieting radio messages were allegedly received: 'Everything is wrong . . . strange. We can't be sure of any direction. Even the ocean doesn't look as it should . . .' But this 'quote' was actually made up by an early writer on the case. The snatches of genuine radio messages which have survived indicate that Lieutenant Charles Carroll Taylor, leading the aircraft, reported that both of his compasses had simultaneously gone out of action. Being unfamiliar to the area he mistook his position, thinking he was near the Florida Keys when he was actually close to the Bahamas. With faulty equipment and a darkening sky he simply flew off in the wrong direction. Eventually, the hopelessly lost Avengers ran out of fuel. In his final, tragic

LOST SQUADRON Torpedo bomber No. 28 and her crew – one of the five planes that made up Flight 19, which vanished in 1945.

THE WALLS OF ATLANTIS

Lying in the Bermuda Triangle the small island group of Bimini near the Bahamas became the focus of intense interest in 1968 when aircraft pilots glimpsed what seemed to be giant submerged stonework in the sea off the north island. Divers exploring the site reported colossal blocks of square-cut masonry 35 ft (10.5 m) underwater, which were thought to be the top of some massive wall, or perhaps the foundation of a vanished building. Were these relics of Atlantis – the lost island civilisation in the Atlantic of which Plato wrote 2400 years ago? The notion excited followers of the American psychic Edgar Cayce, who had predicted in 1940 that the drowned civilisation would rise up again in 1968 or 1969, somewhere in the Bahamas.

Sadly for the enthusiasts, scientists believed that the Bimini formations were natural rock features, resulting from faulting of the seabed – though tourist maps of the holiday islands still advertise them as the Walls of Atlantis.

MISSING SHIP The USS *Cyclops* disappeared without trace on a journey to the West Indies in 1918.

transmission, Taylor called for all planes to close into a tight formation and prepare to ditch into the sea: 'When the first man gets down to 10 gallons we will all land in the water together.'

Perhaps the question of what happened to Flight 19 is partially answered, but why did two compasses which had just passed pre-flight tests fail simultaneously?

Despite the *Deep See*'s find, the final resting place of the unlucky bombers and their crews remains a mystery. The five planes found by the treasure-hunters were not the missing Avengers of Flight 19 after all. The site turned out to be an old bombing practice range, where planes had been regularly ditched between 1943 and 1945. The US Navy revealed that Lt Taylor's plane bore the

1900   1950

1902 German ship *Freya* found abandoned   1918 USS *Cyclops* disappears   1940 Yacht *Gloria Colite* found drifting abandoned
                                                               1944 *Rubicon* ghost ship found
                                                               1945 Flight 19 disappears

same number as a plane which had already been lost in the waters of the Bermuda Triangle long before he even took off on his own mission to nowhere.

Hurricanes take the blame

Ships and their crews have also disappeared in the Triangle, and one natural phenomenon which is certainly responsible for such mysteries is the tropical hurricane. In a famous 'ghost ship' case of October 1944, the Cuban freighter *Rubicon* was found drifting off Florida's east coast. A dog was found to be the only living thing on board. What had happened to the crew? The ship was seaworthy, and everything aboard was intact but for one missing lifeboat and a broken hawser.

Light was shed on the mystery by National Oceanographic and Atmospheric Administration records. That month a ferocious hurricane had ravaged the area with winds of up to 158 mph (254 km/h). It is presumed that the *Rubicon's* broken hawser had secured a sea anchor which got severed in the storm. The crew panicked as the freighter ran adrift

HOODOO SEA About 1000 airmen, sailors and passengers in over 100 different aircraft and ships are alleged to have disappeared in the Bermuda Triangle.

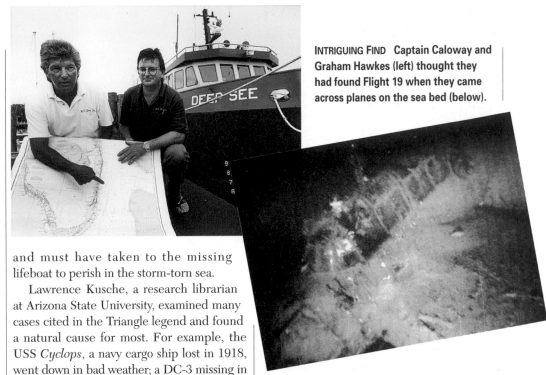

INTRIGUING FIND Captain Caloway and Graham Hawkes (left) thought they had found Flight 19 when they came across planes on the sea bed (below).

and must have taken to the missing lifeboat to perish in the storm-torn sea.

Lawrence Kusche, a research librarian at Arizona State University, examined many cases cited in the Triangle legend and found a natural cause for most. For example, the USS *Cyclops*, a navy cargo ship lost in 1918, went down in bad weather; a DC-3 missing in 1948 made a navigational error; another plane, a British troop transporter that disappeared in 1953, probably crashed in a storm some 900 miles (1440 km) north of the Triangle.

Patiently examined one by one, disappearances in the Triangle have not been especially mysterious. Weather conditions, equipment failure, and human error seem to be able to explain most of the tragedies, not

something from the supernatural. Even the frequency of accidents in the area is not unusual. In fact, as science fiction writer Arthur C. Clarke once said: 'It is a considerable tribute to the Florida Coastguard that there are so few disappearances in this busy area, among the legions of amateur sailors and weekend pilots who venture out across it, often with totally inadequate preparation.'

1973 Freighter *Anita* disappears with 32 aboard

1963 Two new US Air Force stratotankers disappear 300 miles south-west of the Bahamas.

1945 Five US Navy bombers (Flight 19) disappear

1948 DC-3 private charter lost with 32 passengers on board

1963 Freighter *Marine Sulphur Queen* vanishes. No wreckage ever found

1949 *Star Ariel*, sister plane of *Star Tiger*, which vanished in 1948, disappears

1965 *Flying Boxcar* lost near the Bahamas with ten aboard

1950 Freighter SS *Sandra* vanishes without trace

1955 Yacht *Connemara IV* abandoned

1967 Yacht *Revonoc* disappears within sight of land

1974 Cabin cruiser *Witchcraft* and crew vanish while moored at a harbour buoy one mile from Miami

THE COMING OF THE FLYING SAUCERS

DO UNIDENTIFIED OBJECTS IN THE SKY REALLY INDICATE THE EXISTENCE OF ALIEN LIFEFORMS?

An American search and rescue pilot flying on a mission over the Cascade Mountains on June 24, 1947, had a very peculiar experience. The weather was fine, and the visibility excellent, when suddenly a flash lit the inside of Kenneth Arnold's plane. He then saw what he described as a formation of nine bright objects coming from the direction of Mount Baker, flying close to the mountain tops at a phenomenal speed. From his knowledge of the area, Arnold

FIRST-HAND ACCOUNT Arnold published a book about his experience called *The Coming of the Saucers.*

was able to calculate that they were travelling at no less than 1200 mph (1931 km/h) – more than twice as fast as any known aircraft of his day.

Arnold described the craft as silvery on top and black on the bottom. He said that they travelled in a diagonal formation, flying 'like you'd take a saucer and skip it across the water'. That phrase captured the imagination of the newsmen reporting the strange encounter, and they wrote of 'flying saucers' for the first time.

Earlier strange sightings

Arnold's sighting was by no means the first report of bizarre objects in the skies. References to strange celestial craft are found in mythologies from around the world. Reports even crop up in medieval manuscripts. It is recorded that on January 1, 1254, the monks of St Albans saw in the sky 'a kind of large ship, elegantly shaped, and well equipped and of marvellous colour'.

STRANGE LIGHT A reconstruction, based on contemporary reports, of a wartime bomber sighting one of the 'foo-fighters'.

During the Second World War, Allied pilots on sorties in Europe and the Pacific had reported a new, strange form of German

EVIDENCE This photograph of a classically shaped unidentified flying object was taken in 1967 at East Woonsocket, Rhode Island.

1947 Kenneth Arnold sees 'flying saucers'

air defence, which they named 'foo-fighters'. Typically, foo-fighters manifested themselves as incandescent balls of silvery-white or orange-red light. The foo-fighters would follow an aircraft for a while, as if under intelligent control, and then the strange craft would turn away and vanish into the ether. The odd

ALIENS HAVE CRASH-LANDED

In March 1993 an unusual and alarming police radio message crackled across the airwaves around Warrington in Cheshire. The message reported that a huge, glowing alien spacecraft had crash-landed in a field at Appleton. 'Do not approach. It may be radioactive,' warned the transmission.

Was an alien invasion under way? Not at all: the message was put out by local police in order to trap a group of radio eavesdroppers, who had been illegally tuning in to police frequencies. The unwanted listeners were arrested on arrival at the field, and five people were subsequently prosecuted for telecommunications offences.

thing was that at the same time as the Allies were reporting the foo-fighters, so were the Germans and Japanese. Each side in the

WEIRD EFFIGY Model of a dead alien at the UFO Enigma Museum, Roswell, New Mexico – the site of a controversial UFO incident in 1947.

conflict assumed that the glowing spheres were instruments of war made by the enemy. No one ever found out where the foo-fighters really came from or what their mission was.

Reliable witnesses

It is thought that an unidentified flying object is sighted somewhere on the Earth once every two minutes. Hoaxes, misrepresentation and honest mistakes may account for many of these, but surely not all. Many reports of UFOs are lodged by trained, responsible observers, such as airline pilots and astronauts.

Ed Mitchell, the sixth man on the moon, said: 'I am completely convinced that some UFO sightings are real. The question is not whether there are UFOs, but what they are.'

The most compelling reports of aerial phenomena have been those where human eyewitness testimony is supported by other evidence. Perhaps one of the most convincing sightings occurred on December 31, 1978, in the Antipodean skies.

Following reports of UFOs by six different airline pilots over New Zealand's South Island, an Australian TV crew took to the skies in a cargo plane. The crew retraced the flight path between Wellington and Christchurch, along which unidentified lights had been seen for several weeks.

Something described by the cameraman as having a 'brightly lit base and a sort of transparent dome' approached the cargo plane. The object was picked up by the plane's radar, and using 16 mm colour film the TV crew was able to get

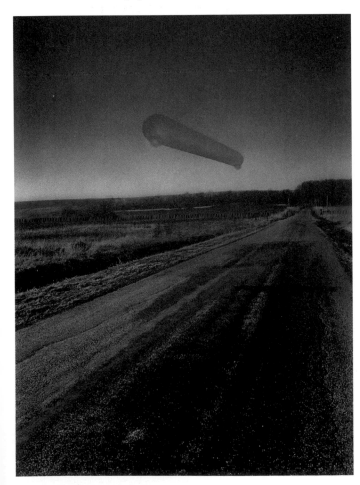

INUNDATED A simulation of an eerie craft seen near Belleville, Wisconsin. The town was plagued by UFO reports in 1987.

footage of it. Meanwhile ground radar confirmed the presence of objects near the plane at that time.

The film, which excited viewers all around the world, and its associated documentation were turned over to a US Navy physicist, Dr Maccabee, for investigation. He estimated that the strange object was about 100 ft (33 m) across and was travelling at about 3000 mph (4800 km/h). Despite rigorous investigation the phenomena caught on film over New Zealand could never be satisfactorily explained; they remain unidentified flying objects.

UFO reports do not always end with strange lights and elusive blips, however. Many people have reported direct encounters with the occupants of alien spacecraft. Some of the reports have come from eyewitnesses

GOVERNOR CARTER'S UFO

Those who believe that the Earth has been visited by alien spacecraft include some impressive names, including Britain's Air Chief Marshal Lord Dowding (the key strategist of the Battle of Britain) and Germany's Professor Hermann Oberth (pioneer of the V-1 rocket). At least one president of the United States has also witnessed a UFO. One evening in 1969, when he was governor of Georgia, Jimmy Carter was standing with about 20 other people at the town of Leary, waiting to address a local meeting, when the group saw something strange in the skies above. Jimmy Carter later said:

'I am convinced that UFOs exist because I've seen one. It was the darndest thing I've ever seen. It was big; it was very bright; it changed colours; and it was about the size of the moon. We watched it for 10 minutes, but none of us could figure out what it was.'

1950   2000

1969 Jimmy Carter sees UFO in Georgia   1978 Australian TV crew films UFO over New Zealand   1994 Lorraine Malcolm films an object above UFO 'hotspot' in Scotland whose testimony would be regarded as reliable under normal circumstances.

In 1964, for example, American police patrolman Lonnie Zamora claimed that he saw a blue, flaming UFO land near the town of Socorro in New Mexico. Speeding to the spot he encountered two weird figures, no more than 4 ft (1.2 m) high, beside a glowing oval vehicle mounted on supporting legs. The figures fled inside and took off, leaving Zamora white and shaken. When another officer arrived at the scene he saw the burning brush, and also square indentations in the ground left, it was presumed, by the spacecraft's landing gear.

Another well-documented case is that of Scottish forestry worker Bob Taylor. In November 1979, while patrolling forests near the M8 motorway at Livingston, he came upon a curious vehicle, like a huge spinning top, with a large flange running

around its rim. As he watched with astonishment, two spiked metal balls emerged from it, bounced towards him, and seemed to tug at his legs. Taylor became aware of a strange smell, then he blacked out. When he recovered some minutes later, he felt 'drained of energy' and believed that he had been gassed.

The police officers assigned to the case did not doubt Taylor's integrity – his thighs were scratched, and his trousers were found to bear long upward tears consistent with having been ripped by spikes as he had described. Police officers investigated the forest clearing and discovered marks in the turf which showed that something had landed heavily. Around the marks were 40 small holes which could have been made by the spiked balls. The marks covered only this patch of turf. How had the vehicle arrived if not from above? Had Bob Taylor been assaulted by aliens?

A UFO hotspot in Scotland

The scene of Bob Taylor's frightening encounter was near Bonnybridge, a small Scottish town where

HOVERING SPACECRAFT? This UFO was photographed in daylight near Albuquerque, New Mexico, on June 16, 1963.

there has been a wave of UFO sightings. Since 1992 about 2000 UFOs have been reported at Bonnybridge – glowing orbs, circles of lights and silver cylinders. About a third of the local population claims to have experienced strange phenomena. In January 1994, for example, a peculiar white light moving in the sky was captured on video by a Bonnybridge housewife, Lorraine Malcolm. She filmed the 18-second video sequence after her shocked husband spotted the object while driving home.

As news of the Bonnybridge phenomena spread around the world, US and Japanese TV crews arrived, and American sci-fi magazines even organised week-long holidays in the town for UFO enthusiasts.

The cover-up theory

In December 1993 a draft report of the European Parliament, drily named DOC/EN/PR/233233, proposed the establishment of a special European Centre for the investigation of UFO sightings. There have been at least two major investigations into UFOs in the United States since 1948. Officialdom, it seems, acknowledges the existence of unidentified flying objects.

Since modern reports of UFOs began, however, there have been accompanying theories that the authorities know far more about UFOs than they reveal to the public. The reasons for such a cover-up

BAFFLING IMAGES Inset: UFO spotted on a Swiss glacier in 1952. Below: four UFOs sighted at Salem, Massachusetts, in 1952.

are as murky as the origins of the UFOs themselves. Perhaps UFOs are part of top-secret national defence systems; or maybe the authorities have proof that UFOs are alien craft and fear the repercussions of making such knowledge public.

After Arnold's first flying-saucer report,

BRIEF ENCOUNTER Bob Taylor at the scene of his strange meeting with the unknown at Livingston, Scotland, in 1979.

eyewitnesses reported a fantastic range of aerial phenomena in the USA. Reports of domed, winged and cigar-shaped craft, as well as flying discs and spheres, raised public concern about the number of supposed visits to the Earth by aliens.

This prompted an official investigation by the US Air Force named *Project Blue Book*. From 1948 to 1969 Blue Book investigated

COMPARISONS Overlaid technical drawings (below) expose the similarity of a flying saucer photographed in California in 1952 (right) and a UFO photographed by a young boy in England in 1954.

12 600 cases. Most could be explained quite easily, as natural occurrences misinterpreted by the observers, such as escaped weather balloons, sightings of planets, cloud formations, or migrating birds. But 701 of the cases defied explanation and were officially classified as Unidentified Flying Objects.

The air force declared the end of *Project Blue Book* in 1969, saying that the results it was yielding were nebulous and did not warrant the continued expense. However, some believe the project is continuing covertly, and the US Government is concealing physical evidence of the existence of alien lifeforms.

In July 1947, a month after Kenneth Arnold's sighting of flying saucers, newspapers reported an extraordinary discovery near Roswell, New Mexico. 'US ARMY TO EXAMINE A FLYING DISC' reported the London *Times*, describing how the Eighth Air Force had confirmed that an object had been found there and was being sent to the research centre at Wright Field, Ohio, for examination. The air force's first press statement said that a flying disc had been recovered. However, a short time later, this was

amended to say that it was in fact the remains of a weather balloon that had been found. Army officers who recovered the debris were placed under strict instructions not to talk to reporters; later at least one repudiated the official weather-balloon story.

Some eyewitness accounts talk of discovering bodies in the desert near Roswell shortly after the crash, and of peculiar air force activity around the site. There is even a film in existence which purports to show the investigation of several dead alien bodies (without hair or facial features) and the wreckage of their craft. The Pentagon dismissed the film as a hoax.

In 1994, the US Air Force admitted that the Roswell Incident, as it had become known, was part of a secret American atomic spying programme. In June 1997, the Pentagon attempted to close the case by reiterating the weather-balloon story and saying any bodies that fell to Earth were dummies. But believers are still unconvinced.

1950   **2000**

1969 Jimmy Carter sees UFO in Georgia   1978 Australian TV crew films UFO over New Zealand   1994 Lorraine Malcolm films an object above UFO 'hotspot' in Scotland

THE CROP CIRCLE CONUNDRUM

**TORNADOES, HEDGEHOGS, ALIEN INVADERS AND HUMAN HOAXERS HAVE ALL BEEN
BLAMED FOR STRANGE PATTERNS IN FIELDS OF GROWING CORN**

GROWING CIRCLES   Formations at Lockeridge, Wiltshire. Corn circles appeared frequently in south-west England in the late 1980s.

Inexplicable circular indentations in reed beds and corn fields have been explained by some as saucer 'nests' – landing sites of alien spacecraft. Back in 1966, Australian farmer George Pedley reported three such nests in the swamps of North Queensland and claimed to have seen a blue-grey spaceship rise from the scene. Investigating the site, he found a flattened circular area about 30 ft (10 m) wide, where the reeds were swirled around clockwise 'as if they had been subjected to some terrific rotary force'.

Sceptics dismiss the circles as the results of atmospheric turbulence. Tornadoes, in particular, have been invoked to explain them. But tornadoes move along the ground and so would leave a furrow, not a circle. Other suggestions range from irregular crop fertilisation to helicopters, hedgehogs and even rutting deer.

In the late 1980s Britain seemed to be overrun by crop circles, some of them comprising elaborate patterns of straight lines as well as circles. Then, on September 9, 1991, newspapers reported the mystery solved. It appeared that making the corn circles had been the hobby of 'two jovial conmen' for 13 years. Doug Bower and David Chorley from Southampton claimed to have been

TOO CLEVER   An elaborately patterned crop circle near Hungerford in Berkshire implies either alien intelligence or a hoax.

responsible for just about all of the classic examples. They confessed to creating the patterns with 'two wooden boards, a piece of string and a bizarre sighting device attached to a baseball cap'.

Immediately there were furious repudiations of the two men's claims. One expert asked: 'Yesterday there were circles discovered on a prairie in Canada. Have these two guys been out there with their board?'

No one could doubt that some circles were the work of hoaxers. But were they all? Dedicated circle-hunters were not put off.

In 1995 Dr William Levengood, a retired biologist from the University of Michigan, announced a method for distinguishing fake circles from authentic ones. He claimed that plants in genuine crop circles undergo changes including a swelling of the nodes, the knuckle-like joints on the plant stems – an effect that no hoaxer could reproduce.

Dr Levengood believes that genuine crop circles are caused by unstable vortices of ions originating in the atmosphere, which reach the ground rather like lightning discharges. In the brief burst of heat that results the plant nodes swell up while the crops are whirled round and laid flat.

THE BESTSELLING TALE OF BRIDEY MURPHY

CAN PEOPLE UNDER HYPNOSIS RE-EXPERIENCE THEIR LIVES IN PREVIOUS INCARNATIONS?

There are many people who believe that people live numerous different lives, one after the other. For some it is a matter of religious faith, whilst others maintain that they can actually remember previous lives.

One of the bestselling books of 1956 in America was called *The Search for Bridey Murphy*. It seemed to prove that some people had past lives. The book was written by amateur hypnotist Morey Bernstein, and described how a Colorado housewife he called 'Ruth Simmons' (real name Virginia Tighe) had been led back in a trance-like state to a past life as an Irish woman of the early 19th century. Under hypnosis she spoke of herself as 'Bridey Murphy' and

MASTER MESMERISER Morey Bernstein, a hypnotist, was at the centre of the Bridey Murphy controversy that rocked the United States from 1956.

described how she had been born in Cork in 1798, daughter of a barrister, Duncan Murphy, and his wife Kathleen. She had lived in a wooden house outside Cork in an area called The Meadows, and recalled a book called *The Green Bay* being read to her. Bridey's story included an account of her marriage and her death, resulting from a fall in 1864, as well as a wealth of fascinating detail about 19th-century Irish life and the Irish coastline. The story was all the more remarkable in that Tighe had been born in 1923 and had never been to Ireland.

Doubts are raised

However, when reporters went to Ireland to try to verify the details of Bridey's story they discovered that places that she had mentioned did not seem to have existed. Local records contained no mention of Bridey's birth or death, there was no record of a wooden house fitting Bridey's description, and no known book of that time called *The Green Bay*. The housewife's narrative seemed to be a mixture of fact and pure fantasy. How had she obtained her memories?

Investigation revealed that Virginia Tighe had an aunt who had been born in Ireland. As a child in Chicago, Virginia had listened

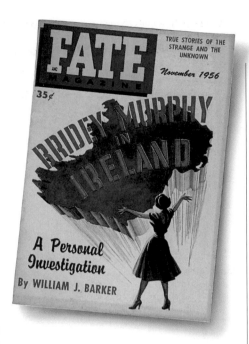

TRANCE TRAVELLER An American magazine investigates the case. Did housewife Virginia Tighe have a past life in Ireland?

to her aunt's tales of her own childhood. Another Irish woman had lived across the street from the young Virginia. The woman's name was Bridie Murphy Corkell.

Sceptics are satisfied that there was no reincarnation. It seems that hypnosis had simply released in the adult Virginia Tighe remarkably detailed memories of conversations heard, or overheard, in her infancy.

The human memory is astonishing in its capabilities. People can retrieve fantastically precise information which they have absorbed casually and unconsciously, perhaps by flicking through a library book

Those who claim to remember their past lives say that it is impossible to prove. If they provide names and dates from the past which are confirmed, critics will suggest that the subjects must have had access to the relevant information.

Believers in reincarnation, however, simply regard the Bridey Murphy case as unproven. The practice of 'regression hypnosis' pioneered by Morey Bernstein is now widespread among those seeking to experience past lives of their own.

1923 Virginia Tighe born

1956 *The Search for Bridey Murphy* published

COULD THIS BE THE FACE OF JESUS CHRIST?

HOW SCIENTISTS INVESTIGATED THE HOLY MYSTERIES OF THE TURIN SHROUD

O n April 21, 1988, under the gaze of delegates from selected laboratories, the Italian professor Giovanni Riggi carefully stripped a 3 in (70 mm) sliver from a corner of the most famous relic in Christendom. With the approval of Church authorities, this fragment of the Turin Shroud was placed on a precision balance, then cut into portions which were put in specially coded and sealed canisters, and finally handed over to the heads of three laboratories in Arizona,

MYSTERY FIGURE A 16th-century painting (above) shows the body being laid in the cloth. Right: the front view of the cloth.

Oxford and Zürich. The purpose was to obtain three independent carbon-dates for this supremely controversial fabric. And the aim was to find out whether it really dated back to the time of Christ – and could, therefore, be the genuine Shroud of Jesus.

A baffling image

Turin Cathedral's extraordinary linen cloth bears the imprint of the body of a bearded man who seems to have been beaten, crowned with thorns and pierced with nails through the wrists and feet. The long rectangle of linen was apparently folded over his body, leaving images of both the front and back of the figure. Only faint outlines are visible to the naked eye, but photographic

1931 Giuseppe Enri is allowed to photograph the Shroud

LABORATORY TESTS Computers enhance the colours (right). Magnified 18 times (above), a bloodstain on the small of the back is visible.

techniques reveal clearer detail: lash marks, for example, inflicted with a scourge – a type of flail – and the mark of a spear wound in the man's side. One scientist reportedly found traces of rare pollen in the cloth which suggested that it had once been in Palestine.

The Shroud is certainly hundreds of years old. In 1502 it was in the possession of the dukes of Savoy, and was kept in the chapel of their chateau at Chambéry. Despite being folded up in a silver casket, it was damaged when fire swept the chapel in 1532. It was moved to Turin Cathedral in 1578.

One of the biggest mysteries surrounding the Shroud is how the image was imprinted on the cloth. Most official investigators have denied the presence of paint or dye on the Shroud, as might be expected if it were the work of a forger. An exception was micro-analyst Walter McCrone, who did claim to find significant amounts of the pigment red ochre and of tempera paint. However, the official Shroud of Turin Research Project refused to endorse his report.

And how was the imprint absorbed? Did strong sunshine create a natural photograph? Was the cloth somehow stained by a vapour from secretions of sweat and body oils combined with ritual burial spices, aloe and myrrh? These are widespread speculations; but attempts to create Shroud-like images by

similar means have yielded disputed results. Besides, as critics have pointed out, corpses do not sweat and give off feverish vapours. The oddest claim made by investigators is that the image appears only on the surface of the material; it seems to have got onto the cloth without penetrating the fibres. According to one popular theory, the image was produced by some supernatural release of energy which scorched the linen. US Air Force scientists have speculated that the figure was formed by a burst of intense radiation which lasted about a microsecond; a side-effect of the Resurrection, perhaps?

However, no satisfactory explanation has yet been found for how the image was formed.

The shocking results

The more that scientists investigated it, the more convincing the Shroud appeared. Then came the bombshell. The 1988 carbon-dating test results dated the cloth to between 1260 and 1390. The Turin Shroud was a medieval fake.

Not everyone accepted the radio-carbon findings. A French priest, Brother Bruno Bonet-Eymard, was among the first to claim

RENAISSANCE MAN Did Italian painter and inventor Leonardo da Vinci, who produced the first-ever design for an aircraft, also create the Shroud image?

that it was the carbon-dating – not the Shroud – which had been faked. An astonishing theory subsequently proposed that the test results had been manipulated by the Church. In *The Jesus Conspiracy*, writers Holger Kersten and Elmer R. Gruber claimed that the real evidence proved that the Shroud was genuine, but implied that Christ had still been alive when laid in the tomb. To protect its central religious doctrine of the Resurrection, the Vatican had had the Shroud dismissed as a fake.

Even if the linen is medieval, many riddles remain. Fake relics were abundant in the 14th century, and manufacturing them was big business. But the figure on the Shroud is much more naturalistic than any of the medieval painters were capable of.

Also, medieval painters always showed the crucified Christ with nails passing through the palms of his hands. A contemporary forger would surely have done the same. In reality, to support the weight of a crucified body, the nails had to pass through the wrists. The figure on the Shroud has wounds at the wrists.

The Leonardo connection

It has been said that if the Shroud was the work of a forger he must have been a genius. In the search for a suitable candidate, the name of Leonardo da Vinci has been raised. The film *The Silent Witness* speculates that Leonardo was the only person who could have created such a forgery.

Supporters of the theory include Lynn Picknett and Clive Prince, whose book, *The Turin Shroud*, proposes that da Vinci improved an ancient fake.

British physician Dr Straiton suggests that the Shroud wrapped the real-life body of a 14th-century crusader who was captured and crucified, in a parody of the death of Christ, by the Saracens.

For those who believe that the Shroud wrapped the body of Jesus, and those who think it is a fake, the question remains – how was the image of a crucified body formed on the Turin Shroud?

1950   2000

1978 Shroud displayed to the public for 42 days   1988 Radio-carbon results announced   1994 *The Turin Shroud* is published

THE THIRSTY STATUES

THE MONTH WHEN EFFIGIES OF HINDU DEITIES APPEARED TO DRINK MILK OFFERINGS WORLDWIDE

Traffic was disrupted across the whole of northern India, and roads were clogged by tens of thousands of people travelling to make offerings of milk to statues. 'MILK-DRINKING DEITIES UNLEASH MASS HYSTERIA,' reported *The Pioneer* newspaper, while the *Indian Express* said that the nation had gone berserk.

It was September 1995, and India's 800 million Hindus were gripped by a frenzy of devotion with reports that statues of the gods – chiefly Siva, his wife Parvati and their elephant-headed son Ganesh – were drinking milk offered to them by worshippers.

The episode seems to have begun on Thursday, September 21, with a report that a statue of Ganesh in a New Delhi suburb had drunk half a cup of milk. Rumours spread that other statues of the Hindu gods in New Delhi were drinking milk. The city was reduced to chaos as crowds bearing milk rushed to the temples to watch the white liquid apparently vanishing before their eyes.

Soon the phenomenon had spread across all of northern India. Queues formed at statues, especially those of Ganesh, god of auspicious beginnings, the most popular of the Hindu pantheon. While milk stalls ran dry and prices soared, the temples of Ganesh were awash.

Mahani Srikant Ravi of the Hanuman temple in central Delhi told a reporter: 'It is magic. The gods have come down to Earth to solve all our problems.' The mahani added that his temple had been under siege since dawn. Over 2500 people had visited by mid-morning, and the crowds had not been disappointed. Parmeesh Soti, a company executive, was just one of the worshippers convinced of the miracle. 'It cannot be a hoax. Where would all that milk go? It just disappears in front of your eyes.'

The gods athirst

Sceptics had their doubts. One theory suggested that the whole phenomenon was a priestly deception wrought with statues containing suction devices, rigged to bring crowds back to the temples. Others saw it as a stunt, worked by the hardline Hindu political parties in India, to whip up faith before a forthcoming general election. But the craze soon spread beyond India to Hindu communities all around the world. Crowds formed at temples in Singapore, Indonesia and Bangkok. In Hong Kong an official claimed that a small silver statue of Ganesh had drunk 40 pints (20 l) of milk. In Long Island and New Jersey in the United States, Hindus said that statues of the gods in family homes were swallowing milk.

In Britain, with 200 centres of worship serving a large Hindu community, eager crowds gathered with milk in cans, cartons and bottles. A supermarket in West London sold out its stock of 28 000 pints (14 000 l) in one morning as the throng converged on the Vishwa Hindu Temple, Southall, where a statue was said to be drinking milk at a phenomenal rate. In 24 hours, 10 000 people reportedly saw the statue drink.

Scientists put the phenomenon down to the way in which plaster and stone can act like blotting paper due to capillary action. Such effigies can be even 'thirstier' if they have a hollow core filled with absorbent materials. However, capillary action cannot so easily explain the many reports of metal Hindu statues 'drinking' the milk.

The whole episode, which lasted only a few days, may have left doubters as dubious as ever, but for believers it was a convincing sign that the coming century would be Hindu in character.

SACRED SIPS Worshippers offer milk to idols of Nandi (above) and Ganesh (below) during the frenzied devotions of 1995.

MANLY DEITY A modern gouache of the four-armed god Siva. In the Hindu religion it is Siva who represents the male principle of generation.

MYSTERIES OF MODERN SCIENCE

FROM THE TITANIC FORCES WHICH DRIVE THE DRIFTING CONTINENTS TO THE MICROSCOPIC MECHANISMS OF GENE-CARRYING CHROMOSOMES, MODERN SCIENCE HAS REVEALED MANY WONDERS IN THE WORLD AROUND US. YET OTHER REALITIES ARE POSSIBLE IN THEORY. BRITAIN'S T.H. HUXLEY, A PHILOSOPHER AND PIONEER OF SCIENTIFIC METHOD, ONCE WROTE: 'I AM TOO MUCH A SCEPTIC TO DENY THE POSSIBILITY OF ANYTHING.'

THE RIDDLE OF HYPNOSIS

TRANCE WITH A STRANGER: UNLOCKING THE SECRETS OF THE DEEPEST PART OF THE MIND

It has been said that one of the great medical questions of the 20th century – what happens under hypnosis – can be answered in three words: 'We don't know.'

Hypnosis is much easier to describe than to explain. People who have been hypnotised enter a sleep-like trance in which the mind remains fully alert yet passive and suggestible. At the hypnotist's command, the subject will carry out instructions; take fantastic suggestions for reality; reveal secrets from the subconscious; and become insensible to pain. Although it is generally held that people cannot be hypnotised into doing things against their will, the dangers inherent in the hypnotist's control are obvious.

An obsession with onions

Effects on memory are particularly eerie. If a stage hypnotist asks subjects to forget everything that has happened during the

HYPNOTIC VISIONARY Medical pioneer Franz Anton Mesmer (1734-1815) used his own theory, known as 'animal magnetism', to cure patients in strange séance-like sessions.

trance they generally do. However, during the period of 'post-hypnotic amnesia' they will respond to suggestions planted during the trance: barking like a dog, say, when the hypnotist gives the previously arranged signal. Casual hypnotism has other perils. In 1994 two drama students in York, England, were hypnotised by a friend who could not then get them out of their trances. Doctors had to call in a hypnotherapist to wake them up.

In Britain and other countries, local authorities have the powers to regulate or prohibit stage hypnosis because of its potential dangers. In November 1994 a woman won an out-of-court settlement of £20 000 after being hypnotised in a Scottish theatre and then falling from the stage and breaking her leg. Dr Prem Misra, a Glasgow specialist in the subject, has described various disorders resulting from sessions, including fits and persistence of hypnotic suggestions. One man became obsessed with eating onions after a stage hypnotist persuaded him during a show that they were Golden Delicious apples.

Medicine and crime

Although 'borrowed' for the stage, the modern techniques of hypnotism were actually developed for healing purposes. The great pioneer was the 18th-century German physician Franz Anton Mesmer, who tried to cure illnesses by conducting séance-like sessions with his patients. Hypnotism (or 'mesmerism') also interested the 19th-century French physiologist Jean-Martin Charcot, under whom Sigmund Freud studied. Revered today as the father of psychoanalysis, Freud used hypnosis to treat his patients in his early days. Working with another physician, Josef Breuer, he probed for emotionally charged repressed memories in his patients while they were in a hypnotic state.

Later, although Freud continued to probe for forgotten memories in his patients, he abandoned hypnosis as a form of treatment. He had deduced that to tell a patient with an affliction such as a twitch to stop when under hypnosis was like trying to cure measles by painting out the spots. The important thing was to get to the underlying

MEETING OF MINDS Patients gathered together for Mesmer's therapeutic sessions in hotels, which sometimes involved sitting round a vat of diluted sulphuric acid.

cause of the disorder, not to erase the symptoms. Besides, Freud had also discovered that not all patients are readily hypnotised.

Nonetheless, hypnosis is still used in medicine – as a technique for inducing relaxation and reducing reaction to pain, and in unlocking the deeper parts of the mind. It is sometimes employed as an alternative to anaesthetics. It can help burns victims feel less pain, and it has also achieved moderate success in treating phobias and addictions. In clinical hypnosis the subject usually remains mentally alert throughout the session.

Attempts to use hypnosis in crime detection have proved more controversial. 'Eyewitness' accounts recovered through hypnosis would be too unreliable to be used as evidence in court, but the police have tried to use it to enhance witnesses' memories of details, such as the registration number of a car seen at the scene of a crime. In one murder case in Britain, in the 1990s, the results were calamitous for the police. Officers arranged for a key witness to be

1918 Hypnosis used to treat neuroses in soldiers after First World War

1945 Hypnosis again used to treat soldiers with neuroses during Second World War

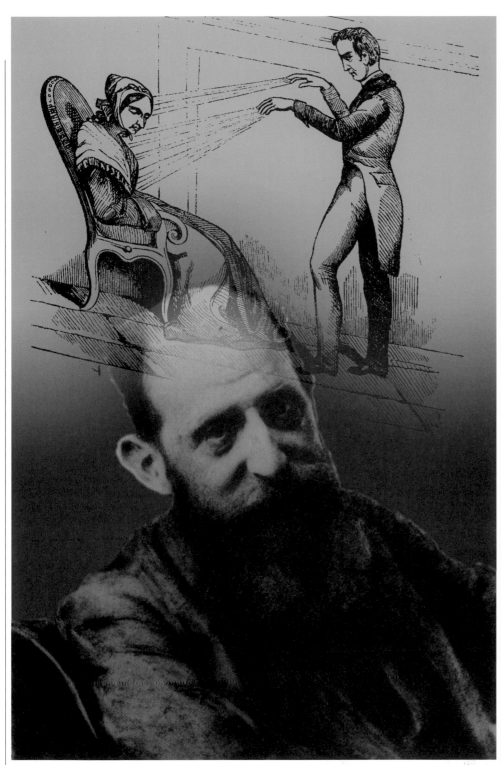

Gradually he or she enters a condition akin to sleep or to day-dreaming, and is ready to accept the hypnotist's influence.

Research suggests that some personalities are more easily hypnotised than others. Creative people make good subjects. Women are slightly easier to hypnotise than men, and children in the 8-12 age range are the best of all. Thereafter, it seems, suggestibility decreases with age.

A special brain state?

Among investigators a hot debate rages between two schools of thought. Some believe that the subjects are basically play-acting – they have agreed to let the hypnotist 'write the script' for them during hypnotism, and are not experiencing anything other than a form of intense concentration. The alternative view holds that hypnotic trance is a special brain state which is cut off, or dissociated, from normal waking consciousness.

The theory of the special brain state appears to have been confirmed by recent experiments carried out in California, USA. Students sat in front of a TV monitor that flashed lights which normally generate electrical discharges in the brain. Hypnotised students, however, had been told that a box was blocking out the lights. As a result, the researchers found, the brainwaves in the visual parts of their brains were significantly reduced. Hypnotism, it seemed, had physically altered brainwave behaviour – but still no one could explain why.

YOU ARE FEELING SLEEPY Mesmerism was a forerunner of psychotherapy, and was used by physicians such as Josef Breuer (above) in conjunction with Sigmund Freud.

hypnotised, but the procedure confused him and led him to make statements damaging to their case against the accused.

In fiction, the glaring-eyed hypnotist may use hocus pocus to put subjects into a trance, but in real life methods are not especially exotic. A hypnotist may, perhaps, start by asking a patient to focus on a fixed point and count backwards from 300. As the patient performs the monotonous task, he or she relaxes; the pulse rate slows, while body temperature and blood pressure both fall.

FREUDIAN SLIP The man himself (right) used hypnosis on patients in his early days, but later abandoned it as a form of treatment in favour of other techniques.

1994 British woman wins out-of-court settlement of £20 000 after breaking her leg during stage hypnosis

SEARCHING FOR ANSWERS TO THE DIVINE QUESTION

EVEN TODAY, THE ANCIENT ART OF DOWSING STILL DEFIES RATIONAL EXPLANATION

Few sights are more curious or bewitching than that of a dowser at work. Clutching a two-pronged, usually hazel, twig, the dowser twitches and jerks towards an unseen quarry under the ground in almost a parody of a cartoon character drawn to a magnet – an image that is strangely at odds with the modern world.

Certainly, dowsing – the traditional method of looking for underground water using a divining rod – is an ancient art form. And when the ability to find water could mean life or death to a whole community, it is not surprising that the art was cherished. By the Middle Ages, dowsing or divining rods were being used in mining and treasure-

AN ANCIENT ART 16th-century dowsers used rods to find veins of metallic ores such as silver. From Georgius Agricola's *De Re Metallica*, Basle, Switzerland, 1556.

hunting to find subterranean minerals, much as metal detectors are today. Even at the end of the 20th century, with the multitude of hi-tech aids available, the services of professional dowsers are still being called upon by farmers, water authorities, oil companies and civil engineers.

These days, their equipment is not much more evolved than the old forked twig, although L-shaped metal rods are also employed. These are held like pistols in the hands, parallel and a few inches apart until they swing across one another. The pendulum is another common dowsing device; it is swung back and forth until the swing changes to a circular motion.

Earth magnetism, cosmic rays

Many researchers believe that dowsers have a special sensitivity to small changes in the Earth's magnetism. The dowser experiences a discernible muscular reaction when tuning in to the fluctuations caused by the presence of water or minerals underground. Perhaps all human beings – and other living things too – have a built-in magnetic detection system which is normally dormant but can be brought into play when necessary. This authentic inner 'sixth sense' – a compass sense – almost certainly plays its part in animal migration.

Earth magnetism – the force that makes a compass needle point north – remains an ill-understood planetary phenomenon with many curious features. It is as if there were a giant bar magnet at the core of the Earth, whose pull, scientists have discovered, has

fluctuated in strength at various times in the past. Astonishingly, the Earth's magnetic field has also reversed itself at intervals in history, so that north became south and vice versa. Scientists

OFF THE MAP Some diviners, such as Andrew Beastley, even claim to be able to make finds without actually visiting the site.

who first made this discovery in the 1950s could hardly believe the evidence of their own investigations, but it was undoubtedly true; studies of rock strata have demonstrated that repeatedly, and for varying periods throughout the Earth's history, the poles have flipped into reverse.

The Earth's magnetic field stretches some way into space and partially deflects incoming cosmic rays. Some recent research into dowsing suggests that attention should be directed toward those incoming cosmic rays rather than the Earth's magnetism. In 1994 Professor Vincent Reddish, a former Astronomer-Royal for Scotland, conducted a series of experiments into dowsing which led him to conclude that the force could not be electrical or electromagnetic.

His theory is that the cosmic radiation field reacts with water or minerals above or below ground to create the energy waves which dowsers detect. The professor found that, while most solid materials conducted the dowsing force, aluminium seemed to

INVESTIGATIVE POWERS Controversy always reigns when the police call in so-called psychic detectives, such as Gerard Croiset, to help locate missing persons.

block the charge. This indicated that the source of the mystery force was not electrical, as aluminium is a very good conductor of electricity. To test his belief, Professor Reddish asked six dowsers in different parts of Britain to try putting aluminium foil over their shoes and walking over water pipes that they already knew about. All reported that the foil eliminated the dowsing effect.

The psychic detectives

Whatever mystery still surrounds the mechanism of dowsing, few people doubt that it works on some basic level. If we are all sensitive to the Earth's magnetism, there is nothing particularly odd in supposing that professional dowsers – whose natural aptitude is enhanced by years of training – should develop highly sophisticated skills. In a different field, wine-tasters have developed the amazing ability to identify the vineyard a

HAND TO MOUTH Science still cannot explain the success of traditional dowsers such as S. J. Searles of Kent.

wine comes from by one sip in a blindfold test. Far more controversial are the claims of those dowsers who profess to make their discoveries at long distance – without visiting sites at all – and have extended their repertoires to include locating missing persons or even dead bodies.

The Dutch clairvoyant Gerard Croiset has gained a reputation for helping police in Europe to locate missing people. He has often offered information simply by dowsing aerial photographs or holding a pendulum over a map and interpreting the response.

Croiset first came to attention in 1959, when he reportedly helped in finding the whereabouts of a Kansas professor's missing daughter. In 1961 he was called in by an official of KLM, the Dutch airline, to help in the case of a missing four-year-old who was eventually found murdered in Brooklyn, New York City. When the killer and the child's body were discovered, some circumstances supposedly matched information supplied by Croiset (although several details were also wrong).

Sceptics remained unconvinced of his psychic powers. In 1978 he was brought in on the British case of the serial killer known as the 'Yorkshire Ripper'. A phoney tape-recorded message

had misled the police into believing that the culprit must come from the north-east, and Croiset focused attention on that area; in fact the killer came from elsewhere. Croiset was also consulted in the same year in the case of missing British schoolgirl Genette Tate. At the time, the police made many references to the help offered by psychics because – knowing the media fascination with all things paranormal – it helped to keep the case before the public eye. Croiset could offer no solution in either case.

Such failures do not, of course, invalidate psychic detection. Remarkable claims have been made for remote viewing by seers and mediums since the dawn of history. Believers point out that the universe is full of information that is beyond the range of our five normal senses. There are sounds too high for us to hear, and colours that are beyond the visible range of the spectrum. Why should we doubt that other information is being transmitted, to which suitably gifted individuals are able to tune in?

MAGNETISM AND MIGRATION

The pinpoint accuracy with which swallows return each spring to the same nest they used last year ... the salmon coming home to find the stream where they were born after journeying thousands of miles ... the skill with which green turtles from the Brazilian coast navigate 1368 miles (2200 km) of ocean to find tiny Ascension Island, a mere pinprick on the vast map of the Atlantic ... These are just a few prodigies of animal migration. Butterflies, bats, lemmings and whales also travel long distances in accordance with seasonal climate changes or breeding cycles.

How do they find their way? Their means of navigation is still only partially understood, but it seems to involve a range of skills. Birds, which have been the subject of careful, extensive research, evidently take sightings of landmarks such as mountains, forests and estuaries. Scientists believe that they also steer by the sun and the stars. (Experiments in a planetarium during the 1950s showed that warblers recognise patterns of stars and use them for orientation.)

But recent theories also indicate that, like dowsers on land, birds are sensitive to the Earth's magnetism. Experiments with homing pigeons have shown that even when fitted with opaque contact lenses that prevent them from seeing more than a few yards ahead, they can still find their way home. However, when small magnets are attached to their heads, the pigeons get lost – presumably because the devices block out the Earth's fainter magnetic signals. Tiny particles of magnetic material have been found in the birds' skulls and neck muscles, which are thought to let them sense the magnetic map of the earth below.

JOURNEYS INTO THE FOURTH DIMENSION

DO BLACK HOLES PROVIDE THE MEANS FOR TRAVELLING THROUGH TIME?

Until 1905, when the brilliant German-born physicist Albert Einstein first formulated his theory of relativity, there was one fundamental concept of time. Known as 'linear time', it is the easily explainable belief that only the present exists. In other words, we cannot go back to the past and relive that time because it has gone. The future does not exist yet, because it has not started. We only live in the time which is happening now.

However, Einstein's work brought about a whole new theory to explain the concept of time. Using highly complex mathematics, he was able to show that the dimensions of time and space are not fixed and separate from one another. They are variable and intimately connected. In this theory, believed by most scientists, both time and space are 'bent' – for example, by the gravity that occurs near large bodies such as stars and planets. According to Einstein, time would slow down for anyone travelling through space at the speed of light but it would carry on at the same pace back on the Earth. A man taking a hypothetical journey lasting 14 years hurtling through space would find that 65 years had gone by on the Earth. Effectively, he would have travelled forwards into the future.

This concept underlies a wealth of fictions, from the British television series *Doctor Who* with its famous 'Tardis' to Steven Spielberg's blockbusting *Back to the Future* series and time-travelling car. Yet the discovery of black holes in space has prompted the idea that vehicles for time travel may already exist as natural features of the universe.

The Hamlet paradox

Scientists believe that a black hole results when a celestial body such as a star dies. The star contracts dramatically, becoming denser, and eventually undergoes such a complete gravitational collapse that no light can escape from it.

Black holes cannot be seen directly, but their presence has been deduced from the movements of other stars which are under the influence of their gravitational fields. A black hole was first identified during the 1970s, and others have since been located at the core of supernova explosions and the centres of certain galaxies. In 1995 a black hole was identified at the centre of our own galaxy, and is believed to be a million times heavier than the Sun.

Scientists theorise that a black hole's gravitational field may be so vast as to reverse the flow of time and tunnel into another dimension. They have even hypothesised about the existence of a 'worm hole': two black holes linked by a funnel, offering mind-bending possibilities. A man time-travelling might disappear into one end and emerge at the other in a

NEW TO THE FAITH Cosmologist and mathematician Stephen Hawking is a recent convert to the possibility of time travel.

different time, or even collide with himself coming the other way. The problem with this is what has been called the Hamlet paradox: a man might go back into the past and kill his own grandfather – and so fail to be born.

Scientists have proposed two ways round this apparent absurdity. The first is a Consistency principle, by which all acts must be consistent with past history (that is, one can go back in time and 'look' but not 'touch'). The second is the Multiverse principle, by which our own universe is one of an infinite number of parallel universes. A man might kill his own grandfather in one universe, and still be born in another.

Some scientists reject time travel as impossible, but there are new converts all the time. Mathematician and cosmologist Stephen Hawking was at one time a disbeliever, but in 1995 called for government funds to research into time travel. 'If you combine Einstein's general theory of relativity with quantum mechanics,' he says, 'it does begin to seem a possibility.'

RELATIVE THEORIES According to the Multiverse principle, Professor Albert Einstein (right) could be alive and well in another universe parallel to our own.

TUNNELS FOR TIME TRAVEL So intense is the gravity within a black hole that it causes time to be 'bent'. It is usually depicted as a 'gravitational well', as below.

1905 Albert Einstein formulates his theory of relativity
1907 German astronomer Karl Schwarzschild predicts the existence of black holes

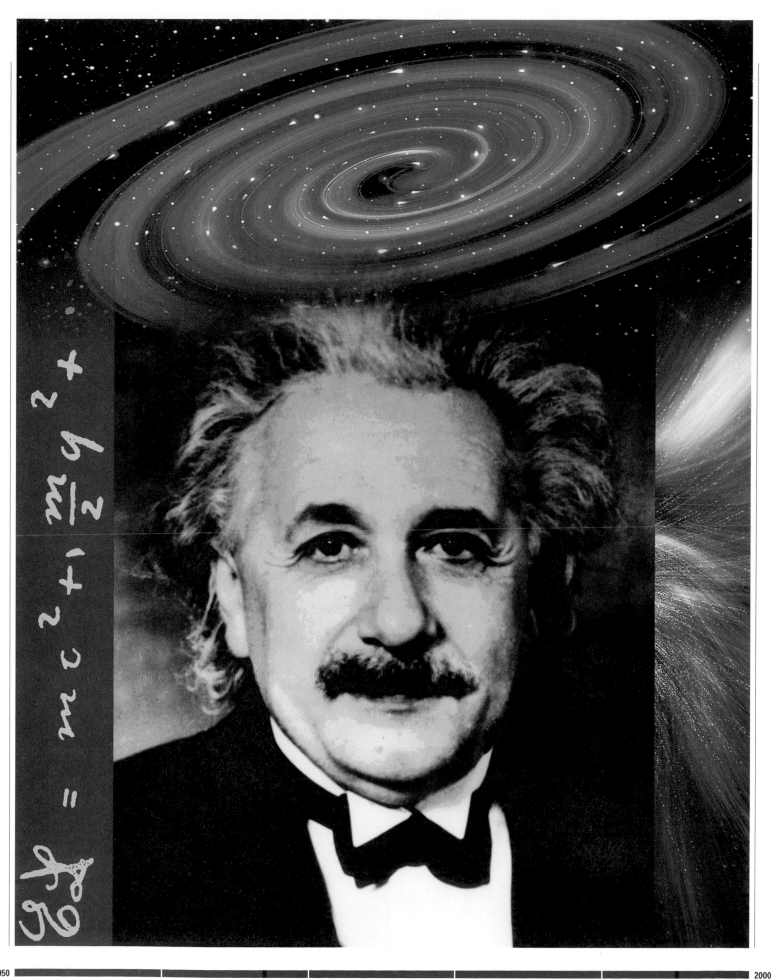

1967 Professor John Wheeler coins
the term 'black hole' in New York
City, USA

1995 A black hole
is identified in the
Milky Way

THE HEALER

WITH THE HELP OF THE SPIRITS, A BRAZILIAN COUNTRY BUMPKIN MADE MEDICAL HISTORY

At the height of his fame in the late 1950s, up to 200 people a day were treated by the Brazilian healer Arigo, who operated on patients while he was in a trance-like state, using no more than a pair of nail scissors or a rusty pocket-knife. He used neither antiseptics nor anaesthetics, and had no formal training; the authorities were so alarmed by his nightmarish procedures that they had him arrested and twice sentenced to jail on the charge of practising illegal medicine.

Yet none of his patients ever brought a complaint against him, and many testified that he had cured them of serious illnesses. After his death in a car accident in January 1971, 20 000 people turned up to mourn at his funeral.

'He just picked up a paring knife'

Born to a farming family in 1918, José Pedro de Freitas was nicknamed Arigo ('country bumpkin') because of his rural background. In his youth he was often disturbed by strange dreams, headaches and hallucinations, and he came to believe that he was possessed by the spirit of a German physicist, Dr Fritz, who had died during the First World War. Arigo thought that the doctor could only find peace by operating through him to relieve the sick and distressed. Witnesses noted that when he performed his 'psychic surgery' Arigo would speak with a German accent and in a sharp, imperious tone very different from his amiable everyday manner.

Eyewitness accounts have survived of the cures he effected in his clinic at Congonhas do Campo, his home town. An American investigator of psychic phenomena, Dr Andrija Puharich, wrote: 'These people step up – they're all sick. One had a big goitre. Arigo just picked up the paring knife, cut it open, popped the goitre out, slapped it in her hand, wiped the opening with a piece of dirty cotton and off she went. It hardly bled at all.' Taking no precautions against infection, Arigo performed an eye operation in the same brusque fashion.

It was an extraordinary feature of all Arigo's reported operations that his incisions hardly bled, and that his patients experienced little or no pain. Puharich later went on to experience the healer's skills for himself, when he agreed to allow Arigo to remove a benign tumour from his arm. This was done with a penknife, and apparently caused no pain or discomfort.

Often, though, Arigo's treatment consisted only of scribbling rapid prescriptions which, on examination, turned out to be medical absurdities: obsolete medicines in weird combinations and sometimes dangerous doses. Yet his cures are alleged to have extended from cysts and small benign

DAMNING EVIDENCE On trial in 1964, Arigo (left) went back to jail for a second time for refusing to stop practising medicine. On his release he simply reopened his surgery.

tumours to virulent cancer. The healer's manner was notably brusque; he made no hypnotic passes over patients. And he himself claimed to know nothing about his miraculous powers, saying only that they were wrought by Jesus and the German doctor whose spirit worked through him. It is said that when, on one occasion, Arigo watched a film of himself performing operations, he fainted.

He treated rich and poor alike and is reported not to have accepted payment for his services; incredibly, he fitted his healing sessions in around a regular day job in a government welfare office. However, not everyone was convinced that Arigo should be allowed to continue with his medical career, and in 1956 the Minas Gerais Medical Association succeeded in having him prosecuted for 'illegal practice of medicine'. He was sentenced to 16 months in prison, but there was such an outcry this was reduced to eight months and a fine. Shortly before he was due to go to jail the Brazilian president, Juscelino Kubitschek, proclaimed a pardon.

In 1964 Arigo's persistent refusal to abandon his illegal practice earned him another jail sentence, which he served in two stretches – first of seven months and then of two.

However, the appeal judge, Filippe Immesi, was much impressed by Arigo. With a friend from the legal profession, he paid an unofficial visit to the healer's surgery and watched him operate with a pair of nail scissors on a woman half-blinded by cataracts. The judge declared himself speechless, amazed: 'She was cured.'

Arigo was examined by the Brazilian Medical Academy, who found that his snap diagnoses matched those of professional doctors in most cases. His ability was tested with X-ray, microscope, film camera and electrocardiogram. No evidence of fraud was ever uncovered. Was he a quack? If so, his deceptions were almost as miraculous as his cures. Arigo was perhaps the 20th century's most celebrated faith healer, and his case must remind all but the most hardened sceptics of how deeply mysterious are the capabilities of the human body and mind.

1918 Birth of José Pedro de Freitas – Arigo – in Brazil

1956 Arigo goes to prison for illegally practising medicine

1971 Arigo dies in car accident

THE WOMAN WHO BURST INTO FLAMES

A CLASSIC CASE OF HUMAN COMBUSTION? THE UNACCOUNTABLE DEATH OF MRS REESER

At 8 am on July 2, 1951, a landlady took a telegram to the door of her tenant, Mrs Mary Reeser, of St Petersburg, Florida, USA. When she put her hand on the doorknob, however, she noticed that it was hot to the touch and called for help. Two painters working nearby ran over, and on opening the door felt a blast of hot air. There was no great conflagration inside, however, just a little smoke and a small flame burning on the beam of a partition dividing the living room from the kitchenette. Mrs Reeser's bed was empty; the 67-year-old widow was nowhere to be seen.

When the firemen arrived they needed only a handpump to put out the feeble flame. But when they tore away the burnt

STRANGE BUT TRUE Officials sift through the charred remains of Mrs Mary Reeser (right), of St Petersburg, Florida – apparently the victim of spontaneous combustion.

partition they found a blackened circle on the floor, little more than 3 ft (1 m) in diameter, in which lay several coiled chair springs, a charred liver attached to a piece of spine, a skull shrunk to the size of an orange, a small heap of ashes and a human foot, burnt off at the ankle but still wearing a satin slipper.

Police, fire officials, insurance men and arson experts were baffled. There seemed to be nothing to explain the cause of the fire. Besides, there was no great damage except around the chair where the woman had died – and there the heat had been extraordinarily intense. The inquest heard that crematoria customarily generate temperatures of 2500°F (1371°C) for as much as four hours to incinerate a body. Even then they would have to use grinders to reduce the remains to the state of Mrs Reeser's residue. The widow, an amply built 12½ stone (80 kg) in weight, had been incinerated into just 8½ lb (4 kg) of ash.

The slippered foot

Despite the phenomenal heat attained, the damage around the small blackened circle was minimal. A wall mirror had cracked

and two pink wax candles on a dressing table had become puddles, but the wall paint adjacent to the chair was only faintly browned, and the carpet where it had rested was not even burnt through. A pile of newspapers just outside the circle was wholly unharmed. The slippered foot also defied belief. It was known that Mrs Reeser experienced some discomfort in her left leg and was in the habit of stretching it out. It looked as if the foot had survived because she had extended it just outside the circle of heat.

Dr Wilton Krogman, a leading authority on deaths by fire, confessed himself mystified. 'They say truth is often stranger than fiction and this case proves it,' he said. And he drew attention to the curiously shrunken state of Mrs Reeser's skull. When a body is burnt in intense heat the skull would normally expand and shatter explosively.

Despite this the FBI released a statement suggesting that the victim had taken her usual sleeping pills and fallen asleep on the chair while smoking a cigarette – although neither her nightgown nor the chair was especially flammable.

Other possibilities were also examined. Death by lightning was dismissed by an expert in such fatalities. Murder and suicide were both rejected; in either case the body would have had to have been doused with petrol or something similar, yet no trace of a chemical agent was found. Besides, the central paradox remained unexplained. How could a fire generate the temperature needed to reduce a body to ash while leaving nearby combustible materials untouched?

The death of Mrs Reeser is often cited as a classic case of spontaneous human combustion – a phenomenon in which a human body appears to ignite and burn of its own accord. Reports of it date back to the 17th century and, although most scientists deny its possibility, many well-documented cases in modern times survive as testimony to a phenomenon that seems to defy analysis. As Dr Krogman said during the Mrs Reeser investigation: 'I regard it as the most amazing thing I've ever seen. As I review it, the short hairs on my neck bristle with vague fear. Were I living in the Middle Ages, I'd mutter something about black magic.'

July 1951 The charred remains of Mrs Mary Reeser are discovered in her apartment in Florida, USA

HUMAN ELECTRICITY

NATURAL FORCES THAT RESULT IN BIZARRE FORMS OF ENERGY

In 1920 a remarkable trend was observed by the chief physician at Clinton Prison in New York. It seemed that 34 convicts suffering from severe food poisoning had somehow become electrically charged. Paper stuck to their hands when they tried to throw it away, compass needles swung wildly in their vicinity, and metal objects were deflected from their grasp. Only when the illness started to ebb did the effects

BIZARRE TALENTS Brian Williams of Cardiff was so full of electricity he could light up a lightbulb just by rubbing it with his hands.

diminish, in a peculiar condition which had also been recorded back in the 19th century. In 1877, in Ontario, Canada, a teenager called Caroline Clare recovering from a wasting disease began to give shocks to anyone who touched her. Pieces of iron stuck to her body and had to be pulled off by force.

Such cases of 'human batteries' are often explained by science as static electricity – although why this should be exacerbated during illness remains unknown. In some cases, such as that of Brian Williams, it is present all the time. Williams had a bizarre

talent for lighting lightbulbs simply by rubbing them with his hands. He had to put rubber grips on the handlebars of his bicycle to stop other people getting shocks.

Freak disturbances

It is accepted that the human body possesses its own electromagnetic field, and that it is susceptible to interference. Franz Mesmer, the pioneer of hypnotism, was among the medical pioneers who tried to use magnets to effect healing. And electro-ailments have recently made headlines, with scientists establishing causal links between overhead power lines and certain cancers.

Freakish electromagnetic disturbances may account for some paranormal phenomena. Cases of poltergeist haunting often occur when a particular person is present – often the focus is female and under the age of 20. Psychic researchers have suggested that the intense anxiety that tends to come with

METAL MAGIC Is it focused electromagnetic turmoil that lets Uri Geller bend all that cutlery, or is it simply trickery?

1920 Convicts at Clinton Prison, New York, become electrically charged while suffering from food poisoning

1934 Worldwide sensation is caused by Italy's luminous woman of Pirano pubescence may find unconscious expression in electromagnetic turmoil around that person. Poltergeist activity is associated with frustrated male adolescents too. Colin Wilson, a prolific writer on the paranormal,

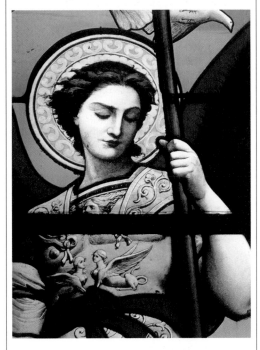

RELIGIOUS AURA   A stained-glass depiction of Saint Michael, in the Basilique du Bois-Chenu, Domrémy, France.

has suggested that many supposed psychics, such as Matthew Manning and Uri Geller, employ controlled poltergeist activity.

Human glow-worms

Human electricity is sometimes associated with radiance, and there have been many curious cases of sick people giving off light. In May 1934, Italy's Luminous Woman of Pirano caused a worldwide press sensation. Signora Anna Monaro, an asthma patient, baffled doctors by emitting a blue glow from her breasts as she slept. Was this, though, an electrical phenomenon? Scientists theorised

---

THE LIGHT OF LIFE

Luminous beings are a fact of nature. Fireflies glow in the dark, as do various other insects, fungi and fish. Their radiance derives from the biochemical oxidation of the compound luciferin. Some scientists believe that occasional reports of sick people with glowing limbs may be prompted by luminous bacteria feeding off the nutrients in human sweat.

KIRLIAN PHOTOGRAPHY: REVEALING THE INVISIBLE TRUTH?

PALM READING   A Kirlian photograph of a human hand shows the glow that surrounds living tissue.

Do human beings possess an aura invisible to the naked eye? Yes, according to believers in Kirlian photography, a technique which claims to reveal a strange, glowing corona around all living things. The process takes its name from the Russian Professor Semyan Kirlian who devised it in the Soviet Union in 1939. Using a high-frequency generator with two metal plates acting as electrodes, he placed a photographic film on one of the plates. Then he placed his hand between the plates and turned on the current. When the film was developed it revealed a remarkable luminous aura around his hand. A live leaf photographed between the plates also showed an aura, but a dead leaf did not. Amazingly, when a torn leaf was photographed the result appeared to show a phantom image of the piece that had been torn away.

When Kirlian's experiments became known to the West in the 1970s they provoked much excitement among students of the paranormal. Here, it seemed, was proof of spiritual reality; a luminous energy uncaged by the form of living things. On Kirlian photographs, psychic healers were said to produce flare-like effects from their fingertips when they were exerting their powers. People speculated that the Turin Shroud's image might have been created by some natural Kirlian process, but scientists were quick to dismiss the results. It was already known that a sudden spurt of voltage could create strange patterned effects on film as tiny particles in the air become ionised, or charged with current. Moreover, when Kirlian apparatus was set up in the West, scientists discovered that they could create all kinds of effects by methods no more 'spiritual' than altering the current. Kirlian photography still has its supporters, but there is no general agreement on precisely what it shows.

IN CLOSE UP   The 'corona' from a fingertip. The image results from interaction between the subject and an applied electric field.

that her weakened state had increased the amount of sulphides (a chemical compound) in her blood. Sulphides can be stimulated into luminescence by ultraviolet radiation, and, since human blood radiates in the ultraviolet range, perhaps this was responsible.

Images of luminosity are widely employed to denote the sacred and the superhuman. Christian saints were portrayed in halos of light, and Mohammed is seen in a golden flame. Are such reports merely symbolic? Or have the world's great spiritual leaders been charged with an inexplicable energy that expresses itself as bodily radiance?

SEEING IS BELIEVING   British healer Matthew Manning treats a patient at a healing demonstration in Germany.

1952 Press attention focuses on Brian Williams's talent for lighting lightbulbs

GREAT BALLS OF FIRE

WITNESSED BY MANY, EXPLAINED BY NONE: THE PECULIAR PHENOMENON OF BALL LIGHTNING

Passengers on board Eastern Airlines Flight 539 flying from New York to Washington in 1963 were astonished when they were treated to an unexpected form of in-flight entertainment. Following a bright crack of lightning, a luminous orb about 8 in

exist – so it was something of an irony that an example should choose to make its presence felt at the Cavendish Laboratories in England, an establishment famed for nurturing Nobel prize-winning scientists. Many of the employees witnessed this phenomenon in August 1982, and eminent physicist Sir Brian Pippard sent off eye-witness accounts to the scientific journal, *Nature*. 'It was most remarkable,' he said. 'It went through a window as a secretary was closing it and passed by without singeing her hair.'

CAUGHT ON FILM? Photograph taken in Castleford, Yorkshire, claiming to show the path and explosion of ball lightning.

(20 cm) in diameter emerged from the door leading to the pilot's cabin. It floated down the aisle to disappear in the direction of the lavatory at the back of the airliner.

What the amazed passengers experienced was ball lightning, the name given to spheres of bright light that hover, bob or bounce around indoors or out, and can pass through doors and windows without causing any damage. They come in varying colours – red, orange, yellow and blue manifestations have been reported – and rarely last longer than a few seconds before disappearing. According to orthodox science, ball lightning cannot

Researchers believe that ball lightning may account for many paranormal phenomena, from luminous apparitions to UFO sightings. The writer Francis Hitching has speculated that large manifestations could account for reports of spontaneous human combustion. Crashing into a human being, ball lightning 'might affect the body in much the same way as a microwave oven would, cooking the tissue inside and leaving the outer covering untouched'.

A faint hissing sound

The problem is that ball lightning is not much more acceptable to scientific thought than spontaneous combustion. Hampered by

the lack of solid physical evidence, scientists are at a loss to explain it. Some have put forward a nuclear radiation theory; others believe that it may be the result of some sort of atmospheric electrical discharge. Another view suggests that it may be due to stored chemical energy in the atmosphere, which is combusting in a similar way to a firework. Eyewitnesses have sometimes reported that the floating orbs appear with a faint hissing sound, and a distinct chemical smell. They often disappear with a loud bang.

In a well-documented case reported by *Nature* in 1976, an English housewife had a close encounter with a luminous ball in her kitchen. When she was examined by a doctor, her clothing was found to be damaged where the orb had hit her, and although her legs were not burnt, they did become red and numb. Apparently the woman had never heard of ball lightning before the incident.

BLAST FROM THE SKY Lightning literally blew a Swedish girl out of her soccer boots and shinpads during a game in July 1994.

1963 Mass sighting on Eastern Airlines flight from New York to Washington

1982 Scientific evidence provided at Cavendish Laboratories

CALLING SPACE: IS THERE ANYBODY OUT THERE?

SEARCHING THE CELESTIAL HEAVENS FOR EVIDENCE OF EXTRATERRESTRIAL LIFE

Sceptics may scoff at some of the wilder UFO reports, but experts do not dismiss the idea of intelligent life in space. In 1993, when the American National Aeronautics & Space Administration (NASA) launched a deep space project designed to seek out extraterrestrial intelligence, bookmakers in Britain cut the odds against its discovery from 500-1 to 33-1. Arnold Wolfendale, Britain's Astronomer-Royal, declared that it was not a crazy bet: 'I feel that there is intelligent life of some sort out there.' His views were echoed by veteran American astronaut Dr Story Musgrove, one of the team involved in repairing the Hubble Space Telescope.

Sadly for believers, NASA withdrew funds from the Search for Extraterrestrial Intelligence (SETI) organisation after criticism in Congress. But the search was resumed in 1995 in a privately funded experiment in

IN SEARCH OF LIFE Storing Earth music and the American flag on Voyager 2 (right); and the Hubble Space Telescope (below).

THE FACE ON MARS

In recent years a growing number of enthusiasts have accused the American space agency, NASA, of covering up astonishing evidence of life on other planets. The Mars Mission is a group of scientists headed by former NASA consultant Richard Hoagland. Its members complain that the space agency is refusing to investigate what looks like a humanoid face carved on the surface of the planet. The 'Face on Mars' was first identified by the Viking orbiters in 1976, and since then it has inspired a small industry of devotees who have written widely and attend conferences on the subject. NASA asserts that the image is no more than a trick of the light created by shadows playing across the planet's rock-scattered terrain.

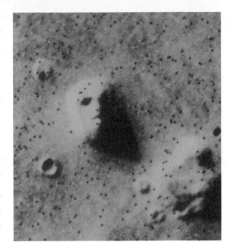

Australia, where 14 scientists scanned the heavens with a 210 ft (64 m) telescope for a five-month period for signs of extraterrestrial life. They also transmitted radio and TV signals to Alpha Centauri which, at 4.25 light years from the Earth, is the star nearest to our own solar system. The messages were expected to reach Alpha Centauri at the turn of the century.

Greetings from Mozart

Since 1960 astronomers have been listening for alien radio messages. The American space probes Pioneer 10 and

Pioneer 11 carried plaques designed for alien eyes, which showed a map of the solar system, the location of our Sun, and representations of two human beings. Voyager 1 and Voyager 2, launched in 1977, carried recorded messages of greeting to any intelligent life form they might meet, with samples of music ranging from Mozart to Chuck Berry.

No acknowledgment from extraterrestrials has been received yet, but the more that scientists learn about space, the more plausible it seems that other life forms exist. During the 1990s experts studying data sent back from the Pioneer 12 spacecraft discovered evidence suggesting that shallow seas once covered the surface of Venus – the planet closest to the Earth and the one it most closely resembles. The seas are thought to have evaporated about 3 billion years ago, under the impact of a runaway greenhouse effect, but they existed long enough for life to have developed. And in 1996 examination of a meteorite from Mars suggested that some form of primitive life may have existed there.

The planets that revolve around our Sun may seem to be inhospitable to life. But there are about 100 000 million other stars in our galaxy alone, and most are likely to have their own orbiting planets. Then there are the galaxies beyond our galaxy. The odds in favour of life elsewhere are overwhelming.

1900   2000

1960 Astronomers start to listen for alien radio messages   1977 Launch of Voyagers 1 and 2   1996 Meteorite from Mars is thought to contain evidence of life on Mars

THE VIRUS OF DEATH

IN THE SHADOW OF A HOLOCAUST: THE NEW DISEASE THAT MAKES AIDS LOOK LIKE A COLD

No one knows where it came from. No one knows where it will turn up next. All that scientists do know is that the mystery virus which first made its appearance on the

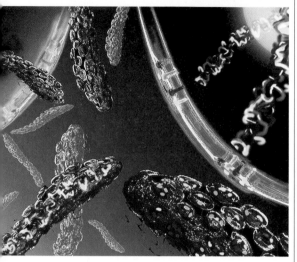

THE ENEMY WITHIN Once the Ebola virus enters a human cell, its ability to multiply is rapid, dramatic and nearly always fatal.

Zaire/Sudan border in 1976 is so lethal and infectious that it has the potential to become the Black Death of the modern world.

Ebola, as the virus is known, kills nine out of ten people whom it infects, wreaking devastation on the body of its victim. It starts with a headache and fever and swiftly moves on to uncontrollable internal bleeding. Within days, organs turn to a jelly-like pulp, which patients expel through every orifice – eventually dying in a massive pool of blood.

So far, the source of Ebola is unknown. Although it has been found in monkeys, the actual reservoirs may be insects, bats or other creatures of its inhospitable jungle home – thought to be somewhere in Africa. The major concern is that jet-age travel means that just one infected person or animal could trigger an epidemic anywhere. This was demonstrated in 1989, when a strain was discovered in monkeys imported

AWAITING THE HOLOCAUST Hospital staff bury the body of the fifth Italian nun to die of Ebola during the 1995 outbreak in Zaire.

from the Philippines for research in the USA – to a laboratory just 10 miles (16 km) from the White House. Extreme measures had to be taken to control the risk of outbreak.

Being a virus, Ebola is extremely difficult to treat medically. Antibiotics are only effective against bacterial infections, and, because viruses actually take over the cells of their victims, it is hard to stop the virus without affecting the other healthy cells at the same time. The usual method is to develop a vaccine, which stimulates the body's own immune system to fight the infection. However, vaccines take time to develop, and the ability of viruses to mutate means that new strains can emerge and make any previous vaccinations ineffective. No vaccine exists for Ebola, but it has already proved cunning in its ability to mutate. It is ferocious, too. It does in ten days what it takes AIDS ten years to do – in scientific terms, a 'biohazard level four', two levels above HIV.

Out of the 'hot zone'

Like AIDS, Ebola is thought to come from central Africa, and it is no coincidence that they have emerged from the same 'hot zone'. The World Health Organisation (WHO) fears that the new settlement of jungle areas, combined with rapid population growth and increased mobility, may be creating the ideal conditions for an explosion of unfamiliar diseases. Dr Ryder, infectious disease specialist at Yale University, says of Ebola: 'It is almost

as if the virus is saying to man, "I'll leave you alone if you leave me alone, but as soon as you step on my turf I'm going to get you." '

A disaster averted

The most recent outbreak, in 1995, was centred on the Zairean city of Kikwit, and at first seemed likely to fulfil all the doomsters' prophecies. Terror spread so fast among the population of 400 000 that people avoided physical contact with each other, and the dead were left where they fell. However, WHO teams were quickly flown in with experts from the American Center for Disease Control (CDC), who wore chemical warfare suits to protect themselves. By imposing quarantine regulations and strict sanitary measures, the experts were able to keep the death toll down. The fatalities strictly attributable to Ebola were given as 79 people.

Each was a horrific death, but the relatively low numbers came as a surprise. One reason is that the known strains of Ebola appear to spread through body fluids but not through the air. Another is connected with the speed of death. The incubation period can be 21 days, but averages about seven to ten and can be as little as two. Basically, Ebola can kill so quickly that the victim does not have time to spread the virus.

Once again, Ebola had vanished as quickly and mysteriously as it had arrived. Now only one question remains: how long will it be before it makes its next appearance?

SOARING BODIES AND SOARING MINDS

SUSPENDING BELIEF: THE STRANGE WORLD OF PHYSICAL AND MENTAL LEVITATION

The geneticist J.B.S. Haldane claimed: 'The universe is not only weirder than we imagine, it is weirder than we can imagine'. His observation was borne out in 1996 when scientists in Geneva announced that

INSIDE STORY   A computer display shows the point of collision between matter and antimatter particles at a Swiss laboratory.

they had created the first antimatter atom – a substance that consists of antiparticles. These antiparticles are like a mirror image of the subatomic particles to which they correspond. They have the same mass, but the opposite electrical charge. Just as atoms of hydrogen exist, nuclear scientists had now created atoms of antihydrogen – making hypothesis reality. The substance was in existence for only a 30 millionth of a second, but its creation opened up new realms of scientific possibility. When particles meet antiparticles they annihilate each other, releasing a burst of energy with unpredictable results on physical forces. In future, antiparticles may be used as fuel, to make a bomb, or to create antigravity – so permitting levitation.

Can humans defy gravity?

Gravitational force is a phenomenon still not wholly understood by science, and oddities have often been reported over the centuries, notably in accounts of human levitation. Some of the most convincing pictures of a

levitation published this century were taken in southern India by English tea planter P.T. Plunkett and appeared in *The Illustrated London News* of June 6, 1936. He recorded a performance by a fakir called Subbayah Pullavar, who laid horizontally about 3 ft (1 m) in the air with his hand resting on a cloth-draped stick. Apparently, he remained there, motionless, for fully four minutes, while photographs were taken from every angle. Plunkett passed a long stick over and under and around the fakir's body, which he reported to be stiff – as if in rigor mortis.

The photographs of Subbayah Pullavar have often been reproduced and sometimes used as proof that humans are capable of levitation. However, evidence published in a subsequent edition of *The Illustrated London News* indicated that it had all been an elaborate – albeit successful – fake.

Out-of-body experiences

Stage magic aside, in most religious traditions physical levitation is a secondary effect of spiritual detachment – the mystic's indifference to the material world. And reports of psychic soaring are much more common than those of physical levitation. At the point of death, many ordinary people have reported a convincing sensation of leaving the body and observing themselves from above (or from a distance). In his book *Life After Life* (1975), physician and psychologist Raymond A. Moody discovered that this was common to all 150 accounts of near-death experience that he analysed, including the now clichéd sensation of entering a long, dark tunnel.

Out-of-body experiences have been reported throughout time – in Ancient Egyptian tomb paintings the *ba*, or soul, is shown hovering bird-like about the body after death. One modern survey records that 34 per cent of undergraduates at Oxford University have at some time experienced looking at themselves from outside their own bodies. Ernest Hemingway, Virginia Woolf, D.H. Lawrence and Arthur Koestler are just some of the 20th-century

FAKE OR FAKIR?   Images of Subbayah Pullavar taken in southern India, 1936, have been used as proof of levitation.

LEVITATION IN THE LUNCHBREAK

In her book *The Decline and Fall of Science*, psychical researcher Celia Green quotes antigravity operating in a manner which is all the more extraordinary because of its mundane setting:

'My only experience of levitation occurred during a lunchtime break at school when I was 17 ... Each girl took her turn lying on a long wooden table at the front of the classroom, with the others gathered tightly around her, so that there were no gaps ... As one lay there, the girls chanted a rhyme – the actual words of which I have forgotten, but which referred to the person on the table looking white, ill and then dead. It was spoken quite slowly and in unison so that its drone-like tone had great depth and was very penetrating.

'Several girls took part before me without much success. Some ... were quite disillusioned. Others, however, did admit to feeling a strange sensation ... and it was this plus the declaration of a friend that she had experienced slight levitation that encouraged me to try it.

'I have absolutely no explanation why I was able to rise approximately 3 ft (1 m) from the table surface. I was perfectly conscious that I was rising and might even have uttered an exclamation of surprise ... The rapidity of the rise and indeed the fact that I had risen at all caused me to jerk my body out of the lying position, and with much commotion the girls cushioned my fall.'

writers who have reported the phenomenon. But does the mind merely compensate for impending death by creating an illusion of detachment, or does the soul really soar?

INDEX

ACKNOWLEDGMENTS

Abbreviations:
T = Top; M = Middle; B = Bottom; R = Right; L = Left

CB = Corbis-Bettmann
FPL = Fortean Picture Library
HG = Hulton Getty
MEPL = Mary Evans Picture Library
MSI = Mirror Syndication International
SPL = Science Photo Library
SSPL = Science & Society Picture Library
TPP = Topham Picturepoint
UB = Ullstein Bilderdienst

3 HG, L; Russian State Library, Moscow, LM; Rex Features, RM; FPL, R. **6** Popperfoto, TR; Magnum/Inge Morath, B. **7** Press Association, TL; Rex Features/Brian Wolfe, TR, BL; Camera Press, MR. **8** SPL/Peter Menzel, TL; SPL/A. Barrington Brown, ML; SPL/Hale Observatories, BR. **9** SPL/Wellcome Dept of Cognitive Neurology, TM; SPL/Philippe Plailly, ML; HG, BR. **10** Times Newspapers Ltd/Martin Beddall, TL; Rex Features Ltd, BR. **11** FPL, MM; Fortean/Llewellyn Publications, MR. **12** FPL/Stephen Pratt, TL; Images Colour Library, TR; TPP, BR. **13** Graphics/Bradbury & Williams; HG, L; Magnum/Eve Arnold, LM; TPP, RM; Sygma/T. Orbau, R. **14** Graphics/Bradbury & Williams, TL; CB, BL, BR. **15** CB, T, BL, BM. **16** CB, TR, BL, BM. **17** CB, TL, TM, TR, BL. **18** Popperfoto, TR; TPP, ML; CB, B. **19** HG, TL; Peter Newark's Western Americana, TM, TR; Popperfoto, MR; CB, BL, BM. **20** TPP, background, TR; CB, foreground, TR; photo montage/Laurence Bradbury, TR; TPP, BL. **21** CB, TL, TR, BR; John Frost Historical Newspaper Service, ML. **22** Image Library, State Library of New South Wales, TM, TR, BL, MM. **23** TPP, TR; Nina Drury/from *White Mischief* by James Fox, published by the Penguin Group, 1984. **24** TPP, TR, BL. **25** TPP, MR; Hugh Dickinson/from *White Mischief* by James Fox, published by the Penguin Group, 1984, BL. **26** HG, ML; CB, TM, BR. **27** CB, TL, TR, BR; AP/Wide World Photos, ML; HG, MR; TPP, BL. **28** Graphics/Bradbury & Williams, BL; AP/Wide World Photos, TR. **29** Popperfoto, TL; CB, BL. **30** HG, ML, BR; Popperfoto, TR. **31** Magnum/Eve Arnold, T; Popperfoto, BR. **32-33** Magnum/Eve Arnold. **33** Magnum/Philippe Halsman, TM; Magnum/Cornell Capa, TR, MR. **34** CB, TL, BR; Cecil Stoughton, Life Magazine © Time Warner Inc/Katz Pictures, TR; TPP, BL. **35** CB,

TR, MR; Popperfoto, BL. **36** CB, BL; John Frost Historical Newspaper Service, TR. **36-37** Illustration Graham White. **37** CB, ML; TPP, MM; HG, BM. **38** TPP, background, BL; CB, foreground, BL; photo montage/Laurence Bradbury, BL; Illustration Graham White, TR. **39** TPP, TL; CB, ML, BM; Popperfoto, MR. **40** Popperfoto, TL, TR; TPP, TM. **41** Magnum/W. Eugene Smith, TR; Magnum/P. Jones Griffiths, MR; MEPL, BL, BM. **42** Sygma/T. Orban, TR; Sygma/Armel Brucelle, MM, BL. **43** Sygma/Armel Brucelle, TL; Sygma/Eric Prean, TR; Sygma, BL. **44** DRK Photo/Peter Vert, TR; National Geographic Society Image Collection/Robert M. Campbell, BL. **45** DRK Photo, TL; Sygma/W. Campbell, TR; National Geographic Society Image Collection/Robert M. Campbell, BL. **46** Gebhardt/Stern/SOA, TM; Stern/SOA, TR; Schmitt/Stern/SOA, BL. **47** Gebhardt/Stern/SOA, TR, BL. **48** Express Newspapers, TR; TPP, MR; Sygma/Frederic De Lafosse, BL. **49** Universal Pictorial Press & Agency Ltd, background, TL; *Daily Mirror*, background, MM; Camera Press/Martin Parr, background, MR; HG, foreground; photo montage/Laurence Bradbury. **50** Gamma/FSP/Esaias Baitel, TR; Gamma/FSP, BL; *Daily Mirror*, BR. **51** Brown Brothers, background; HG, L; Russian State Library, Moscow, LM; TPP, RM; Dennis R. Kromm, R. **52** From *The Fire Came By* by John Baxter & Thomas Atkins, published by Macdonald Jane's, 1976/TBA, TM, BR; TPP, ML. **53** Camera Press/James Pickerell, TR, BL. **54** Dalkeith Publishing Co. Ltd, TR; Illustration Graham White, MM. **54-55** TPP, B. **55** HG, TL; Illustration Graham White, TR; Gamma/FSP, BR. **56** CB, ML; HG, BR. **57** HG, TL; Popperfoto, MM; TBA, BL. **58** Sotheby's/Sygma, TR; Popperfoto, BL. **59** L'Illustration/Sygma, TL; TPP, MM; Camera Press, BR. **60** TPP, TL; Wide World Photos, BL, BM. **61** John Frost Historical Newspaper Service; The Mansell Collection, MR; Popperfoto, MM. **62** Dennis R. Kromm, TM, BL; Popperfoto, BR. **62-63** CB. **63** TPP, TR, BR; The Mansell Collection, MR. **64** CB, TR; Wide World Photos, BL, BR. **65** David King Collection, T; Gamma/FSP, B. **66** John Frost Historical Newspaper Service, background; TPP, foreground; photo montage/Laurence Bradbury. **67** HG, TL; CB, ML. **67-68** From *The Death of Hitler* by Ada Petrova & Peter Watson, published by Richard Cohen Books, 1995/courtesy Ada Petrova & Peter Watson.

68 Illustration by Graham White, BM. **69** Popperfoto, TL, BL; TPP, TR. **70** David King Collection. **71** HG, TL, TM, B; Our Army and Our Country are Strengthened with the Spirit of Stalin!, 1939 poster, V. Deni & N. Dolgorukor, Russian State Library, Moscow, TR. **72** Popperfoto, ML; John Frost Historical Newspaper Service, MR; TPP, BL. **73** TPP, TL, BR; Camera Press/Stern, BL. **74** John Frost Historical Newspaper Service, TR; CB, ML, BR. **75** Abraham Zapruder/Colorific. **76** CB, TL, B; TPP, TR; John Frost Historical Newspaper Service, MR. **77** Illustration Graham White, T; CB, BL. **78** TPP, BL, BM, BR. **79** TPP, TL; HG, BR. **80** AP/Wide World Photos, TR; TPP, ML. **81** John Frost Historical Newspaper Service, TM; AP/Wide World, MM; TPP, BR. **82** John Frost Historical Newspaper Service, TR, BR; Magnum/J.A.F. Collection, ML. **83** John Frost Historical Newspaper Service, TL; Popperfoto, BR. **84** John Frost Historical Newspaper Service, TM; Camera Press, BL; TPP, BR. **85** Illustration Graham White, T; Camera Press, ML, BR. **86** Associated Press, TL; Sygma/T. Franck, BM. **86-87** Sygma/T. Franck. **87** Rex Features Ltd, TR, MR. **88** Sygma/Perscal le Segretain, TR; Marc Deville/Gamma/FSP, ML; Camera Press/Benoit Gysembergh, BR. **89** Laurence Bradbury; TPP, L, LM; HG, RM; CB, R. **90** Camera Press/Bassano, TR; HG, B. **91** CB, TL; National Center for Missing & Exploited Children, BR. **92** The Mansell Collection, background, TR; AP/Wide World Photos, foreground, TR; photo montage/Laurence Bradbury. **93** Associated Press, TR; CB, ML, MR, BL. **94** CB, TR; TPP, ML, B. **95** Illustration Graham White, TR; AP/Wide World, TL; HG, MR; TPP, BM. **96** Chattanooga Choo Choo, TBA, background, TR; CB, background, TR; TPP, foreground, TR; photo montage/Laurence Bradbury. **97** Sygma/Keystone, TR; Popperfoto, ML; HG, MR; Camera Press, BL. **98** HG, TR; Popperfoto, BL; TPP, BM; TBA, BR. **99** Sygma/David Gamble, TR; Popperfoto, ML; TPP, BM. **100** Camera Press, TR; AP/Wide World Photos, MR; TPP, B. **101** Magnum/ Peter Marlow, T; Cadres Decide Everything, 1988, poster, Alexander Konduvov, from *The Posters of Glasnost and Perestroika*, published by Sovietsky Khndozhnik Publishers, Moscow, 1989, MR; Novosti (London), BL. **102** HG, ML; TPP, BM, BR. **103** TPP, TR, B. **104** TPP, TR; HG, BL; John

Frost Historical Newspaper Service, BM. **105** AP/Wide World Photos, TR, BL. **106** AP/Wide World Photos, ML; Gamma/FSP/R. Neven, MM. **107** TPP, TL, B. **108** Camera Press, TM; AP/Wide World Photos, MM, MR; TPP, BL. **109** Illustration Rob Williams. **110** Illustration Graham White, TR; TPP, MR. **111** CB, TR, BL; Camera Press, MR. **112** Allsport/Steve Powell, MR; Allsport, BL. **113** SPL; Rex Features Ltd, L; MEPL, LM; Jürgen Liepe, RM, FPL, R. **114** Images Colour Library Ltd, TR, BL. **115** TPP, TR; FPL, ML; CB, BM. **116** Popperfoto, background, R; HG, foreground, R; photo montage/Laurence Bradbury; Popperfoto, BL. **117** MEPL, TM, TR; CB, BL. **118** TPP, BM. **118-19** From *The Wolf Children*, Charles Maclean, Allen Lane, Penguin Books Ltd/Mrs P.L. Jana, ML. **120** Rex Features/Leo Dickinson, TR; Popperfoto, BL; TPP, BM. **121** MSI, TM; FPL/René Dahinden, TL; Filmworks/From Arthur C. Clarke's *A-Z of Mysteries: From Atlantis to Zombies* by Simon Welfare & John Fairley, HarperCollins, BR. **122** Jürgen Liepe, TR; MSI, BL; HG, MR. **123** Highclere Castle, TM; CB, BL; BPK/Egyptian Museum Berlin/Jürgen Liepe, BR. **124** MEPL, ML, BR. **125** Ann Ronan Picture Library/Image Select, TR; MEPL, ML; TPP, BM. **126** MSI, background, TR; FPL, foreground, TR; Photo montage/Laurence Bradbury; MEPL, BL, BM. **127** MEPL, TL; HG, BL; FPL, BR. **128** MEPL, ML; Popperfoto, B. **129** FPL, TR, MM; MSI/Academy of Applied Science, Boston. **130** AP/Wide World Photos, BL; TPP, BR. **131** AP/Wide World Photos, TM, TR; Illustration Graham White. **132** Images Colour Library Ltd, TR, B; MEPL, BL. **133** FPL, TR; SPL, BL. **134** FPL, TR; Images Colour Library Ltd, ML; TPP, BL. **135** FPL, TL, BR; Popperfoto, BM. **136** SPL/David Parker, T, B. **137** FPL/Llewellyn Publications, TR; Popperfoto, BL. **138** TPP, ML; Popperfoto, R. **139** TPP, TL, TM; MEPL, BR. **140** Popperfoto, TR; Rex Features Ltd, MR; Images Colour Library Ltd, BL. **141** SPL, background, L, RM; TPP, LM; MSI, R. **142** MEPL, TR; Images Colour Library, BL. **143** TPP, background, TL; CB, foreground, TL; Photo montage/Laurence Bradbury; MEPL, BR. **144** Popperfoto, TM; TPP, MR; Images Colour Library, BL. **145** TPP, TM, BL. **146** MSI, TR; SPL, BL. **147** SPL, background; TPP, foreground; Photo montage/Laurence Bradbury. **148** TPP. **149** FPL,

MR, BL. **150** MSI, ML, BR. **151** Images Colour Library, ML; SPL, TM, MR; FPL, BM. **152** FLPA, TL; Popperfoto, BR. **153** SPL, TR, MM, BL. **154** SPL, TL; Popperfoto, BR. **155** SPL, TL; MEPL, BR.

Front Cover: SPL, T; Laurence Bradbury, B; Jürgen Liepe, L; HG, LM; Dennis R. Kromm, RM; Press Association, R.

Back Cover: SPL, T; Laurence Bradbury, B; David King Collection, TL; Camera Press, TR; SPL background, BL; TPP foreground, BL; CB background BR; AP/Wide World Photos, foreground, BR.

Endpapers: John Frost Historical News Archives

The editors are grateful to the following publishers for their kind permission to quote passages from the books below:

Bantam Press, *A Conspiracy of Crowns*, Alfred de Marigny, 1990
Bloomsbury, *Kiss the Boys Goodbye*, Monika Jensen Stevenson and William Stevenson, 1980
Jonathan Cape, *No Other Choice*, George Blake, 1990
Faber and Faber Inc., *Tom Slick and the Search for the Yeti*, Loren Coleman, 1989
Facts on File, *The Guinness Encyclopedia of Ghosts and Spirits*, Rosemary Ellen Guiley, 1992
HarperCollins, *Arthur C. Clarke's Mysterious World*, Simon Welfare and John Fairly, 1980
HarperCollins, *Mysteries*, Colin Wilson, 1979
Headline, *Lord Lucan – What Really Happened?*, James Ruddick, 1994
Inverness Courier, May 2, 1933
McGraw-Hill, *The Kennedy Conspiracy*, Anthony Summers, 1980
John Miles, *The Story of the Secret Service*, Richard Rowan, 1938
Penguin, *Hitler – A Study in Tyranny*, Alan Bullock, 1962
Piatkus, *Strange but True?*, Jenny Randles and Peter Hough, 1994
Thames & Hudson, *Phenomena – a Book of Wonders*, John Michell and Robert J.M. Rickard, 1977
Yale University Press, *Fall of the Romanovs*, Mark D. Steinberg and Vladimir M. Khrustalëv, 1995.

78-002-2

34 KILLED!

Zep Crash Shocks World

BELG...
MURD...
EARL'S

Riddle
of the
'cosmic' cornfields

Daily
No. 24522.   LONDON, SATURDAY, OCTOBER 25, 1924.

By JOHN STEVENS, ROB...
MURDER SQUAD de...
39-year-...

RED PLOT AGAINST B...

SENSATIONAL EXPOSURE.

RUSSIAN INSTRUCTIONS SENT TO THE BRIT...
COMMUNIST PARTY.

DAILY Mirror

Wednesday, August 7, 1996   HONESTY, QUALITY, EXCELLENCE   June daily sale 3,129,289 (INCORPORATING THE DAILY REPORTS)   30p

...RY CAMP.
...nd to Know
Means.
...Thous...
...PLEDGES.

WEATHER
Today: Cloudy and mild with afternoon showers.
Tomorrow: Fair, windy and colder.
TEMPERATURE RANGE
Yesterday: 53-64; Today: 54-62
HUMIDITY
Yesterday: 3 P. M. 42%; Today: 65-75.
Reports and Maps—Page 24

...OLUTION   NEW

Herald

VOL. CXXIII No. 42,611

230 West 41st Street, New York 10036, N. Y.
Telephone PEnnsylvania 6-4000

Established 123 Years Ago. A Europe...

SATURDAY, NO...

DRAMATIC STATEMENT FROM NASA

LIFE ON MARS

Kennedy A...

JOHNSON SWOR...

Daily Mail
News Chronicle
FOR QUEEN AND COMMONWEALTH
NO 20,343

TUESDAY, SEPTEMBER 19, 1961

AMELIA EA...
RED
LINE   BA...

VOL. LVII—NO. 45

Airliner mystery of flashes in sky

HOW DID DAG DIE?

HEAR...

Comment   THE SHOCK   Lord

untess runs out screami

AVIA
ER AT
HOME

McGOWAN and ROGER BRAY

ives today wo
Lord '
FINAL

OLYMPIA STAND No 205

MIDGLEY CAR LIGHTING CO. LTD
Oceanic House, 1a, Cockspur Street, London, S.W.1

ONE PENNY.

TITAIN.
Bandleader's
mysterious
disappearance

ORK ── dis-

Tribune

n Is Published Daily in Paris
R 23, 1963

© 1963, New York
Herald Tribune Inc.

ssassinated

broad-
ber 12,
single-
aircraft
days lat-

AS PRESIDENT

ART MISSING IN
erald Chicago Examiner
RIOT FILM IN CHICAGO

MONDAY──JULY 5, 1937

ELIA'S FAINT CALLS

VOL. LXI...No. 19,802.

NEW YORK, TUESDAY, APRIL 16, 1912.──TWENTY-FOUR PAGES.

ONE CENT In Greater New York, Jersey City, and Newark.

TITANIC SINKS FOUR HOURS AFTER HITTING ICEBERG;
866 RESCUED BY CARPATHIA, PROBABLY 1250 PERISH
ISMAY SAFE, MRS. ASTOR MAYBE, NOTED NAMES MISSI

Col. Astor and Bride,
Isidor Straus and Wife,
and Maj. Butt Aboard.

"RULE OF SEA" FOLLOWED

omen and Children Put Over
n Lifeboats and Are Supposed
to be Safe on Carpathia.

KED UP AFTER 8 HOURS

Biggest Liner
to the Bo
at 2:20 A.

RESCUERS THERE

ick up the
tho Took
lifeboats.

CHILD

rpathia
rk wil
vivors.

Sta
king
Ra

THE
Sun
Maxwell
mystery

Wednesday, November 6, 1991 **25p** Audited daily sale for September 3,762,151 Today's TV: Pages 28 and 29

DID HE FALL..

LOST AND FOUND IN THE BERMUDA TRIANGLE, THE ILL-FATED SQUADRON 19

The deadly Hoodoo Sea

From **IVOR KEY**
in New York

AT 2pm on December 5 1945, 15 aviators in five Navy Avenger torpedo bombers took off in perfect flying weather on a routine training mission over the Atlantic from Fort Lauderdale, Florida.

Less than two hours later, the flight commander radioed he was "completely lost" and then there was silence.

A rescue plane carrying a crew of 12 went out to look for them the same day. It never ame back. Despite one of his ost extensive searches, the craft and doz were not

U.S.
Ft. Lauderdale
Miami
BERMUDA
Bermuda Triangle
Atlantic Ocean
CUBA
PUERTO RICO
Caribbean Sea

WRECKAGE FOUND OFF THE COAST OF
FORT LAUDERDALE, FLORIDA, MAY BE
FIVE NAVY AVENGERS LOST ON A
TRAINING MISSION IN 1945.

DISAPPEARING ACT:
Members of Squadron 19
pictured at Fort
Lauderdale, Florida, with
one of the five Avenger
torpedo bombers which
went missing
today.

Cap'n Bob.. Robert Maxwell on t

DID HE JUMP:
Tycoon found dead in sea

HUGHES and IAN HEPBURN
axwell was found
st night ── 14

id he jump to his death

I have plunged over the 3ft rails surrounding the deck of his 450-ton yacht after he from his cabin at 4:45am ight sleeper who often rs while at sea

well said there were no signs of v
the body
SUICIDE? Personal and busines
had mounted on 20 stone Maxwel
weeks. Debts of the huge re
Maxwell firms is much greater
counts of his public companies
revealed in a Financial Times r

The total debt could have been
billion early this year.
Maxwell, famous for his hou
nally lost £98 million
── Page Thr

SUNDAY EXPRESS

OCTOBER 23 1966 Lighting-up Time 5.21 p.m. to 6.9 p.m. (Mon.) Founded by LORD BEAVERBROOK Moon C Rises 3.32 p.m. Sets 12.47 a.m. (Mon.) PRIC

DOUBLE-SPY BLAKE
ESCAPES FROM JAIL

Two Sections──Part I──THREE Ce.

The mothers who wanted action

Liner
Chann
rescue

drama